Rhetoric & Composition
PhD Program

PROGRAM
Pioneering program honoring the rhetorical tradition through scholarly innovation, excellent job placement record, well-endowed library, state-of-the-art New Media Writing Studio, and graduate certificates in new media and women's studies.

TEACHING
1-1 teaching loads, small classes, extensive pedagogy and technology training, and administrative fellowships in writing program administration and new media.

FACULTY
Nationally recognized teacher-scholars in history of rhetoric, modern rhetoric, women's rhetoric, digital rhetoric, composition studies, and writing program administration.

FUNDING
Generous four-year graduate instructorships, competitive stipends, travel support, and several prestigious fellowship opportunities.

EXPERIENCE
Mid-sized liberal arts university setting nestled in the vibrant, culturally-rich Dallas-Fort Worth metroplex.

English
DEPARTMENT
Contact Dr. Mona Narain
m.narain@tcu.edu
eng.tcu.edu

Illustration by Ian Golding.

composition STUDIES

Volume 43, Number 2
Fall 2015

Editor
Laura R. Micciche

Book Review Editor
Kelly Kinney

Editorial Assistants
Christina M. LaVecchia
Janine Morris

Former Editors
Gary Tate
Robert Mayberry
Christina Murphy
Peter Vandenberg
Ann George
Carrie Leverenz
Brad E. Lucas
Jennifer Clary-Lemon

Advisory Board

Linda Adler-Kassner
*University of California,
Santa Barbara*

Tom Amorose
Seattle Pacific University

Chris Anson
North Carolina State University

Valerie Balester
Texas A&M University

Robert Brooke
University of Nebraska, Lincoln

Sidney Dobrin
University of Florida

Lisa Ede
Oregon State University

Paul Heilker
*Virginia Polytechnic Institute
and State University*

Peggy O'Neill
Loyola College

Victor Villanueva
Washington State University

SUBSCRIPTIONS
Composition Studies is published twice each year (May and November). Annual subscription rates: Individuals $25 (Domestic), $30 (International), and $15 (Students). To subsccribe online, please visit http://www.uc.edu/journals/composition-studies/subscriptions.html

BACK ISSUES
Back issues, five years prior to the present, are freely accessible on our website at http://www.uc.edu/journals/composition-studies/issues/archives.html. If you don't see what you're looking for, contact us. Also, recent back issues are now available through Amazon.com. To find issues, use the advanced search feature and search on "Composition Studies" (title) and "Parlor Press" (publisher).

BOOK REVIEWS
Assignments are made from a file of potential book reviewers. If you are interested in writing a review, please contact our Book Review editor at kkinney@uwyo.edu.

JOURNAL SCOPE
The oldest independent periodical in the field, *Composition Studies* publishes original articles relevant to rhetoric and composition, including those that address teaching college writing; theorizing rhetoric and composing; administering writing programs; and, among other topics, preparing the field's future teacher-scholars. All perspectives and topics of general interest to the profession are welcome. We also publish Course Designs, which contextualize, theorize, and reflect on the content and pedagogy of a course. Contributions to Composing With are invited by the editor, though queries are welcome (send to compstudies@uc.edu). Cfps, announcements, and letters to the editor are most welcome. *Composition Studies* does not consider previously published manuscripts, unrevised conference papers, or unrevised dissertation chapters.

SUBMISSIONS
For submission information and guidelines, see http://www.uc.edu/journals/composition-studies/submissions/overview.html.

Direct all correspondence to:

> Laura Micciche, Editor
> Department of English
> University of Cincinnati
> PO Box 210069
> Cincinnati, OH 45221–0069
> compstudies@uc.edu

Composition Studies is grateful for the support of the University of Cincinnati.

© 2015 by Laura Micciche, Editor
Production and printing is managed by Parlor Press, www.parlorpress.com.
ISSN 1534–9322.
Cover art and design by Gary Weissman.

http://www.uc.edu/journals/composition-studies.html

composition STUDIES

Volume 43, Number 2
Fall 2015

From the Editor   10

Composing With   13

   Composing With Sound   13
      Steph Ceraso and Kati Fargo Ahern

   Imagine That   19
      Edward Jacobs

Articles   22

   Communists and the Classroom: Radicals in
   U.S. Education, 1930–1960   22
      Jonathan Hunt

   From Story to Analysis: Reflection and Uptake in the Literacy Narrative
   Assignment   43
      Kara Poe Alexander

   Gloria Anzaldúa's Rhetoric of Ambiguity and Antiracist Teaching   72
      Sarah Klotz and Carl Whithaus

   An Intimate Discipline? Writing Studies, Undergraduate Majors, and
   Relational Labor   92
      T J Geiger II

   Writing the Personal in an Outcomes-Based World   113
      Elizabeth Kimball, Emily Schnee, and Liesl Schwabe

Course Design   132

   Collaborative Course Design in Scientific Writing: Experimentation and
   Productive Failure   132
      D. Shane Combs, Erin A. Frost, and Michelle F. Eble

   Working with Disciplinary Artifacts: An Introductory Writing Studies
   Course for Writing Majors   150
      Lori Ostergaard

Where We Are: Undergraduate Writing Majors & Concentrations   172

Coauthoring the Curriculum: Student Voices and the Writing Major   172
Erin Bradley, Melissa Davis, Michelle Dierlof, Keith Dmochowski, John Gangi, Laurie Grobman, Kristy Offenback, and Melissa Wilk

Stone Soup: Establishing an HBCU Writing Concentration   177
Collie Fulford and Aaron Dial

If You Build Online Classes (And Empower Faculty to Teach Them), Non-Traditional Students Will Come: One Student's Journey through the Professional and Technical Writing Program at the University of Arkansas at Little Rock   182
Heidi Skurat Harris and Wendy McCloud

Looking Into Writing   186
Cami Sylvia and Michael J. Michaud

The Evolving Identity of an Undergraduate Major in Writing and Linguistics   190
Barbara Jayne McGaughey, Aleyna Rentz, and Jessica Nastal-Dema

English Majors are Professionals, Too: Liberal Arts and Vocation in the English Writing Major   193
Michelle Smith and Michelle Costello

Major Affordances: Collaborative Scholarship in a Department of Writing and Rhetoric Studies   197
Christie Toth, Mitchell Reber, and Aaron Clark

Book Reviews   201

Multimodality in Composition, Rhetoric, and English Studies: Praxis and Practicalities   201
Reviewed by Kirsti Cole
Review of *Cultivating Ecologies for Digital Media Work,* by Catherine C. Braun; *Multimodal Composition: A Critical Sourcebook,* edited by Claire Lutkewitte; *Remixing Composition: A History of Multimodal Writing Pedagogy*

Embracing the Challenges of Conventional Practices, Program Inquiry, and New Media in Writing Center Theory and Research **208**
> Reviewed by Harry Denny, Cara Messina, and Michael Reich
> *Peripheral Visions for Writing Centers,* by Jackie Grutsch McKinney;
> *Building Writing Center Assessments that Matter,* by Ellen Schendel and William J. Macauley, Jr.; *The Routledge Reader on Writing Centers and New Media,* edited by Sohui Lee and Russell Carpenter.

Christian Rhetorics: Toward a Hopeful Future **216**
> Reviewed by T J Geiger II, Lamar University, and Melody Pugh
> *Mapping Christian Rhetorics: Connecting Conversations, Charting New Territories,* edited by Michael-John DePalma and Jeffrey M. Ringer;
> *Renovating Rhetoric in Christian Tradition,* edited by Elizabeth Vander Lei, Thomas Amorose, Beth Daniell, and Anne Ruggles Gere;

Teaching Arguments: Rhetorical Comprehension, Critique, and Response, by Jennifer Fletcher **225**
> Reviewed by Glen McClish

Rewriting Success in Rhetoric and Composition Careers, edited by Amy Goodburn, Donna LeCourt, and Carrie Leverenz **229**
> Reviewed by Beth L. Hewett

Other People's English: Code-Meshing, Code-Switching, and African-American Literacy, by Vershawn Ashanti Young, Rusty Barrett, Y'Shanda Young-Rivera, and Kim Brian Lovejoy **234**
> Reviewed by Jenny Krichevsky

The Open Hand: Arguing as an Art of Peace, by Barry M. Kroll.
> Reviewed by Rachel Griffo **238**

Contributors **243**

From the Editor

Before you get here, you will have seen an illustration of metaphors for writing that emerge in the first half or so of Peter Elbow's *Writing Without Teachers*. This playful, striking drawing by Ian Golding, a doctoral student in rhetoric and composition at the University of Cincinnati, was produced as part of his presentation on Elbow's book during my Theories of Composing class this term. I was so taken with his rendering of Elbow's work that I asked Ian's permission to include it in this issue. I hope you will share my appreciation of Ian's visual take on Elbow's classic exhortation to keep writing, above all else.

This issue begins with two Composing With selections that address sound as a powerful mode of composition. In the first piece, Steph Ceraso and Kati Fargo Ahern describe an approach to sonic composition in the classroom that aims for "greater material and spatial opportunities" than those afforded by linear uses of sound. To get a better feel for these opportunities, access the online version of their piece on our website, which includes embedded sound clips. In the next selection, musical composer Edward Jacobs's "Imagine that" might be read as an extended illustration of the sort of open, ungrounded use of sound that Ceraso and Ahern advocate. While Jacobs reflects on how and why he composes, he also develops a theory of listening that informs his composing stance: "Through their unique perceptions, each listener becomes a sound-organizer—a composer—in a very real sense."

An attentive listener himself, Jonathan Hunt, in "Communists and the Classroom," uses interviews and archival research to construct a largely untold history of Communist educators working in and outside classrooms. As Hunt contributes to the field's history of radical educators, he reminds us that political activism takes many forms, not all of which can be measured by classroom practices. Exploring the political implications of reflective writing assignments, Kara Poe Alexander draws on qualitative research to argue for refining what we mean by "reflection" in literacy narratives, ultimately contending that such refining can lead to better articulated criteria and more democratic classrooms. This theme continues in "Gloria Anzaldúa's Rhetoric of Ambiguity and Antiracist Teaching," in which Sarah Klotz and Carl Whithaus reveal how their students resisted binary constructions of race, which were modeled in a text they selected for their co-taught course, and developed instead an intersectional understanding of racial identities based on a "rhetoric of ambiguity."

T J Geiger develops a disciplinary study that refreshingly encourages us to see our classrooms from students' perspectives. Building on survey and interview data about the disciplinary work of writing studies, Geiger finds that, more than content knowledge, student respondents emphasized the importance of relationships with teachers and teachers' expressions of care toward students. Geiger encourages us to think about the productive potential of care while acknowledging the gendered history in writing instruction that has made women, in particular, suspicious of expectations surrounding care delivery. Also within the realm of productive care, Elizabeth Kimball, Emily Schnee, and Liesl Schwabe examine one particular effect of the learning outcomes assessment (LOA) movement: the banishment of personal narrative from academic writing. Drawing on their experiences at a selective liberal arts college, an urban community college, and a private religious college, the authors argue that the widespread adoption of LOA has led to a lack of nuance in uptake that deserves our attention and interrogation.

We include two get-the-wheels-turning Course Designs in this issue. The first, by D. Shane Combs, Erin A. Frost, and Michelle F. Eble, documents a collaborative scientific writing course that incorporates an innovative writing mentor component into the design. The authors reveal what worked, of course, but also show how failures led to important pedagogical and curricular insights. Also highlighting the value of course revision, Lori Ostergaard outlines a 300-level writing studies course that emphasizes disciplinary knowledge as developed through first-hand archival research rather than through histories of the field. When I read course design submissions, I hope to get agitated by good ideas, to think immediately of how I might re-make one of my own courses. The two course designs included in this issue fit the bill; I hope you'll find them as generative as I do.

In Where We Are: Undergraduate Writing Majors & Concentrations, faculty and undergraduate students write collaboratively about their experiences and revelations. These pieces add much-needed student perspectives to the discipline's accounting of undergraduate writing programs' goals and results. In addition to teaching us something about student experiences, these essays might also be valuable reading for students in introductory writing major and concentration courses.

Finally, I am thrilled to include three review essays—two of them collaboratively written—and four book reviews. Collectively these reviews address a stunning array of topics: multimodality, writing centers and new media, Christian rhetorics, peaceful argumentation and argumentation grounded in ancient rhetoric, rhetoric and composition training for diverse careers, and African American literacy practices. I'm grateful to Kelly Kinney for supporting our reviewers, who offer thoughtful and substantive writing about important currents in our field.

Our next issue, spring 44.1, will be a special issue on Composition's Global Turn: Writing Instruction in Multilingual/Translingual and Transnational Contexts, guest edited by Brian Ray and Connie Kendall Theado. The issue will feature articles by Lisa Arnold; Cynthia Selfe, Kaitlin Clinnin, Ben McCorkle, and Kay Halasek; Bruce Horner and Laura Tetreault; Julia Kiernan, Joyce Meier, and Xiqiao Wang; and Shawna Shapiro, Gail Shuck, Michelle Cox, and Emily Simnitt. We hope you'll look for 44.1 in May and consider the issue for course adoptions, which we are happy to facilitate for any issue.

For complete submission and subscription information, visit our website at http://tinyurl.com/pjezb2o. Also find us on Facebook and Twitter, where we're always looking for new friends.

L.M.
Cincinnati, Ohio
September 2015

Composing With

Composing With Sound

Steph Ceraso and Kati Fargo Ahern

Often when rhetoric and composition scholars talk about composing with sound, it is with the assumption that sound will be used to create linear, narrative-driven texts like audio essays or musical soundtracks. In contrast, the following two projects offer ideas for assignments that make composing with sound open to greater material and spatial opportunities. We share these abbreviated examples in an effort to further discussions about the possibilities of sonic composition.

The Sonic Object (Steph)

To defamiliarize the usual ways of working with sound in multimodal composition courses, such as recording and editing scripted podcasts, I have been experimenting with assignments that encourage students to approach their interactions with sound holistically—to pay attention to how sound shapes and is shaped by different contexts, material objects, and embodied, multisensory experiences. One assignment, based on what I call a "Sonic Object," focuses on an object that uses sound to enhance a user's overall experience. This project requires students to design their own sonic objects by sketching a model and talking through how it would work, as well as creating the distinct sounds for their object in an audio editor.

At CCCC 2014 in Indianapolis, I had a chance to test run a version of this assignment during a Sonic Pedagogy Workshop (due to time constraints, the workshop only dealt with the design phase of the project). One of the many interesting sonic objects designed in the workshop was a "Toy Fruit Basket."

Christopher Potts and Lisa Phillips invented a baby toy they described as "a fruit basket that comes alive" (see fig. 1). They explained that each piece of toy fruit in the basket would respond sonically to touch. Each unique kind of touch—rubbing, scratching, squishing—would trigger a unique corresponding sound. Their design plan indicated that the pieces of fruit would be white to start, and then, as the baby interacts with them, the fruit would become colorful, make sounds, and release smells. Compared to simplistic kinds of children's toys (e.g., press a button on the toy and hear the same sound every time), the toy that they imagined integrates sound with visual, tactile, and olfactory elements of the design in complex ways. In short, the fruit basket uses sound as a key part of the immersive, holistic sensory experience of the toy.

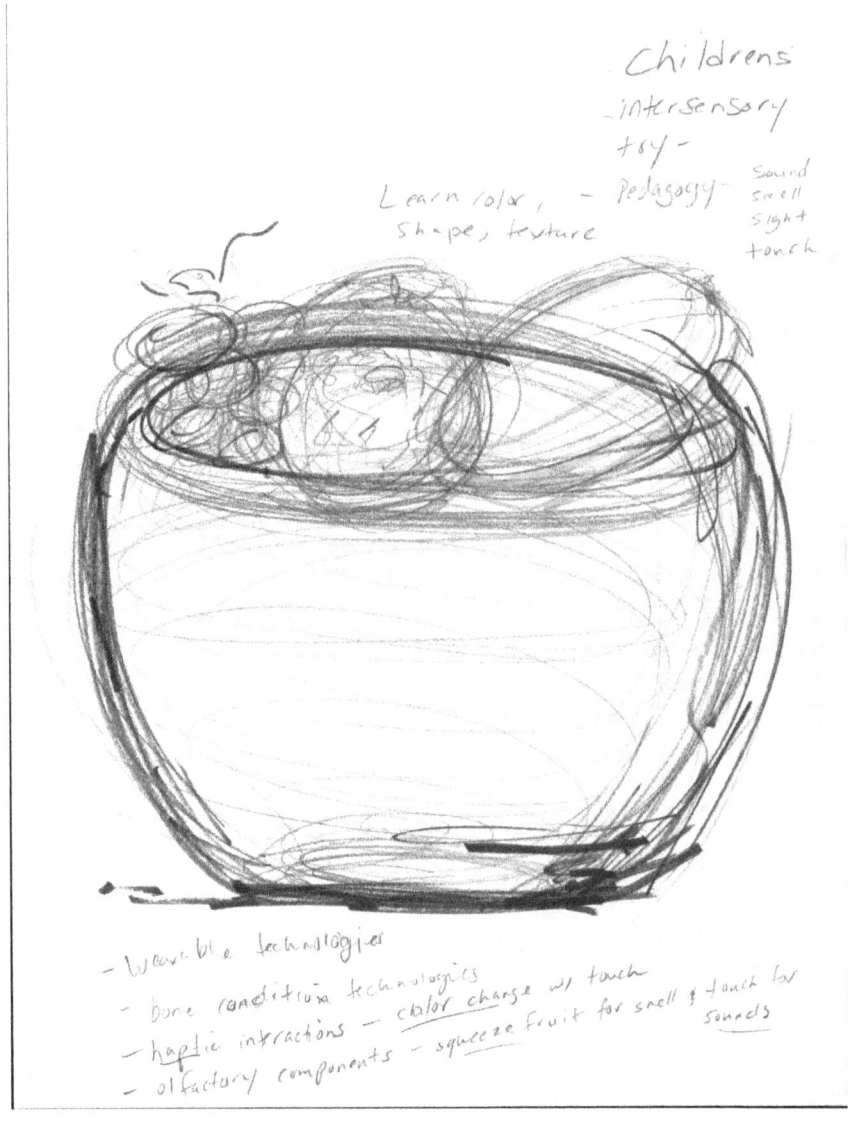

Figure 1. Toy Fruit Basket.

What I found most interesting while listening to workshop participants talk about and develop their sonic object designs was how different their approach to this assignment was from how my students typically talk about planning a podcast. Rather than asking themselves questions about the structure and meaning of their sonic compositions, participants wrestled with another set of questions: How does the use of sound make me feel and behave? How does the sound contribute to my experience as a whole? What are the various possibilities and limitations of sound in this situation? How does sound work with other material and sensory elements of the design?

Considering the increasing popularity of sound design and "sonic branding" in the products we interact with every day—from household appliances to the packaging of food—such questions are critical for helping students understand how sonic composition works in a range of experiences beyond the classroom. Whether or not others choose to experiment with the sonic object assignment, rhetoric and composition scholars need to develop more sonic composing projects that aim to (1) enrich students' understanding of how sound affects audiences in different contexts, not just digital ones; (2) teach students to attend to how sound works with and against other sensory modes and materials; and (3) create opportunities for students to explore and reflect on how embodied interaction figures into and shapes multimodal experience.

Embodied Soundscape Design (Kati)

I asked students in a spring 2014 digital writing and multimodal composing class to engage in an activity of embodied soundscape design in order to complicate their preconceptions of composing with sound. A soundscape can be defined as a landscape made of sound, a sonic "field," or an arrangement of simultaneous and spatially situated sounds. Soundscapes can potentially draw together music, speech, and nonverbal sound. Because composing a soundscape involves situating sounds in spaces rather than on paper or in linear arrangement, designing a soundscape causes participants to attend to sound as a range of possibilities where sound is spatial, dynamic, situated, and involves an intervention not only in our lived-in spaces but also our presumptions concerning what it means to be a listener.

In this activity, students begin by choosing a sound to make in our classroom space and writing the name (or description) of that sound on a notecard. They then choose a point in the room to stand and begin making their sound (see fig. 2).

The notecards provide a way for participants to commit to a sound and to visually map the soundscape so that participants with listening differences can also experience the soundscape through a preferred modality. The combination of all the sounds being made in our space formed the first version of our soundscape design (listen to audio clip 1 at http://bit.ly/1vlG0uA).

Figure 2. Students arranged in classroom.

Next, I asked students to alter the soundscape by varying the pitch, volume, speed, and position of their sounds (and thus their bodies) by moving around the space (listen to audio clip 2 at http://bit.ly/1F48TLq). Audio clips 1 and 2 are meant to illustrate some of the differences in the soundscape as students alter their sounds, although listening to and producing a soundscape in a space is experientially different from listening to audio recorded from one vantage point. After engaging in the extemporaneous soundscape design, we designed a soundscape by creating a soundmap—a visual map of the room showing descriptions and drawings of sounds (see figs. 3 and 4 for soundmap variations).

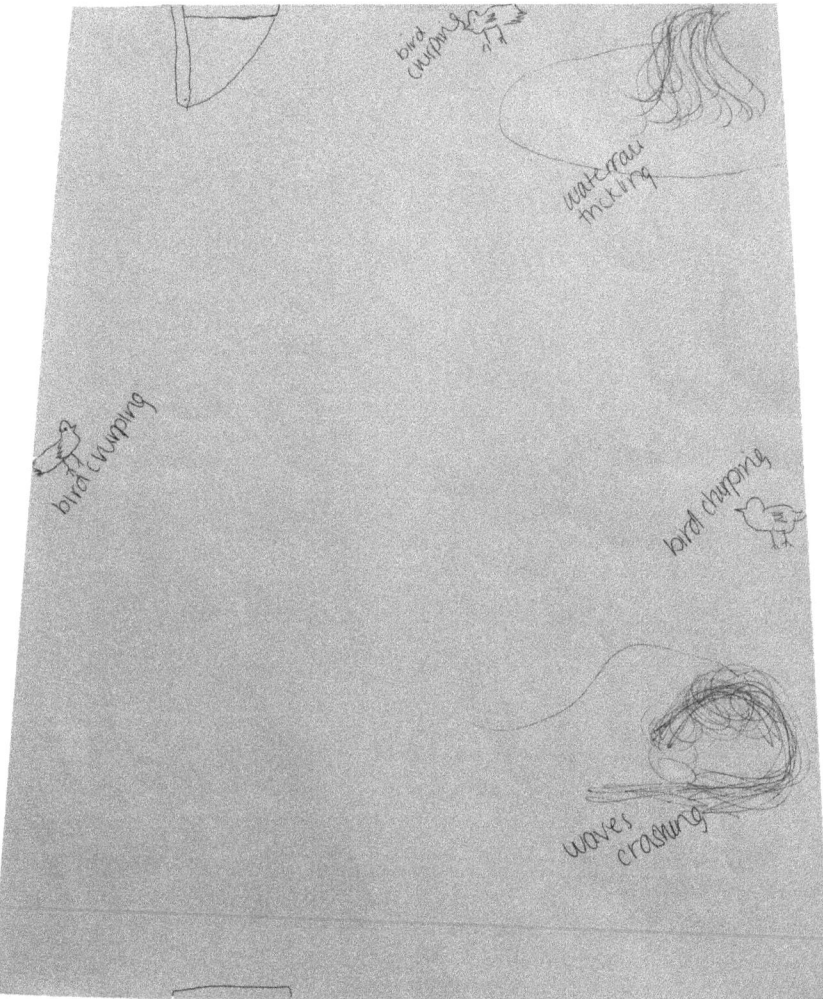

Figure 3. Soundmap variation.

In order to create embodied soundscapes from soundmaps, students were each assigned a new sound, either to make or to find and play using YouTube and mobile devices. Each person was arranged in the room based on one of the soundmaps. In this way, we composed the newly designed soundscape, person by person, sound by sound (listen to audio clip 3 at http://bit.ly/1DB6MSt). In audio clip 3, students composed a soundscape based on a soundmap designed to make the classroom more tranquil through the arrangement of sounds of silence, birds, water, and wind.

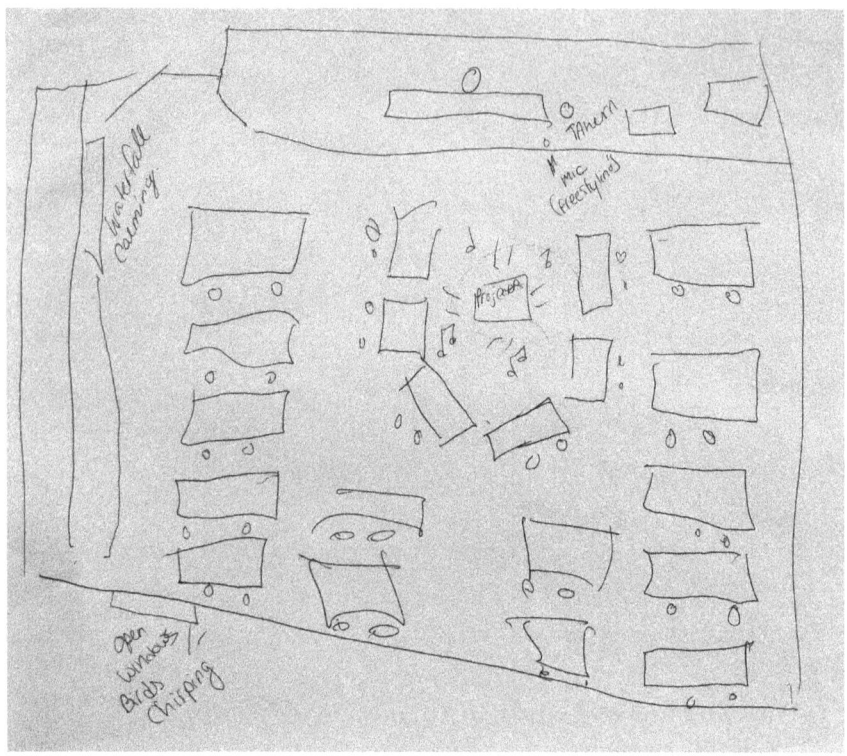

Figure 4. Soundmap variation.

This act of composing with sound may feel impermanent, but it allows participants to trace changes in arrangements of sound, become more aware of embodied, individual listening differences, and bring the experience of composing with sound into other acts of multimodal and material compositions.

Acknowledgments

Steph extends special thanks to those who participated in the CCCC Sonic Pedagogy Workshop: Jon Stone, Kati Fargo Ahern, Jordan Frith, Amy Riordan, Lisa Phillips, Christopher Potts, and Crystal VanKooten. Kati thanks soundscape participants: Jeremiah Aviles, Alexis Cobb, Ed Costa, Dan Duffey, Alyssa Economos, Yumi Hanamura, Ashley Henry, Joe Jenkins, Christina King, Aimee Leon, Melissa Nosel, Staci Palacino, Ashley Pottinger, Christa Speranza, Melanie Wagner, and Marc Williams.

Imagine That

Edward Jacobs

My musical compositions begin with aural fantasies. What I hear in my mind is often veiled, yet its impression vivid—closer to memories than to anything tangible. The striving to articulate these sounds often feels like grasping at wisps of smoke, or recalling the sights, sounds, or smells of long departed experiences and friends. I work with sound because aural visions demand my imagination's attention; the sounds in my mind's ear are eager to be transformed into vibrations beyond the privacy of my mind.

I cannot resist the chase to capture, or recapture, ineffable mental impressions and the lure to shape them into expressions that might become memories for others. The phases of my compositional process *seem* straightforward enough: determine how an imagined sound might be generated in a shared world; discover the world whose drama might be implied by such sounds; and devise instructions for musicians to re-create that sound world. But working with the sound objects of this imagined aural world is like searching for metaphors.

An initial image might take many forms: the sound of spoken words, the rhythm of a dancer's movements, the stillness of a fog-laden morning, the energy of a terrifying storm, or the warm voice of a loving friend. Such images arise, and then prompt a coaxing from my mind to a shareable sensory world. I transcribe what lives *in* my ear into a form that can be interpreted by performers and then experienced by others. What follows are steps continually taken and retraced: selecting sounds that might grow into larger musical stories, evaluating their generative potential, and then considering (and rejecting most) paths of possible evolution that seem dramatically inevitable. Some ideas will remain in this fantastical playground, demanding adventure; others will fade.

In this work I am trying to discover the world in which a heard idea lives; to find and describe the environs where these imagined birds sing, the context in which they live. I am trying to perceive, understand and portray a world I do not yet know, a world hinted at by the few sounds legible to me. As fertile initial ideas reveal details and suggest relationships, multiple contexts bloom, one of which will offer particularly alluring charms. From fragments of thought, memory, retelling, and re-hearing, a landscape emerges, and musical events find significance through their unique interconnections.

Composing is forming groups of sculpted sounds, sequences of events—none of which have intrinsic meaning. Composing is forming relationships between and among moments and phrases that can create cohesiveness and comprehensibility. Composing is making these events feel inevitably linked.

The result builds expectations and drama emerges from satisfying (or not satisfying) those expectations, which are born from each listener's background and approach to listening—an intriguing complication for a composer.

That each listener constructs their aural experiences differently leads to interesting possibilities. Imagine allowing the random sounds around you (e.g., traffic, or coffee shop conversations) to occupy the foreground of your mind's attention.[1] If you subsequently imply patterns, connections, and relationships among those utterly random events, have you transformed these sounds into a "piece"? Through their unique perceptions, each listener becomes a sound-organizer—a composer—in a very real sense.

Who, then, is the real organizer of events? Attentive listeners hear and shape what they are willing and able to perceive. Each hearer attends to different degrees of detail and uniquely comprehends what has occurred—regardless of a composer's instructions, or a performer's execution of those instructions. In my work as a composer, I may create patterns, but the only patterns that *truly* exist (in each hearing) are the ones perceived by listeners.

The truth, then, is that what I write isn't necessarily what you hear[2]. I know that my work will be filtered through a broad array of sensitivities, inclinations, translations, and signifiers—no different than artists of any other medium. I compose with full knowledge and acceptance that an audience's responses—even those with a personalized extra-musical narrative—are neither controllable nor predictable. Consequently, what drives my pursuit is the desire to hear a sound vibrate in a performance space beyond my mind, and my criteria is no more than, and no less than, what works for me as a satisfying and engaging—musically, expressively, logically—momentum filled drama-in-sound[3].

To compose is to construct a suggestion whose ideal forms in my mind's ear. It is to sketch the game plan for a drama that I hope performers and engaged audiences will find as enticing as I do. The game's "play"—the real interaction of ideas—is in performance and in a listener's hearing. To compose is to make a plan, cede control of its realization, revel in the variety of results, and then find another fantasy to chase.

****

For more about Jacobs and samples of his work, please visit www.edwardjacobs.org or soundcloud.com/edjacobs.

Notes

1. The works of John Cage are illustrative and enlightening in this regard. George Leonard writes that "when Harvard University Press called [Cage], in a 1990 book advertisement, 'without a doubt the most influential composer of the last half-century,' amazingly, that was too modest" (120).

2. Undoubtedly, a sentence with which any writer/artist, in any medium, might agree.

3. This, of course, is a luxury that comes with not relying on commercial success for a living.

Works Cited

Leonard, George J. *Into the Light of Things: The Art of the Commonplace from Wordsworth to John Cage.* Chicago: U of Chicago P, 1995. Print.

Articles

Communists and the Classroom: Radicals in U.S. Education, 1930–1960

Jonathan Hunt

Concern about Communists in education was a central preoccupation in the U.S. through the middle decades of the twentieth century. Focusing on post-secondary and adult education and on fields related to composition and rhetoric, this essay offers an overview of the surprisingly diverse contexts in which Communist educators worked. Some who taught in Communist-sponsored "separatist" institutions pioneered the kinds of radical pedagogical theories now most often attributed to Paulo Freire. Communist educators who taught in "mainstream" institutions, however, less often saw their pedagogy as a mode of political action; their activism was deployed mainly in civic life rather than the classroom. Awareness of this complex history may help current educators appreciate a wider range of possibilities for thinking about the relationships between politics, pedagogy, and professionalism.

Our field, like the teaching profession more broadly, has a long tradition of debating the complex relationships between politics, pedagogy, and professionalism. While the strident exchanges of critical pedagogy's heyday have waned, at least in the pages of our journals, the issues raised by this pedagogy remain alive for every composition instructor who hopes that teaching writing can empower students to intervene positively in their own lives and in their communities, however defined: what forms of political belief and practice are essential to pedagogy and professionalism, as we understand them, and what forms are anathema? This issue periodically surges into the headlines, as in the recent case of Steven Salaita, inviting each of us to not only think deeply about our own individual practices (both in the classroom and out), but also to take part and to become involved—to sign this or that petition, to pressure our professional organizations to take a stand (or not), to repost a link on Facebook, or compose an op-ed or essay.

This essay looks to the past to help us consider our present responses to the complex challenge of political commitments in the writing classroom and in the profession of teaching. The past I propose to investigate is the messy and in some ways still-controversial context of radical educators in the Cold-War-era

U.S. And by "radical," I mean in the Old Left sense of the word. Alice McGrath, a Communist lawyer who was the basis for the character Alice Bloomfield in Luis Valdez's play and film *Zoot Suit*, described the term in an interview with another radical, Studs Terkel, as follows:

> The word "liberal," when I was young, meant somebody who was scared of his own shadow. Today, it means somebody of the extreme left. The *L* word of the '80s is what the *C* word—*C* for Communist—was in the '50s. You talk about the "radical right" today. That's a phrase we never would have used in the '30s and '40s. "Radical" always referred to the Left beyond liberalism. (Terkel 364)

In short, the radical educators I'll discuss were—for part of their professional lives, at least—Communists.

The issue of Communism overshadowed most of the history of the twentieth century in the U.S., particularly the decades following World War II: no social or political movement could be understood independently from the question of Communism, no cultural product went unscrutinized in the search for Communist propaganda; the question of Communism (or more accurately, anti-Communism) was central to American identity. Radical (again, meaning Communist) pedagogy in the U.S. from the 1920s through the 1960s was hotly debated in daily newspapers as well as scholarly journals, and in the halls of academe as well as the halls of legislature—it was a consuming topic of interest not only for teachers and students in the classroom, but also for trustees and administrators, law enforcement officers, political parties, and professional associations. Even now, decades after the end of the Cold War and the collapse of the Soviet Union, conversations about American Communists are politically charged and haunted by deep historical scars.

How can the study of this context help us today? Not in any simple way, unfortunately. Or rather, the value of this history is precisely its complexity and diversity. The people I'll discuss—"Red-ucators," as they were dubbed by anti-Communist discourse of the time—were individual educators making practical decisions about politics and pedagogy, and often doing so in the context of membership in the Communist Party. The Party, for many, both gave meaning to and, for some, betrayed their efforts as teachers.

The educators I discuss came from divergent backgrounds, played a range of different roles in the Communist Party, and participated in the Party in very different historical moments. Although today we might not consider all of these people to be compositionists, they each taught courses that in the twenty-first century would fall under the broad umbrella of composition and rhetoric or writing studies, courses intended to build rhetorical effectiveness in various contexts, to develop school and community literacies, and to increase critical thinking and civic engagement. Some taught first-year writing or public speaking in the same institutions where many of us work today. And like us, they had to decide when and how to bring their varying, contested, and evolving politics into their professions and their classrooms.

Varieties of Rhetorical Education and the Mid-Century Radical Left

Through the middle decades of the twentieth century, hundreds of thousands of Americans were drawn, in one way or another, to the Communist Party. Precise numbers are hard to come by, both because the Party itself was highly secretive and because claims about its size or influence were (and remain) highly politicized. Anti-Communist historian Harvey Klehr states that membership peaked at about 100,000 in 1939, while Alan Wald asserts that up to a million people "passed directly through membership"; both agree that up to five times the membership were close to the Communist Party as "fellow travelers" (Wald 71). At the height of the Red Scare, long-time FBI Director J. Edgar Hoover placed the number of fellow travelers somewhat higher: "for every Party member ten others are ready, willing, and able to do the Party's work" (5). In absence of an archival record of membership, assertions about the Party's membership or influence usually tell us more about the rhetorical purpose of the claimant (pro or con) than about the Party itself.

Anti-Communist discourse of the period argued that any member of the Communist Party ceded all independence and free will, becoming instead a disciplined agent of Joseph Stalin. This idea was central to the logic of loyalty oaths for academics: academic freedom, it was argued, could not be applied to someone who had surrendered her freedom to Communism. In fact, many former Communists have reported in memoirs that they felt their integrity was severely compromised by the demands of Party discipline. Yet as Wald and others have definitively shown, Communism and the Communist Party were also hotly contested arenas of thought and action, where a diversity of voices, intentions, strategies, and aims circulated and competed. The case of long-time Communist organizer Dorothy Healey is illustrative. In her autobiography, Healey observes that strong discipline contributed to the effectiveness of the Party and the identity of its members, but it also "leaves a false impression to say we changed directions only because of orders from Moscow" (Healey and Isserman 58). Healey argues that organizers on the ground had to make their own decisions: "The United States was a long way from the Soviet Union, and California was a long way from national Party headquarters in New York, and I [. . .] was a long way from state Party headquarters in San Francisco" (58). In short, as is the case with institutional forms ranging from representative government to corporate management structure to the governance of the modern university, the Communist Party as an institution was varied and contested. As Wald puts it, "what actually happens in a trade union or on the pages of a novel is usually far more dependent on matters such as the personalities and abilities of those who are the human agents, and the context in which those agents are active" (74).

In the case of U.S. Communism, the diversity of human agents and contexts corresponds to the diversity of the United States: Communists were migrant farm workers and movie stars, plumbers and diplomats; they were immigrants and native born; they came from every region, ethnicity, religious background, income bracket, and educational level. Thousands were teachers and scholars working in every discipline. Many taught at what Susan Kates calls "separatist" institutions on the Left, such as Brookwood Labor College, which Kates describes vividly in her 2001 book *Activist Rhetorics and American Higher Education, 1885–1937*; other separatist institutions deserving our attention include the nonsectarian Highlander Folk School and the socialist People's College, co-founded by Helen Keller and directed by Arthur Le Sueur, father of Communist author Meridel Le Sueur (whose 1984 memoir *Crusaders* focuses on the political and personal legacies of her parents and includes an account of the school). Many more taught at the Communist-run Workers Schools and their successors, such as San Francisco's California Labor School, where PhDs taught alongside dockworkers. Most, however, occupied posts in public and private institutions of learning ranging from Midwestern elementary schools to Harvard University.

It is impossible to determine how many educators were Communists—at the time, the FBI and congressional investigating committees made every effort to find out, but because being a member of the Communist Party was actually illegal for much of the mid-century, and because any teacher identified as a Communist would almost certainly be fired, few were willing to stand up and be counted. Historian Ellen Schrecker has observed that the investigating committees of the McCarthy era were particularly interested in education: she calculates that "almost 20 percent of the witnesses called before congressional and state investigating committees were college teachers or graduate students" and observes that "most of the academic witnesses who did not clear themselves with the committees lost their jobs" (*No Ivory Tower* 10). These penalties for membership in the Communist Party were such that "it became possible and often desirable to be a member in practice with no material evidence" (Wald 75).

Even with the opening of the Communist Party archives, donated in 2006 to New York University's Tamiment Library, we cannot determine with any accuracy the number of educators involved in the Communist Party; as one commentator in the 1950s wryly put it, "the number of Communists on university faculties is not, of course, a matter of statistical record" (Hultzen 425). But Lee Hultzen and others estimate that Communist Party membership among higher education faculty was probably not more than one percent: energetic investigation at the University of Washington revealed two Communists among 1,397 full- and part-time faculty members (Hultzen 425); 12 Communists were discovered among Harvard's roughly 2,000 faculty members; and the Rapp-Coudert Committee named 63 "confirmed" Communists among more than 10,000 teachers in the New York City area (Iverson 162, 219). For the FBI and congressional investigating committees, however, this paucity of results only provided greater evidence of Communists' cunning skills at infiltration.

Like others on the Left, some educators remained "fellow travelers," close allies of the Communist Party but never joining, such as philosophy professor Melvin Rader of the University of Washington. Rader characterized his thinking in a 1969 memoir: "Like millions of others, I reasoned that a good cause should not be deserted merely because Communists supported it. . . . It seemed apparent that if I refused to function in an organization simply because Communists were in it, I would be stymied, unable to effectively support the very causes I *knew* to be right" (31). Other educators were members, either in secret or openly, for a few years or for decades. Some joined the Party as adults: W.E.B. Du Bois famously joined in 1961 at the age of 93, half a century after his days in the Sociology Department at Atlanta University. Others were practically born into the Party: Sovietologist Bill Mandel, probably the only person to have served as an instructor at the Communist Party's New York Workers School and as a Fellow at Stanford University's Hoover Institution, was raised in the Communist subculture of the 1920s and for a time attended university in Moscow (on this early generation of "red diaper babies" see Paul Mishler's *Raising Reds*).

Some left the Party in protest, some left quietly, some were expelled (as was Mandel), and some lived out their lives as Communists. Of those who left the Communist Party, many stayed loyal to what they saw as its principles, and remained active in what they called the "non-sectarian" left. This trajectory, in fact, was probably the most common. Others left the Communist Party altogether, disillusioned with progressive politics, and took a hard turn to the right; for example, Frank S. Meyer, an instructor at the Communist Party's Workers Schools in Chicago and New York in the 1930s, left the Communist Party to help William F. Buckley found the *National Review*, and, as the author of *In Defense of Freedom: A Conservative Credo*, is considered by some to be one of the primary architects of late twentieth-century conservatism. Many Communists or suspected Communists were fired, some went to prison or into exile; others laid low, signed loyalty oaths, and struggled to live out their beliefs in a time of massive state repression in both the U.S. and the USSR.

In the U.S., the state abuses of power known colloquially as McCarthyism are well known, in spite of attempts by pundit Ann Coulter and others to rehabilitate the senator from Wisconsin. Coulter's 2003 book *Treason: Liberal Treachery from the Cold War to the War on Terrorism* reprises the rhetorical stance of Joseph McCarthy and the House Committee on Un-American Activities (HUAC). More recently, David Horowitz has attempted to keep the Cold War alive under the guise of "ideological diversity" and a "student's Bill of Rights." Horowitz, stumping for his 2006 book *The Professors*, told Fox News host Sean Hannity that the University of California at Santa Cruz is ideologically the "worst school in America," citing as evidence the presence of feminist and "well-known American Communist" Bettina Aptheker on the faculty ("Worst"). By her own account, Aptheker was a Party member for almost 20 years but resigned her membership in 1981 after experiencing "a sense of overwhelming betrayal by the party," which would not accept her feminism, her sexuality, or the scholarship these informed (Aptheker, *Intimate* 403).

It is important to remember, though, that while McCarthy names an era, his career as a red-hunter was short-lived (1950–54). Yet Communist teachers faced federal and state legislative and criminal investigations long before and well after McCarthy's brief heyday: throughout the 1920s, '30s, '40s, and '50s, the "Old Left" in education was the subject of surveillance, scrutiny, and blacklisting. We remember the institutions of this repression: the HUAC and the many "little HUACs" at the state level, such as (to mention just a few) the Rapp-Coudert investigations in New York, Washington's Canwell Committee, and the Tenney Committee in California, which brought about the Loyalty Oath that I shame-facedly signed in 1989 in order to work as a teaching assistant at the University of California. We invoke this history when academic freedom or civil liberties are threatened.

Context 1: Rhetorical Education and Communist "Separatist" Institutions

Given this history, it is perhaps unsurprising that the pedagogical practices, the theoretical positions, and the lived politics of U.S. Communist educators were as diverse as those educators themselves, a fact that makes it difficult to draw clear historical lessons from their experiences. Nonetheless, some general claims about these educators are permissible. Notably, they did all the same things we do as citizens and professionals: attended faculty meetings and perhaps union meetings, joined the PTA or ran for City Council, coached baseball, donated to causes or raised funds for them, wrote letters to the editor and submitted manuscripts to *College English*, signed petitions, planned or participated in demonstrations or read about them in the newspaper, voted. Yet they also did things differently—differences enabled, in part, by their awareness of and participation in a global political movement. This movement sponsored a massive network, now entirely defunct, of separatist educational institutions whose central goal was activist organization and rhetorical training. These institutions provided very different contexts from those in which most of us now teach, and were in fact different from the mainstream institutions where most Communists taught. In these separatist contexts, Communist educators struggled with limited resources to enact visionary pedagogies they believed would help transform the world. However, in mainstream academic professional and pedagogical contexts—the contexts most familiar to us, which I discuss in the next section—they generally took care to moderate their political behavior. But *outside* the academic context they often put enormous effort into fundraising and political causes.

While discussing the work of Communist educators in the context of separatist institutions and other forms of explicit activist-rhetorical education and sponsorship, I combine two borrowed concepts: Susan Kates's concept of activist rhetorical education and Deborah Brandt's concept of sponsors of literacy. Kates's notion of activist rhetoric applies clearly to Party-sponsored schools; in its briefest formulation, an activist rhetoric "pursues the relationship between language and identity, makes civic issues a theme in the rhetoric classroom, and emphasizes the responsibility of community service as part of the writing and speaking curriculum" (xi). The Party also pursued activist rhetorical education outside the classroom, playing the role of a literacy sponsor. For Brandt, sponsors of literacy are "any agents, local or distant, concrete or abstract, who enable, support, teach, and model, as well as recruit, regulate, suppress, or withhold, literacy—and gain advantage by it in some way" (19). She explicitly notes that sponsors "represent the causes into which people's literacy usually gets recruited"—an apt description of the goals of Party-sponsored rhetorical education.

A brief survey of Communists in these separatist or alternative educational contexts reveals that a full treatment of them would require several volumes, and some of these volumes have already been written. They include Communist apostate Frank S. Meyer's *The Moulding of Communists* (1961) and life-long Communist (and former NCTE President) Holland Roberts's unpublished memoir *The Dangerous School: An Autobiography* (1971), as well as more recent texts by historians, such as Schrecker's *No Ivory Tower: McCarthyism and the Universities* (1986) and Richard J. Altenbaugh's *Education for Struggle: The American Labor Colleges of the 1920s and 1930s* (1990). Other histories are in the works, such as Marvin Gettleman's *"Training for the Class Struggle": Communist Education in the U.S.* and Jess Rigelhaupt's as yet unpublished dissertation on the California Labor School. These studies show that, in spite of a few clear directives in the Marxist-Leninist canon, pedagogical practices in Communist-run or sponsored institutions were widely divergent. It is notable, by the way, that these works are authored either by participants (Meyer; Roberts) or historians (Altenbaugh; Gettleman; Rigelhaupt; Schrecker); in our own field, as I have mentioned, disciplinary histories of the last decade have often brushed up against the Communist Party without treating it explicitly.

The now-forgotten Workers Schools and their World War II-era incarnations such as the "Jeff School" and the California Labor School were laboratories for many of the pedagogical methods, curricular features, and institutional structures that many composition teachers value today. These schools were student-centered in complex and ambivalent ways; Communists of the mid-century who survived to witness the late-century enthusiasm for Paulo Freire's work often remarked that they had pioneered similar ideas in the '30s and '40s (see Le Sueur; Roberts). Unlike most labor colleges, the left-separatist institutions of the mid-century were open admissions and free (or nearly free) to attend. They were desegregated and antiracist, coeducational and antisexist, and they focused on student learning and not on quantified assessment. As Altenbaugh puts it in his description of labor colleges, they "served liberatory rather than adjustive outcomes, addressing the cognitive domain of human agency" (4). Particularly in the late 1930s and 1940s, leftist schools paired a broad cultural curriculum with activist rhetoric.

From the perspective of the Communist Party, these schools were established to build working class culture and to pursue political goals, including support for the labor movement, civil rights struggles, feminism, and a pro-Soviet foreign policy. Earl Browder, the head of the Communist Party from 1930 to 1945, who shepherded it into the moderate Popular Front period and coined the slogan "Communism is Twentieth-Century Americanism," testified before a legislative committee in 1935 that "the Communist Party has its own educational work, with its own educational institutions" (Iverson 61). It was no secret that the Communist Party operated the schools; particularly in their early period, they were often housed under the same roof as Communist Party offices. Gettleman confirms that "North American Communists between 1923 and 1957 created a network of adult labor schools which was perhaps the most extensive program of adult education carried out anywhere in the Americas before regular colleges discovered the cash cow of continuing education."

The enormous resources put into these schools indicate that the Communist Party and its members did not focus—or, in any case, did not focus *primarily*—on "infiltrating" mainstream schools. Browder himself explained part of the rationale for this in the Communist-influenced progressive educational journal *Social Frontier* in 1935, observing that "bankers and lawyers make up about 95% of all controlling boards in the educational system and it is utopian to expect to change the situation fundamentally until bankers and lawyers are in general expelled from seats of power" (qtd. in Eagan 140).

We may certainly view a Communist Party leader's remarks with suspicion, as candor was not a hallmark of Party leadership. But in spite of occasional calls for Communist teachers to use the classroom to revolutionize students, Browder's arguments were widely accepted. There was a general sense in the Communist Party that the marginalized groups it most wanted to reach—workers, racial minorities, immigrants, women—were underrepresented or neglected in mainstream schools, and that the schools themselves were not structured to privilege the knowledge of people belonging to these overlapping groups. As historian Eileen Eagan puts it, "Believing in the primacy of the working class in efforts to overthrow capitalism, Marxists tended to downplay the role of educators and intellectuals" (139-40); Schrecker concurs, observing that the Communist Party "had never been eager to recruit professors. It wanted workers" (*No Ivory Tower* 46).

This view was widely held, confirms Jane Dawson, Party organizer in Chicago and then Los Angeles from the mid-1930s to the mid-1950s. Dawson's FBI file, which she obtained through the Freedom of Information Act, includes a page from the 1938 course catalog of the Chicago Workers School, indicating that she taught a course entitled "The Woman Question" (in an interview with me, she says that she ultimately did not teach the course, but does not recall why). As a professional organizer for the Communist Party, however, she was familiar with the broad educational theories in place within the Party: "there was a feeling that a trade unionist would be more likely to understand capitalism than a learned, middle-class person, . . . that if you were a worker, you would understand what oppression was, whereas if you were middle class, you'd have a hard time understanding it" (Dawson). Students in the universities, particularly, were not the audience sought by the Communist Party, and—in spite of Vladimir Lenin and Stalin's various pronouncements on the role of the teacher—the Communist Party considered it unlikely that a few "subversive" instructors could change the situation. Surveying his time at Rensselaer Polytechnic Institute (RPI) and Harvard, Communist Granville Hicks observed, "Even if I had done my level best to convert my students, how much headway could I have made against the several hundred members of the faculty who were thoroughly committed to the capitalist system?" (*Where* 63).

In addition to the Workers Schools that could be found in most cities and many large towns, the Party ran training schools for Party organizers and leaders, as well as initiatives directed at the rank and file, such as literacy-oriented immigrant solidarity clubs based on national or regional origin, known as *landsmanshaft*s. These groups, says Dawson, "weren't necessarily Communist, but there were a lot of Communists there, and probably, because Communists worked harder and stayed longer, they dominated them to some extent." The Communist Party's John Reed Clubs fostered proletarian writers—and in the

1930s "writing" meant not just fiction or poetry, but also "the (overlapping) genres of documentary, ethnography, oral history, folklore, journalism [and] reality-based fiction" characteristic of the period (Staub 1). The Communist Party's Popular Front-era successor to the John Reed Clubs, the League of American Writers, put less emphasis on fostering proletarian culture, but nonetheless (according to Communist Frank Folsom) "maintained close contact" with the National Council of Teachers of English (NCTE) and sponsored writing classes ("Finding Yourself in Writing" was the title of one 1939 offering) and Writers Schools in several cities (Folsom 78). Here, Folsom alludes to the influence of Holland Roberts, a specialist in literacy and a Communist who, at the time, was an associate professor of education at Stanford, a frequent contributor to and assistant editor of the *English Journal* in the '20s and '30s and president of NCTE in 1936–37 (see also Roberts).

These outreach or sponsorship efforts often served Communists and non-Communists alike, and were accompanied by literacy-oriented and activist rhetorical activities aimed specifically at members: Party membership included involvement in a small group (called a "cell" by the anti-subversives). This group would meet periodically to discuss readings and current events and to plan fundraisers and other events—it was essentially a politically active book club. As Hollywood script writer Jean Rouverol notes in her memoir of the period, "these once- or twice-a-month meetings at someone's house with 8 or 10 friends sitting about a living room, fueled by coffee and Danish and discussing dialectical materialism, were an intriguing experience" (23). Hicks, for his part, characterized such meetings as "dull as dishwater[: . . .] An ordinary meeting of the branch of the Party I belonged to in Troy was more like a meeting of the Roxborough Parent-Teacher Association or the Roxborough Volunteer Fire Company than it was like a meeting of conspirators" (*Where* 43).

The local Party organizer (Dawson was one of thousands) would usually attend group meetings to listen in on conversations and guide discussions of theory and doctrine. The local groups were often sites of the kind of discussion and critique that the late twentieth-century Right would call "political correctness." In a revealing moment, Frank S. Meyer, the former Workers School instructor who became a prominent conservative, decried the educational component that accompanied Communist Party activities, complaining that "even common expressions must be carefully watched [. . . as] the last word of the harried male, 'That's just like a woman,' has more than once been seized upon as a pernicious sign of 'male chauvinism'" (29). Finally, the Party mounted *ad hoc* efforts in the midst of other struggles and campaigns; in her memoir, for example, Dorothy Healey remembers one-on-one literacy work with African American Communists in the South (Healey and Isserman; for a more detailed description of literacy efforts in the South, where even many organizers were not literate, see Kelley 93-99).

These many and varied contexts of activist rhetorical education, from massive schools with extensive curricula and thousands of students to small clubs and discussion groups, have been extensively documented by historians as well as in FBI files, legislative committee investigative reports, sensational anti-Red screeds, and, usually obliquely, in dozens of memoirs of Communists.

Context 2: Activist Rhetorical Education in "Mainstream" Schools

We have seen that radical pedagogues were at work in a wide range of contexts during the 1930s and '40s. But what of those who taught in mainstream schools, particularly the colleges and universities that (unlike the Workers Schools and labor colleges) still stand today? That is the situation for most of us now. We (probably) will not get fired for assigning Marx in our classrooms (by the early 1960s even conservatives began to argue that Communism should be taught in U.S. schools in a know-your-enemy policy; see Iverson; Seymour). Our academic freedom is generally more secure, although recent efforts by David Horowitz and others on the Right to "save" academic freedom follow quite closely the logic of the anti-Communist purges of the post-World War II period, when Sidney Hook (a former Communist) and others redefined the term "academic freedom" so that instead of protecting teachers with radical politics, it became the rationale for excluding them (see Horowitz, *Indoctrination*; Schrecker, *No Ivory Tower* 105-12). So long as we have no real or imagined financial ties to Al Qaeda or refrain from tweeting too aggressively on political topics, we are reasonably free to belong to any political party we choose (Jaschik). But we have neither the option nor, for most of us, the courage, to teach in the kind of radical "separatist" political contexts described above—Worker's Schools, labor colleges, activist training schools, etc. In other words—and this is a key point—any decisions made by Communist teachers working in mainstream institutions in the middle decades of the twentieth century need to be understood in a larger context informed by an awareness of and (sometimes) participation in a broad, varied, organized, and politically radical program of free education.

Like most of us today, most teachers who were Communists taught in "public schools, private schools, and church schools, from kindergartens to colleges," and these were the primary concern for congressional investigating committees and other professional anti-Communists, as well as for concerned parents (Stripling 206). While Communist educational institutions such as the Workers Schools that were found in most large cities were looked upon with concern, the real fear was of the "infiltrator," a teacher in a mainstream classroom who would secretly indoctrinate America's youth in an *Invasion of the*

Body Snatchers-style scenario, turning them into robots controlled by Moscow. According to Robert Stripling, chief investigator for the HUAC from 1938 to 1948, these Red teachers operated by "slipping propaganda into classroom work and textbooks and by leading gullible students into Red-sponsored campus activities" (201). Once "snared," the "girl or boy who falls under Communist influence is in danger of losing his whole future as an independent, American citizen" and becoming subject to "absolute obedience in all things to Party orders" (200-01). Here we can see the basis for the logic that purging Communists would protect, rather than jeopardize, academic freedom.

Yet if successful in firing hundreds of teachers who were Communists or suspected Communists, investigating committees and even the FBI were hard pressed to provide examples of actual subversion or indoctrination in the classroom. Schrecker observes, "Had the colleges and universities who sought these dismissals possessed any information that the teachers they were trying to oust had proselytized in class, they certainly would have produced it. But they had none. . . . Despite all the Cold War rhetoric about Communist teachers indoctrinating their students, there is no evidence that they did" (*No Ivory Tower* 44). In the perverse logic of the times, though, this absence of evidence was itself taken as proof of the enemy's skill. Congressional investigating committees and anti-communist witnesses who appeared before them were obsessed with the idea that, even if no explicit instruction in Communism were given, some form of indoctrination would take place. After all, Communists were, in the words of J. Edgar Hoover, "masters of deceit"—this phrase became the title of his own book-length anti-Communist screed, *Masters of Deceit: The Story of Communism in America and How to Fight It* (1958).

Other semi-official anti-Communist texts similarly emphasized the slipperiness of the Communist threat: the suspected will not admit to being Communists, but if they do admit it, they will not admit to indoctrinating students; and if no evidence of indoctrination can be found, that just proves how wily they are. Semi-official texts along these lines include Stripling's *The Red Plot Against America* (1949) and California Senator Jack Tenney's *Red Fascism: Boring from Within by the Subversive Forces of Communism* (1947); spanning the decades, other notable examples include Fascist sympathizer Elizabeth Dilling's *The Red Network* (1934), conspiracy theorist Eugene Lyons's *The Red Decade* (1941), Harry and Bonaro Overstreet's *What We Must Know About Communism* (1958), and former Communist Frank S. Meyer's *The Moulding of Communists* (1961), as well as a volley of titles from Louis Budenz, a Brookwood Labor College instructor turned professional witness: *Men without Faces* (1950), *The Cry Is Peace* (1952), *The Techniques of Communism* (1954). Budenz famously declared, "Every Communist educator or Red sympathizer in education is an active agent of the conspiracy, whose orders it is his duty to obey. In his own field, he is just as dangerous as a Soviet espionage agent" (*Cry* 156).

Every scholar who has looked at the question of Communist practices in the classroom has noted that our project is similar to that of the FBI and the investigating committees of the mid-century era. And like the committees, "we know surprisingly little about the CP's [Communist Party's] activities within the academic community" (Schrecker, *No Ivory Tower* 24-5). I asked Dawson about the practices of Communist teachers that she knew through her Party work. Her reply to my question showed a rhetorical perspective: "Well, they did pretty much what you do, probably—a little more emphasis on civil rights, something about the poor or about industrial working conditions. They didn't come right out with Marx and Lenin. You had to think about your audience" (Dawson).

Dawson's observation brings to mind Karen Kopelson's rhetorically minded critique of the critical-pedagogical imperative that the instructor's politics must be staged in the classroom. Drawing on the ancient Greek rhetorical concept of *mêtis* or "cunning," Kopelson argues that an instructor's "performance of the very neutrality that students expect from their (composition) instructors, and from education more generally, can become a rhetorically savvy, politically responsive and respon*sible* pedagogical tactic" (Kopelson 118, emphasis in original). In other words, Kopelson argues not that instructors should abandon political commitments, but that a strategic, audience-aware performance of political neutrality is a way to "negotiate students' resistance" and thus help students wrestle productively with politically volatile or sensitive topics.

While Communists' pedagogical goals may have involved changing students' minds, there is considerable evidence that they nonetheless did not see a politicized classroom as the best path to this end. To depart momentarily from the post-secondary and adult education worlds, the case of David Friedman is illustrative. Friedman, who joined the Communist Party after becoming a substitute teacher in Harlem, never mentions students or the classroom in his account of his activities as a Communist teacher. When he was hired, Friedman "was appalled" by the conditions in Harlem schools, which, as he says, "were considered a place where you didn't worry too much about the quality of education" (qtd. in Schrecker, *Age* 112). The teachers' union seemed to him to be the only active force for change, getting parents involved and pressuring the board of education to address the high ratio of substitutes, scarcity and antiquity of textbooks, and poor condition of the facilities. Friedman was drawn to the Party through his involvement in the union. He observed that the most active and dedicated members of the union were Communists: "the ones who would sweat it out all kinds of hours and come in on Saturdays and would work the mimeograph machine or writing statements or trying to mobilize committees all hours of the late afternoon and evening" (133). His admiration for these activists led him to the Party: "I realized that these were the kind of people I was glad to work with" (133). Friedman's remark aligns with Jane Dawson's observation that Communists "infiltrated" organizations like unions by working harder and staying later than others.

Significantly, though, in describing his work, Friedman *never once* mentions the pedagogical strategies he pursued in the classroom. The "tremendous energy" and "tremendous activity" (his words) of Communists in the union was devoted to organizing teachers and parents; selling the Communist Party's newspaper, *The Daily Worker*; raising money for other unions such as auto workers' and steel workers'; and raising consciousness about the dangers of fascism. It may well be that Friedman and his colleagues engaged in some form of Communist-influenced pedagogy (the worst fear of Congress and, apparently, much of the public), but his reminiscences indicate clearly that he imagined his primary sphere of activity as located outside the classroom. His students were not the target of his activist rhetoric.

Across both higher education institutions and public schools, New York City had the highest number of Communist teachers (and the same is true of staff members, who were subject to the same repressive measures). Of particular concern to investigators was The City College of New York (CCNY), whose large population of dispossessed students was seen as a potential breeding ground for Communists. While the evidence suggests that it *was* such a breeding ground, the fear that teachers were indoctrinating students was misplaced. In fact, *students* were the most active recruiters: most Communists on the teaching staff had been radicalized by other students during their own undergraduate years. In a detailed and carefully documented 1959 monograph on Communism in U.S. schools, Robert Iverson wrote:

> The idea that a handful of Communist teachers launched students on the road to Communism must be laid to rest. The Communist student movement antedated any activity among professors. There was not a single Communist teacher on the staff of the New York City colleges when the Communist student movement began. . . . By 1938, enough young instructors, tutors, and graduate students had emerged from the student movement to provide faculty support. (142)

Bill Mandel, the instructor at the Communist Party's New York Workers School who later went on to be a fellow at Stanford's Hoover Institution, was a part of the student movement described by Iverson. Mandel attended City College before being expelled in 1933 for involvement in student antimilitarism demonstrations. His account of the Communist presence at City College does not quite fit with Iverson's, though: according to Mandel, students demonstrated as early as 1932 in defense of an English instructor, Oakley Johnson, fired for being a Communist. But if Mandel's autobiography challenges Iverson's claim that "there was not a single Communist teacher on the staff," it nonetheless confirms the general thrust of Iverson's argument: the Communist student movement did not come out of the classroom. Like David Friedman, the Harlem substitute teacher interviewed by Schrecker (*Age*), Communist students at City College devoted their energy primarily to raising money and organizing protests. Mandel even goes so far as to say he has "only one memory of my classes" at City College.

This memory is of a moment when Mandel, as a *student*, did try to bring communism into the classroom. He reports that an English instructor assigned the class to choose a passage to read aloud. Mandel, whose middle name is Marx, chose a passage from *The Communist Manifesto*, expecting to provoke other students and the genteel Southern instructor. According to Mandel, the instructor "listened courteously, and properly confined his comments to manner of delivery and enunciation" (62). It was only later, when the instructor joined the Abraham Lincoln Brigade and was killed in the Spanish Civil War, that Mandel realized he must have been a Communist. Mandel does not identify the instructor by name in his memoir, but I believe he must have been Ralph Wardlaw (1907-38), a Georgia native and instructor in CCNY's Department of Public Speaking (see Watt 104-05 for an account of Wardlaw's death).

It might seem surprising that an instructor so dedicated to a political cause would keep his opinions to himself, and in fact, Leon Wofsy, another red-diaper baby and active Communist who attended CCNY in the late '30s, told Marvin Gettleman of his surprise at learning which of his professors had also been in the Party (Schrecker, *No Ivory Tower* 42). Yet this seems to have been the dominant practice of Communist teachers. Most sought to keep their Party membership secret, because open admission of Communist Party membership was generally cause for immediate dismissal and even, for much of the 1940s and 1950s, imprisonment under the Smith Act. But this constraint was not the only reason for discretion: for most, "professionalism as well as prudence encouraged [Communist educators] to separate their politics from their teaching. They were, after all, highly trained scholars who, despite their radicalism, shared their colleagues' commitment to the standards of their calling" (Schrecker, *No Ivory Tower* 43). Most saw their primary sphere of activity as Communists as being *outside* the classroom, in study groups, unions, organizing meetings, fundraisers, demonstrations, and the like.

The most prominent Communist in education during this period was Granville Hicks, who was among the few members of the Communist Party to be relatively open about membership, and one of many intellectuals who joined the Party during the Popular Front period in the middle and late 1930s—a time when, in the words of his Harvard colleague Daniel Aaron, "a communist seemed hardly more exotic than [. . .] a Republican or Elk" (qtd. in Levenson and Natterstad 110). The Harvard-educated Hicks first became widely known during the 1930s as an essayist and literary critic whose work appeared in such periodicals as *The Nation*, *The New Republic*, *SAQ*, *American Literature*, H.L. Mencken's *American Mercury*, and other magazines and journals, including *College English*. As he moved to the left through the 1930s, Hicks became a contributor to and, subsequently, literary editor of *The New Masses*. He was fired from the English Department at RPI in 1935, most probably due to his radical political associations and his published work, which included *The Great Tradition* (1933), an openly Marxist rereading of the U.S. literary canon. While openly a Communist, he was employed at Harvard on a one-year contract in 1938-39. Along with many others, he left the Party in the fall of 1939, as a result of the Nazi-Soviet Non-Aggression Pact of that year.

At Harvard, Hicks was a "counselor," associated with a residential house rather than an academic department. He did not, in other words, teach writing, composition, rhetoric, or literature, but instead led reading and discussion groups, advised undergraduates and graduate students on academic matters such as theses, and arranged lecture series. However, Hicks's case is illustrative of the perceived stakes of political radicals in education. The appointment of an unashamed Communist Party member to the faculty of (arguably) the nation's most prestigious university was controversial, unleashing considerable debate on campus and in the pages of local and national newspapers. Eventually, after the war, Hicks drew the attention of the HUAC; having left the Party, he appeared as a "friendly" witness in 1953. At stake was the question of propaganda or bias in the classroom.

There was no shortage of canonical Marxist works asserting the power of education in bringing about revolution—Lenin's writings, in particular, offered a vision of teachers as sowing the seeds of a revolutionary future. Hicks, however, asserted that he "leaned over backward to keep my biases out of the classroom, and [. . .] called attention to them when they forced their way in" (*Where* 63). In Hicks's view, his primary contribution to the Party was in his writing and public speaking; in other words, in his role as *rhetor*, not as pedagogue. He also brought to the Party (as Party head Earl Browder confirmed later) his protestant New England heritage. Although he was willing to risk and ultimately sacrificed his academic career for his beliefs, he did not see the classroom as an appropriate arena of political activity.

Though the vision of the Left educator as a pedagogical fifth columnist haunted discussions of American education through the twentieth century and continues to haunt us today, we see again and again evidence that suggests that most radical educators in "mainstream" contexts sought to make political impacts *outside* the classroom, either in Party-sponsored alternative educational contexts or in civil society, in the practices we associate with the duties and pleasures of citizenship. Their main strategy for "infiltration" in these civil society contexts—and this is a motif in Communist memoirs—was not brainwashing but simply working harder and staying longer (as both Dawson and Friedman emphasize). In fact, Schrecker notes that many academics who drifted away from the Party in the 1940s did so not because of political objections to a Party line but because involvement in the Party was simply *so much work* (*No Ivory Tower* 57). And, as Schrecker's point illustrates, most Communists did not make a life-long commitment to the Party, even if they remained committed, in multivalent ways, to the Left.

Conclusion: Betrayal and Promise

This brief survey of radical educators demonstrates the rich variety of positions and activities available in negotiating Left political and professional identities, a variety that runs counter to grim visions of rigid conformity to a Party line and a relentless agenda of subversion. These visions remind us of the fact that histories are never neutral; they are, as Jeanne Gunner puts it, "interested rhetorical forms, and our work should include examination of whose interests are being served by them" (264). When we bury a rich, varied, and problematic history behind thin but powerful stereotypes, we allow not only our past but also our present to be commandeered.

The educators discussed here, working in a range of related fields, thought carefully and often rhetorically about the intersections of their politics, their professionalism, and their pedagogies. This rhetorical thinking led radical educators to a wide range of conclusions about the intersections of their politics and their work as educators. The Cold War stereotypes of the doctrinaire Stalinist or the insidious spy were but two of the many possible roles available to Left educators, though some people did actually adopt them (as some educators do today). Most, however, seemed to have tried, as we do today, to maintain a capacity for aspiration in the face of very real political and institutional challenges, a capacity that was often bolstered and sometimes hindered by the context of an organized, international Left centered on the Soviet Union.

I opened this essay with the observation that for many radical educators, the Communist Party both gave meaning to and also betrayed their efforts as educators. The notion that the Party betrayed its own adherents is a common motif in the historiography of Communism in the U.S., and an often-poignant feature of Communist memoirs (or, more accurately, ex-Communist memoirs, since most authors of such memoirs were no longer in the Party at the time of writing). A clear example comes from Hope Hale Davis, who was a member of the Communist Party in the 1930s, along with her husband Robert Gorham Davis, the noted author, literary critic, essayist, and professor. Near the conclusion of her memoir *Great Day Coming*, Hope Hale Davis describes the continuing shame at this betrayal she felt at having her struggle for a more just world hijacked by Stalinism:

> Not shame that we joined in the fight, which indeed must be renewed and renewed, as long as people are still ill-fed, ill-clothed, ill-housed, and brutally tortured. My shame is in the terms of my joining: I forfeited for the cause my most essential freedom, to think for myself. Instead of keeping my wits about me, I gave them over to others, believing big lies and rejecting truths as big as millions starving. No excuse can lighten the knowledge that I used my brain and talents in defense of Stalin. (336)

This shame has, I think, occluded our field's knowledge of the past in a way that undermines Hope Hale Davis's main goal: to "renew and renew" the fight. Such a renewal depends on confronting this radical past, so that we may "truly overcome [its] grave errors and yet still draw sustenance from real glories" (Wald 81).

Yet if shame and betrayal are motifs in our understanding of Communism, Communists are certainly not the only educators who have felt betrayed in their political lives and their professional work. I point to Richard Ohmann's 1976 *English in America: A Radical View of the Profession*, of enduring interest to disciplinary history in rhetoric and composition, as well as to activist rhetoricians. I do not know if Ohmann ever joined the Communist Party; I am assuming that he uses the term "radical" in its post-1968 sense, no longer as a synonym for Communist. In his 1995 introduction to the book, Ohmann opens with the observation that the "anger" of the book was "closely linked to a feeling of having been deceived and of having collaborated in the deception" (xii)—a familiar motif, but Ohmann's collaboration was not with Stalin. It was, rather, with liberal humanism. If ex-Communist Hicks could write that "the great evil of Communism is not that it uses vicious persons, as it sometimes does, but that it corrupts good ones" (47), the same must certainly be said of liberal humanism and its institutional forms, including the disciplines in which we work and the colleges and universities that house them.

Our field has energetically explored its past—or, more accurately, pasts—and hosted vigorous and eloquent discussions of the value of this exploration. It is now time to include in this discussion an exploration of our Communist past. Burying our Communist past will not save us from a sense of betrayal by the groups to which we belong and the institutions in which we labor. Recovering this radical past may, in fact, enrich our understanding of the possibilities before us. In language that would not have been out of place in the 1930s, Richard Miller has recently observed that "it is not difficult to imagine a preferable world, one where students come to college to learn how to work collectively on solving the major problems of the twenty-first century" (*Writing* 173; see also *As If Learning Mattered*). Studying the "Red-ucators" of the twentieth century—their vision and their errors, their vigorous debates and energetic citizenship as well as their excesses and failures—may help us to "renew and renew the fight," to be more effective in our struggle not only to imagine but to realize a preferable world.

Works Cited

Altenbaugh, Richard J. *Education for Struggle: The American Labor Colleges of the 1920s and 1930s*. Philadelphia: Temple UP, 1990. Print.

Aptheker, Bettina F. *Intimate Politics: How I Grew Up Red, Fought for Free Speech, and Became a Feminist Rebel*. Emeryville: Seal, 2006. Print.

---. "Mary Church Terrell and Ida B. Wells: A Comparative Rhetorical/Historical Analysis from 1890-1920." Master's thesis, San José State U, 1976.

---. *Women's Legacy: Essays on Race, Sex, and Class in American History*. Amherst: U Massachussetts P, 1982. Print.

Brandt, Deborah. *Literacy in American Lives*. Cambridge: Cambridge UP, 2001. Print.

Budenz, Louis. *The Cry Is Peace*. Chicago: Henry Regnery, 1952. Print.

---. *Men without Faces*. New York: Harper, 1950. Print.

---. *The Techniques of Communism*. Chicago: Henry Regnery, 1954. Print.

Coulter, Ann. *Treason: Liberal Treachery from the Cold War to the War on Terrorism*. New York: Crown, 2003. Print.

Davis, Hope Hale. *Great Day Coming: A Memoir of the 1930s*. South Royalton: Steerforth P, 1994. Print.

Dawson, Jane. Personal interview. 1 Sept. 2004.

Dilling, Elizabeth. *The Red Network: A 'Who's Who' of Radicalism for Patriots*. Kenilworth: E. Dilling, 1934. Print.

Eagan, Eileen. *Class, Culture, and Classroom: The Student Peace Movement of the 1930s*. Philadelphia: Temple UP, 1981. Print.

Folsom, Franklin. *Days of Anger, Days of Hope: A Memoir of the League of American Writers, 1937-1942*. Niwot: U Colorado P, 1994. Print.

Freire, Paulo. *Pedagogy of the Oppressed*. Trans. Myra Bergman Ramos. New York: Continuum, 2000. Print.

Gettleman, Marvin E. "The Triumph of Exegesis over Praxis and History." Rev. of *Gramsci and Education*, ed. Carmel Borg, Joseph Buttigieg, and Peter Mayo. *H-Education*. July 2003. *H-Net Reviews*. Web. 17 Aug. 2004. <http://www.h-net.msu.edu/reviews/showrev.cgi?path=112801061285203>.

Gunner, Jeanne. "Doomed to Repeat It?: A Needed Space for Critique in Historical Recovery." *Historical Studies of Writing Program Administration: Individuals, Communities, and the Formation of a Discipline*. Ed. Barbara L'Eplattenier and Lisa Mastrangelo. West Lafayette: Parlor P, 2004. 263-78. Print.

Healey, Dorothy, and Maurice Isserman. *Dorothy Healey Remembers: A Life in the American Communist Party*. New York: Oxford, 1990. Print.

Hicks, Granville. *The Great Tradition: An Interpretation of American Literature since the Civil War*. New York: Macmillan, 1933. Print.

---. *Where We Came Out*. New York: Viking, 1954. Print.

Hoover, J. Edgar. *Masters of Deceit: The Story of Communism in America and How to Fight It*. New York: Henry Holt, 1958. Print.

Horowitz, David. *Indoctrination U.: The Left's War against Academic Freedom*. New York: Encounter, 2007. Print.

---. *The Professors: The 101 Most Dangerous Academics in America*. Washington, D.C.: Regnery, 2006. Print.

Hultzen, Lee S. "Communists on the University Faculty." *The Journal of Higher Education* 21.8 (1950): 423-29. Print.

Iverson, Robert W. *The Communists and the Schools*. New York: Harcourt Brace, 1959. Print.

Jaschik, Scott. "Out of a Job." *Inside Higher Ed*. 6 Aug. 2014. Web. 14 Aug. 2014. <https://www.insidehighered.com/news/2014/08/06/u-illinois-apparently-revokes-job-offer-controversial-scholar>.

Kates, Susan. *Activist Rhetorics and American Higher Education, 1885-1937*. Carbondale: SIUP, 2001. Print.

Kelley, Robin D. G. *Hammer and Hoe: Alabama Communists During the Great Depression*. Chapel Hill: U of North Carolina P, 1990. Print.

Klehr, Harvey. *The Heyday of American Communism: The Depression Decade*. New York: Basic, 1984. Print.

Kopelson, Karen. "Rhetoric on the Edge of Cunning; Or, The Performance of Neutrality (Re)Considered as a Composition Pedagogy for Student Resistance." *CCC* 55.1 (2003): 115-46. Print.

Le Sueur, Meridel. *Crusaders*. New York: Blue Heron, 1955. Print.

Levenson, Leah, and Jerry Natterstad. *Granville Hicks: The Intellectual in Mass Society*. Philadelphia: Temple UP, 1993. Print.

Lyons, Eugene. *The Red Decade: The Stalinist Penetration of America*. New York: Bobbs-Merrill, 1941. Print.

Mandel, William. Personal interview. 20 Sept. 2006.

---. *Saying No to Power: Autobiography of a 20th-Century Activist and Thinker*. Berkeley: Creative Arts, 1999. Print.

Meyer, Frank S. *In Defense of Freedom: A Conservative Credo*. Washington, D.C.: H. Regnery Co., 1962. Print.

---. *The Moulding of Communists: The Training of the Communist Cadre*. New York: Harcourt Brace, 1961. Print.

Miller, Richard E. *As if Learning Mattered: Reforming Higher Education*. Ithaca: Cornell UP, 1998. Print.

---. *Writing at the End of the World*. Pittsburgh: U Pittsburgh P, 2005. Print.
Mishler, Paul C. *Raising Reds: The Young Pioneers, Radical Summer Camps, and Communist Political Culture in the United States*. New York: Columbia UP, 1999. Print.
Ohmann, Richard. *English in America: A Radical View of the Profession*. 1976. Hanover: Wesleyan UP/UP of New England, 1995. Print.
Overstreet, Harry, and Bonaro Overstreet. *What We Must Know about Communism*. New York: Norton, 1958. Print.
Rader, Melvin. *False Witness*. Seattle: U of Washington P, 1969. Print.
Rigelhaupt, Jesse. "'Education for Action': The California Labor School, Radical Unionism, Civil Rights, and Progressive Coalition Building in the San Francisco Bay Area, 1934-1970." Diss. U of Michigan, 2005. Ann Arbor: UMI, 2005. Print.
Roberts, Holland. "The Dangerous School: An Autobiography." 1971. MS. San Francisco State U Labor Archives and Research Center, San Francisco. N. pag.
Rouverol, Jean. *Refugees from Hollywood: A Journal of the Blacklist Years*. Albuquerque: U New Mexico P, 2000. Print.
Schrecker, Ellen W. *The Age of McCarthyism: A Brief History with Documents*. New York: Bedford/St. Martin's, 2002. Print.
---. *No Ivory Tower: McCarthyism and the Universities*. New York: Oxford UP, 1986. Print.
Seymour, Harold. "A Communist in the Classroom: 'Competition for Men's Minds Begins When They Are Students'." *The Journal of Higher Education* 31.7 (Oct. 1960): 369-75. Print.
Staub, Michael E. *Voices of Persuasion: Politics of Representation in 1930s America*. Cambridge: Cambridge UP, 1994. Print.
Stripling, Robert. *The Red Plot Against America*. Drexel: Bell, 1949. Print.
Tenney, Jack. *Red Fascism: Boring from Within by the Subversive Forces of Communism*. Los Angeles: Federal, 1947. Print.
Terkel, Studs. *Coming of Age: The Story of Our Century by Those Who've Lived It*. New York: New P, 1995. Print.
Wald, Alan M. *Writing from the Left: New Essays on Radical Culture and Politics*. New York: Verso, 1994. Print.
Watt, George. *The Comet Connection: Escape from Hitler's Europe*. Lexington: UP of Kentucky, 1990. Print.
"Worst School in America?" *Hannity & Colmes*. FOX News Network. 8 Sep. 2007. *FOX News.com*. Web. 1 June 2010. <https://www.youtube.com/watch?v=9Y676GIDIJI>.

From Story to Analysis: Reflection and Uptake in the Literacy Narrative Assignment

Kara Poe Alexander

The literacy narrative assignment is popular with composition instructors because of the reflection it encourages in students. Previously, scholars have claimed that students demonstrate reflection in literacy narratives when they critique dominant ideologies. Largely absent, however, is research on what other elements might indicate reflection and thus inspire "instructor uptake," defined here as a positive response by an instructor to regard some part of the text as reflection. This essay therefore seeks to discover the core composition features that stimulate instructor uptake by examining what elements instructors identify as reflection in student literacy narratives. Think-aloud protocols were conducted with seven instructors and findings showed that three elements generate instructor uptake: analytical moves of cause-effect and evaluation (69%); vivid, metaphoric language (20%); and ideological critiques (11%). Findings also revealed that when instructors observed ideological critiques as reflection, they were more apt to amplify the reflection for students. These data underscore the need for revamping our literacy narrative pedagogies to more adequately emphasize critical analysis and evaluation rather than ideological critique. By clarifying what composition instructors mean by reflection, we can design equitable writing assignments, begin to defend against our own biases, and foster more democratic classrooms.

The literacy narrative assignment, though certainly not new, has gained in popularity in recent years as more scholarly research on the genre has been conducted and as more composition textbooks have begun to include chapters, readings, and assignments on the genre.[1] In general, the classroom-based literacy narrative assignment asks students to explore and reflect upon their past experiences with language, schooling, education, and/or learning to better understand how these past encounters have formed them into the literate beings they are today. These literacy narratives also attempt to chart the writer's processes (Carpenter and Falbo; Ryden; Scott), reveal what happens when the writer acquires written and/or spoken language (Soliday), and act as sites of "self-translation" (Soliday 511). Literacy narratives are "not simply stories about learning to read and write; they are attempts to define who we are and what we want to become, both as individuals and as a community" (Young 26).

A major commonality in the research and in textbooks is the importance placed on reflection in the assignment. Richard Bullock's chapter on the literacy narrative in *The Norton Field Guide to Writing*; John Trimbur's literacy narrative assignment in *The Call to Write*; and Duane Roen, Gregory R. Glau, and Barry M. Maid's *The McGraw-Hill Guide* are full of injunctions for students to "reflect." Likewise, in *Joining the Conversation*, Mike Palmquist includes two literacy narrative assignments in his chapter "Writing to Reflect," and Thomas Deans' assignment asks students "to adopt a self-reflective posture" (27). Other textbooks imply an expectation for reflection when they ask students to examine the "significance" of their experiences (Kutz; Ramage, Bean, and Johnson; Yagelski).

In addition to textbooks, in their scholarly work, both Wendy Ryden and Stephanie Paterson describe reflection as a major goal and assessment measure of the literacy narrative assignment. Ryden argues that the literacy narrative is a "metacognitive genre" concerned with students' reflections on the process of becoming literate (86). Paterson similarly notes that in literacy narratives, students "reflect both consciously and maybe unconsciously about emotional, intellectual, and social benefits that are accrued through literate practices," and she hopes students will use literacy narratives to "reflectively examine the structures of their [literate] expression" (3). I, too, have found in my own research that reflection is a primary goal of literacy narrative assignments. In a survey I distributed to one hundred instructors who assign literacy narratives, reflection was ranked as the most important purpose of the assignment (out of 10 options) and the second most important evaluation criteria (out of 32 options).[2] In diverse composition circles, then, reflection is viewed as a goal and assessment tool of the school-based literacy narrative assignment.

Reflection is a major goal of the assignment because of the purported outcomes fostered through the process of reflecting, including increased self-awareness as writers, readers, and thinkers (Ryden 85). Scholar-teachers argue that reflection in the literacy narrative can cultivate:

- A greater sense of self-awareness about one's literacy processes and experiences (Brown 403; Carpenter and Falbo 25; Fox 19; Paterson 57-58; Sandman and Weiser 21; Scott 111; Soliday 511; Webb 33; Williams 343).
- Critical analysis of schooling, education, and sanctioned notions of literacy, discourse, identity, and the "literacy myth" (Brown 403; Eldred and Mortensen 513-14; Franzosa 410; Paterson 8-9; Scott 112; Soliday 520; Young 9).

- Examination into social, cultural, and political issues involved in acquiring language (Clark and Medina 69; Eldred and Mortensen 523-24; Pratt 34; S. Rose 245; Young 112).
- Ethnic and cultural understanding and diversity (Brodkey 139; Meyers 4; Soliday 511; Wallace 435-36; Young 7-30).

These outcomes show major potential for the literacy narrative assignment. However, while many scholars view the reflection associated with literacy narratives as accomplishing the goals listed above—noble goals for sure—published research is seldom clear about how teachers can assess reflective content in student products. Reflection, of course, is an internal process of thinking not readily available for examination by others (see Dewey; Higgins, Flower, and Petraglia; Schön; Yancey); it is the process and product "by which we know what we have accomplished and by which we articulate accomplishment" (Yancey 6). Thus, there is no way an instructor can know for certain whether or not a student actually reflected in the process of completing an assignment. Yet, in evaluating essays for evidence of reflection, instructors imply that some manifestations of this internal process can be identified and measured. But what exactly are these manifestations? Our textbooks suggest that a good literacy narrative requires "a well-told story," "vivid detail," and "some indication of the narrative's significance" (Bullock; Lunsford, et al.). This last criterion in particular seems related to reflection, but it can also lead students to produce clichéd life lessons that are not particularly reflective. In fact, recent research on the dominance of the success master narrative in student writing—where literacy is some kind of panacea—supports this conclusion (see Alexander; Carpenter and Falbo; Fox; Williams) and might preclude the kind of critical reflection that scholars such as J. Blake Scott, Mary Soliday, and Morris Young claim the literacy narrative assignment fosters. In short, although evidence indicates that teachers value reflection in the literacy narrative assignment and agree that it is a goal worth pursuing, research is less clear on how instructors in their actual practice of reading student writing recognize reflection when they see it.

One way to examine this question of how instructors characterize reflection is through the lens of uptake. Uptake is a concept used in genre theory that accounts for the response a certain genre generates when it moves and mediates between texts and utterances (Bawarshi; Freadman), thereby defining, coordinating, and sanctioning the genre (Bawarshi 653). Uptake does not naturally occur as a result of writing in a specific genre but instead occurs when genres are taken up, or translated, across boundaries (Freadman 43). Uptake thus relies on selection and response—the selection of material that makes it appropriate to the rhetorical situation and the response from an interpreter that reacts to it (Freadman 48). Uptake also depends in large part on memory and translation (Bawarshi; Freadman; Kill). Memory is important in that prior experience informs the understanding "of what to take up, how and when," and translation is significant because it is the principle device through which genres move (Bawarshi 653), thus stimulating certain responses. In sum, uptake is a "a deeply intertextual space that not only translates new genres from memories and repertoires of genre knowledge, but also folds that translation into what is meaningful within that current repertoire through active knowledge construction" (Rounsaville).

When viewed through the frame of uptake, the literacy narrative can be said to produce "instructor uptake" when an instructor evaluates the text or parts of the text as reflection based on what he/she views as reflective writing, thus confirming, altering, or denying the uptake. We might then ask: What are the generic elements of reflection in the school-based literacy narrative that will produce the desired uptake in the reader/instructor?

Published research on literacy narratives indicates that instructors characterize reflection as ideological critiques (e.g., Anderson; Clark and Medina; Paterson; Soliday; Webb; Young). Janet C. Eldred and Peter Mortensen, for instance, connect reflection to critiques of the "literacy myth,"[3] and J. Blake Scott views reflection as critique of the individualist ideology that leads to an emphasis on "the social relatedness of language" (112). This view of reflection as ideological critique has even been said to be particularly beneficial for racially and socioeconomically disadvantaged students. For these students, critiquing prevailing ideologies empowers them to transform literacy for their own purposes and to resist and revise dominant narratives on literacy, race, and education (Ferretti; Fox; Green; Reid). As an example, Soliday finds through her case study of one African-American student, Alisha, that minority students often use literacy narratives to navigate between language worlds and to "perform imaginative acts of self-representation" (522). She argues that assigning literacy narratives can "enhance [students'] personal success as writers in the university […], deepen their teachers' understanding of difference, and shape responses to today's competing versions of multiculturalism" (522), thus leading to more multicultural and democratic classrooms. In addition, Eileen Ferretti argues that literacy narratives can be beneficial for working-class students because they "illuminate the unique cultural conflicts of upwardly-mobile working-class students" (70-71) and "provide critical insights about [students'] gendered/classed position and its relation to issues of culture and social class" (84). These examples demonstrate that ideological critiques would produce desired instructor uptake in terms of reflection.

Research on the working class, however, also indicates that working-class students might be less equipped to make the kinds of ideological reflections that instructors value. Scholars have found, for instance, that working-class students often have difficulty negotiating the codes and language of the academy (Giroux; Marinara; Nagle; Pratt) and have to "invent" the university (Bartholomae). A growing body of research therefore argues for the explicit teaching of ideological values to working-class students in order to prepare and equip such students to be successful in college and beyond (see Adler-Kassner 99-105; Brooks 9, 12; Green 18-19; Royster 221).

Other than ideological critiques, however, we do not yet know what additional elements might produce such instructor uptake. This project is therefore a study based on the concept of instructor uptake. Specifically, I look for elements in student literacy narratives that produce the desired uptake in instructors—in this case, the instructor evaluating the text as "reflective." This question of the generic elements of reflection in the literacy narrative is important because the answer can help us better teach the literacy narrative genre and design fair assignments. This study may also reveal important insights about ourselves as the discourse community of instructors who are the primary audiences for this genre. Furthermore, this project helps us recognize that when we ask our students to reflect, we may in fact be asking them to perform particular subjectivities that they may or may not be prepared (or willing) to perform. In fact, certain power dynamics and personal biases might need to be accounted for when we ask for reflection, including what we assume our students know and do not know, our own positionality, and our willingness to engage our students' positions (see Caywood and Overing; Haswell and Haswell). When we understand what produces the desired instructor uptake for reflection, we can then reveal this to our students so they can be more equipped to meet the goals we set for them. The absence of specific criteria for what we mean by reflection in the literacy narrative is potentially unfair to students who do not have the educational background or the prior knowledge or experience to understand what reflection means or how to meet this goal in their writing (Bawarshi; Kill). Ultimately, I hope to lay a framework for others to investigate how literacy narratives are being taught in the classroom and what potential biases instructors might bring to the responding and evaluating of student texts. Since genres carry with them ideological values that instructors may not fully recognize (see Beebee; Coe, Lingard, and Teslenko; Devitt), by using literacy narratives more carefully and by clarifying what constitutes reflection in this genre we can design equitable writing assignments that enable students from all backgrounds to understand and meet our goals for reflective writing.

It is important to note that it is not my intention to examine whether or not students actually reflect (which we can never truly know); instead, my aim through this project is to determine what specific elements of the school-based literacy narrative genre instructors view as reflection. By doing this, we can come to a better understanding of the generic features of the literacy narrative and the aspects of reflection that lead to instructor uptake.

Methods of Instructor Analysis of Reflection

To obtain a closer look at what reflective elements in student literacy narratives generate instructor uptake, I conducted think-aloud protocols with seven composition instructors from a large Midwestern university where approximately 55% of first-year writing sections assigned the genre.[4] All instructors had previously assigned the literacy narrative genre at least four times, and all of them viewed reflection as an important component of the assignment. This value of reflection was evidenced from their responses to the aforementioned survey that I distributed to one hundred composition instructors prior to participation in the protocols. In this survey examining why instructors assign the literacy narrative genre, six of the respondents ranked reflection as both the most important purpose of and the main assessment criteria for the literacy narrative assignment (Parts II and III); one ranked it second in both instances. Instructors participating in the think alouds varied by age (ranging from 24 years of age to over 55) and teaching experience (from 2 to 23 years), with the average teaching time being 7 years. Three of the instructors were graduate students, two were full-time lecturers, and two were tenured faculty. Coincidentally, all instructors were white females.

To permit observation of the instructors' immediate processing of reflection as it was embedded within the student essays, instructors were asked to "think aloud by saying whatever pops into their mind" and to "underline passages that suggest reflection by marking the smallest unit possible of the reflective moment (i.e., a word, a phrase, a sentence, or an entire paragraph)." Eleven essays were randomly selected from a larger sample of sixty for use in the think alouds.[5] Each essay was read by two instructors, and each instructor read at least two essays, spending between 35 to 45 minutes on each. Instructors did not read their own students' work. Instructors were also given a copy of the original instructor assignment that went with each essay to provide some context. I remained silent during the sessions, except when I needed to prompt the participant to think aloud. Afterwards, instructors took part in a brief follow-up interview. The think alouds and interviews were audio-taped and transcribed.[6]

I coded the eleven literacy narratives used in the think alouds five times. First, each essay was coded into "episodes" that represented a paragraph unit with a recognizable beginning, middle, and end (see Barton and Hamilton; Marshall, Smagorinsky, and Smith). The eleven essays contained 320 episodes. Second, each episode was coded to see how often students invoke each of three ideological values frequently discussed in published scholarship on literacy:

literacy equals success, anti-academic appeals, and literacy as a shared activity (see Table 1).[7]

Table 1: Coding Scheme for Ideological Critique Invoked

Ideological Value Invoked (Published scholars who discuss value)	**Description of Value**
Literacy Equals Success (Alexander; Carpenter and Falbo; Eldred and Mortensen; Fox; Paterson; Ryden; Williams)	The notion that literacy leads to success, progress, and upward mobility and that it can ultimately transform lives and society.
Anti-Academic Appeals (Clark and Medina; Eldred and Mortensen; Fox; Paterson; M. Rose; Scott; Soliday; Webb; Young)	Critiques of academia, standardized testing, and school-based reading and writing practices and pedagogies.
Literacy as a Shared Activity (Chandler; Clark and Medina; Eldred and Mortensen; Sandman and Weiser; Selfe and Hawisher; S. Rose; Scott; Soliday; Webb; Young)	The idea that literacy is a social, relational, and communal occurrence where many people and factors influence one's literacy development.

Third, I marked whether an instructor noted an episode as "having reflection" or "not having reflection." Fourth, I assigned each episode a "proportional reflection score," which considered what percentage of the episode the instructor underlined as reflection.[8] Finally, I coded each episode according to the reason instructors gave for marking the text as reflection. Through grounded theory analysis (see Glaser and Strauss), I classified their reasons into three broad categories:

1. Logical, analytic moves (cause/effect and evaluation)
2. Metaphoric language (vivid, evocative, or metaphoric language)
3. Ideological critiques (mentioning of values or inserting critiques)

If the instructor noted more than one of these reasons for underlining a single episode as reflection, it was coded accordingly.[9]

Generic Elements of Reflection and Instructor Uptake

Results from the seven think-aloud protocols show that three specific elements generate instructor uptake: analytical reasoning moves of cause-effect and evaluation (69%); vivid, metaphoric language (20%); and ideological critiques (11%).[10] While instructors in this study define reflection as ideological critiques—as previous research indicated (i.e., Clark and Medina; Paterson;

Soliday; Webb; Young)—these critiques were not the primary ways instructors defined reflection in student writing. Instead, instructors mostly viewed logical, analytical moves as reflection, which means that this composition feature produces the greatest instructor uptake. These findings are important because they can help instructors design equitable writing assignments that allow all students to successfully meet the goal of reflection.

Logical, Analytic Structure as Reflection

By and large, this research suggests that in their evaluation of reflection in the literacy narrative genre, the logical, analytic structure of the text was the primary element that indicated reflection and thus led to instructor uptake. In fact, over two-thirds of the time instructors cited reflection, they noted the logical structure. Many instructors mentioned that they would not have been able to characterize reflection in this way beforehand but, after looking for evidence of reflection in the context of student writing, they came to this conclusion.

Causal and evaluative elements are the two primary logical moves that led to instructor uptake. The following comment by instructor Sarah emphasizes this point: "Cause-effect statements signify reflection because they indicate an examining of circumstances and then drawing conclusions from them. Also, evaluating a past event means reflection because you have to think about how something has influenced you."

Cause-Effect Moves

Instructors perceive cause-effect statements as evidence of reflection. All instructors mentioned cause-effect multiple times and viewed it as an important component of reflection, making it the number-one cited composition element that leads to instructor uptake. Take the instructors' responses to Lisa's episode as an example. Lisa writes,[11]

> Entering the confusing days of middle school, I was no longer given the opportunity to choose the books I read, so I slowly had to say goodbye to the page-turning days of *The Babysitters Club*, *The Boxcar Children*, and *Goosebumps*. Books for social studies, math, and English all took their place, and <u>as they did, my interest in furthering my literacy diminished</u>.

Both instructors underlined the last phrase as reflection. Instructor Becky claimed, "This student is connecting the curricular change to her diminished love of reading. That's cause-effect. That's reflection." Likewise, instructor

Kelly noted the causal elements as reflection because "the student is critiquing and interpreting old feelings about past events from a present perspective."

Another student wrote about how her cousins made fun of her because of a speech problem that prevented her from correctly pronouncing the letter "r." The student wrote, "<u>I never really enjoyed reading out loud in class until I started seeing a special teacher for my problem.</u>" One instructor commented, "She's reflecting on the fact that the speech impediment caused her to not really enjoy reading out loud in class." This instructor equated reflection to the student's clear explanation of the problem (or cause) and the resulting consequences (or effects) and commented later that this instance "indicated a sort of drawing together, of making connections." The other instructor who read this student's text also viewed the cause-effect inference as reflection, claiming, "She realizes the root of one of her attitudes. She doesn't just say, 'I never enjoyed reading out loud in class.' Instead, she says, 'I never enjoyed reading because,' which, to me, is a clear indicator of reflection." Several other instructors noted reflection in phrases that linked causes to effects, such as "Consequently," "Due to these experiences," or "Although I didn't realize it at the time."

In sum, cause-effect performances clearly led to instructor uptake in definitions of reflection. Trisha's response sums it up nicely: "To me, cause-effect statements are reflective. I don't know that I could have articulated it before, but that's obviously one of my criteria for reflection. Explaining past events and including strong cause-effect statements amounts to reflection for me."

Evaluation

In addition to cause-effect sentence structures leading to instructor uptake, evaluation—or when students drew conclusions or generalized from their experiences—also signified reflection to instructors. Instructors were particularly apt to cite evaluation as reflection when it was tied to the cause-effect structure: writing about the cause led to the effect, which, in turn, resulted in an evaluation of the event. In the following example, both instructors who read Matt's essay appreciated how he evaluates the reasons he does not enjoy reading and noted the last two sentences as reflection. Matt writes:

> Teachers always chose the books we read. Usually these novels depicted the tale of a child undergoing difficult circumstances—stories that left me so depressed I wanted to scream at the teacher for making me read them. <u>Because of such reading assignments, reading a book has always seemed to me a chore and strictly school related. Thus, today I have no desire to read a book that hasn't been assigned by a class in school.</u>

Instructor Julie explains why she marked these passages as reflection: "The student is generalizing and making evaluations. It's reflection in that he's re-evaluating the event now." Instructor Sarah similarly notes, "The student is drawing conclusions and evaluating, reflecting in the sense of evaluating this event today, having a new perspective today on something that happened to him in the past and thinking about the event in a different way today." The student's evaluation is closely tied to the preceding causal clause, which led to the desired instructor uptake.

Instructors also viewed evaluative moments as reflection if the evaluative move appeared to "sum up" experiences. Jeremy, for instance, incorporates a summing-up statement into his conclusion: "Luckily, the joys that reading offered prevailed in the end after being burned out by reading so much literature that didn't interest me." Michelle viewed the entire sentence as reflection, remarking that the sentence is "racking up in the reflective kind of way"—good evidence that instructors perceive the summing-up function of evaluation as reflection.

Overall, these examples demonstrate that instructors equate logical, analytic elements to their assessments of reflection in student literacy narratives. Particularly, they regard as reflection cause-effect sentence structures and evaluative, summing-up moves.

Metaphoric Language as Reflection

Even though logical, analytical elements are what produced the greatest instructor uptake in terms of reflection within student writing (69%), two other features also led to instructor uptake but to a much lesser extent: metaphoric language (20%) and ideological critiques (11%). Twenty percent of the time instructors marked a passage as reflection because of the language students invoked, which may not be surprising given the literacy narrative is a personal writing genre. Instructors often noted expressive words, such as "neglected," "haunted," "cowered," and "annoying," as reflection. In one instance, student Rachel incorporates vivid words to describe negative experiences with college. She writes: "After a year of breezing through classes in high school, college came as a brick wall—I couldn't go through it, under it or around it. Reading and writing were daily tasks to maintain and I was used to them on a bi-weekly basis. I didn't know what to do." The instructor responded that she particularly liked the phrase "brick wall—I couldn't go through it, under it or around it" and states, "The descriptive language this writer uses creates an evocative moment that is stronger than just recounting the event." Here, poignant language caused instructor uptake.

In addition to vivid descriptive elements, instructors also defined reflection as emotional accounts that encourage, according to one instructor, "visceral" responses. One instructor viewed Jocelyn's narrative as reflection specifically for such a reason: "The new way of writing I was learning bothered me. It always felt like someone was forcing me to write their way and if it wasn't the way they wanted it to be, it was incorrect. But my main question was how? How can you tell me what I'm writing is wrong? It is my opinion; it's what I think." Instructor Trisha marked the emotional content in this passage as reflection ("bothered me," "felt like," "forcing") because "they are emotionally-charged words." She also underlined the rhetorical questions this student poses because of "the emotion these questions evoke" in the reader. Trisha's assessment demonstrates that evocative, emotional words are clear signs of reflection that lead to instructor uptake.

Instructors also viewed reflection as metaphor, particularly the "journey towards literacy brings success" motif in which students detailed how their experiences with literacy have brought them success and accomplishment. In the introduction to her essay, student Rachel incorporates this journey metaphor:

> Literacy for me is not a destination, but a journey that began earlier than my memories and hopefully will never end. My journey can be compared to an uphill hike. There are no times during this journey that I ever regress, but some instances weren't as steep as others. It is in those steeper moments that a sponsor has impacted my reading and writing. Combining the experiences […] will best explain my literacy journey.

Both instructors who read Rachel's essay underlined this entire episode as reflection. Instructor Julie remarked, "Journey is a word I associate with reflection, and I guess I associate reflection with metaphor, especially personal journey metaphors." Even though this metaphor is a common cliché in literacy narrative scholarship, it produced the desired instructor uptake: instructors in fact viewed this moment as "strong reflection." In short, vivid, descriptive, and metaphoric language produces instructor uptake.

Ideological Critiques as Reflection

Ideological critiques also led to instructor uptake within this study, which confirms the published research stating that reflection in literacy narratives equals ideological critiques. However, ideological critiques were not marked as often as we might suppose. In fact, out of everything instructors marked as reflection, ideological critiques were only given as the reason 11% of the time (a significant difference). This composition feature did not lead to instructor uptake as much as the other two categories.

Instructors equated reflection with three ideological critiques incorporated into their literacy narratives: anti-academic appeals, literacy as a shared activity, and literacy equals success. In response to these value critiques, instructors often made comments, such as "Yes, definitely," "I agree," or "I feel that way, too." One instructor even stated the following about a student's essay: "Those sentences are reflective. I definitely agree. Nice. Very nice." These comments suggest that instructors equate reflection with certain ideological critiques and, often, ones with which they tended to agree. Table 2 shows that all ideological critiques were seen as reflective a large percentage of the time and that anti-academic appeals produced the most instructor uptake.

Table 2: Reflection Level of Ideological Critique

Value	% of Episodes Marked as Reflection n=320	Proportional Reflection Score
Anti-Academic Appeals	78%	1.32
Literacy as a Shared Activity	75%	0.93
Literacy Equals Success	69%	0.87

Anti-Academic Appeals

Critiques of school-based literacy practices—or what I am calling "anti-academic appeals"—generated the most instructor uptake for what counts as reflection. Anti-academic appeals were marked as reflection over three-fourths of the time (78%) and carried an extremely high proportional reflection score (1.32; i.e., instructors underlined more than half the episode as reflection). The most common anti-academic appeals were aimed at school-based literacy practices, such as "required" reading and writing, Accelerated Reader, book reports, research papers, and academic writing.

Some readers might at first think that anti-academic appeals contradict instructor values because of this value's negative assessment of academic literacy practices. While it is possible that teachers might feel allegiance to schooling and the pedagogical practices employed there, research also shows that teachers equate these kinds of moves with reflection (e.g., Paterson; Soliday). In fact, some scholars are invested in seeing traditional school assignments and current-traditional pedagogies as stifling, painful, constraining, or outdated (see Bizzell, Schroeder, and Fox; Selfe). Colin Lankshear, for instance, critiques dominant school-based literacy because it "undermines independent thought" and "create[s] logical hierarchies" that become naturalized through ideological discourses (5). In addition, many of the most popular published literacy narratives contain similar anti-academic appeals (e.g., Gilyard; M. Rose; Villanueva). Anti-academic appeals thus seem valued as legitimate critiques in literacy narratives.

Instructor Michelle greatly values these critiques. In her response to Kristy's literacy narrative, she clearly equates anti-academic appeals to reflection. The student wrote: "I still continue to love to write, but <u>my aspirations to become a writer drifted after starting high school for the simple reason that I felt like I couldn't really write what I wanted to write.</u> I <u>had</u> to write about <u>what was assigned.</u> I couldn't just <u>let my mind go free. The required course materials are what tore down my love for writing</u>." Though this episode contains both analytical and literary elements that typically produced instructor uptake, Michelle does not mention these elements. Instead, she responds to the critique of academic writing and views the episode as reflection because of the perspective offered:

> I think this situation would be common for students since, in my opinion, school kind of kills our creativity, and this person felt the same way. She wanted to be a writer, but maybe, as she advanced through the school system, wasn't told that it was a practical occupation and lost her desire to become a writer. What I'm underlining as reflection are the instances where this student highlights specific things that tore down her love for writing.

We might even surmise that Michelle focuses on the student's anti-academic account rather than the logical move or the vivid language because she agrees with the position expressed. In this case, the student effectively plays to this instructor's desires to see traditional school writing as stifling, even though the student did not know Michelle or her ideological leanings. In short, incorporating an anti-academic viewpoint challenged the cultural notion of the literacy myth and thus led to instructor uptake.

Literacy as a Shared Activity

Appeals to the belief in literacy as a shared activity, or the notion that literacy is a social occurrence influenced by diverse factors and people, also generated instructor uptake. This ideological value was marked as reflection three-fourths of the time and also carried a high proportional reflection score (0.93). This value appeal produced instructor uptake when students incorporated social commentary or explored how they were part of a "global community." Instructors singled out phrases such as "togetherness," "openness," "community," and "diversity," all values highly regarded in composition studies.

Instructor Nina marked the following in Terrence's paper as reflection: "<u>I attended a debate institute at my school and this was my turning point. I finally had a teacher who would allow me to rebel, but also taught me how to 'play school.' She gave me the tools to be an independent thinker</u> but operate in the "norms" of school." Nina responded:

> I think this student is smart. He understands that school is a game, a social game in a sense, where his teacher has influenced him. It is not necessarily always about learning the things you think you should be learning but rather learning how to be a student, learning how to be a learner. And debate is a structured and rigorous activity, and the student is acknowledging, reflecting on, how that's what school is as well. I think that's a key moment of reflection.

Nina's remarks indicate that she equates reflection to this student's ideological critique of literacy as a shared activity. Her comment, "It is not necessarily always about learning," implies that she agrees with Terrence's position expressed.

Literacy Equals Success

Instructors also regarded literacy-equals-success appeals as reflection but somewhat less often than they did the other two critiques (Table 2). Still, this ideological appeal led to instructor uptake almost three-fourths of the time (69%) and carried a relatively high proportional reflection score (0.87). This ideological critique might have appealed to instructors because it promotes many of the same beliefs writing instructors hold about literacy and education. Although we want students to question the notion that literacy leads to success, as many advocates of the literacy narrative assignment have pointed out, we still believe that literacy and education matter. We want students to become literate, get an education, and use their knowledge and learning to change the world, which might be why this ideological value generated instructor uptake.

Instructor Cheryl, for instance, views the literacy-as-success part of Laura's episode as reflection. Laura writes, "Throughout my four years, I grew more confident by building upon my literacy skills, even though it was through countless essays that were forced out of me, and reading books that were far less appealing than [books I read as a kid]. <u>It all benefited me in the end.</u>" Cheryl commented, "What I underlined is reflection in that it's reflecting on how all of it put together worked together to benefit this student, as literacy can do for people, although it doesn't go into reflection. It just kind of gives us a broad statement." Although Cheryl remarks that the final sentence "doesn't go into reflection," she still marks it as reflection perhaps because of the ideological value expressed in this student's essay.

Amplifying Reflection in Ideological Critiques

That instructors equate reflection with ideological critiques is not surprising; we can never truly escape ourselves as we read. Also, proponents of reflection tend to want to see certain ideological critiques in student writing. Nevertheless, it is interesting that instructors in this study were more apt to amplify and infer the reflection for students in ideological critiques, especially when the analytic structure—which was most often the main determinant of reflection—was weak or underdeveloped. These amplification inferences were most obvious in anti-academic appeals and literacy as a shared activity appeals.

One example of how instructors amplified anti-academic appeals can be seen in Michelle's response to Kristy. In the following episode, Kristy expresses nostalgia for the time when writing was not mandatory and instead creative and imaginative: "Writing is something I enjoy doing when I get the time. I would love to be able to just sit down somewhere quiet and write; get back to my childhood imagination. However, writing for me can be very difficult now that I am in college and have grown up." Instructor Michelle viewed the last two sentences as reflection and asserted,

> This person is working within these boundaries of school writing, and she's able to be successful, but I'm not sure she gets pleasure out of it except for the fact that she's making good grades, so she gets extrinsic pleasure from that but not really intrinsic pleasure from the writing. She's forced to write for teachers, but she really desires to write for herself and what's important to her. [...] She must want to be a creative writer and perhaps she could have been if that desire was fostered a little more.

Note how much Michelle amplifies the analytic moves for the student in her response to the reflection in the text. She even contends that the student wants to be a creative writer because of the expressed desire to return to her "childhood imagination." Michelle seems to infer reflection and elaborate on this reflection because of this student's critique of academic writing. While Michelle's inferences are not farfetched, the assumptions she makes about the student's experiences go beyond what is actually written in the text, a point evident in her remark that "school kind of kills our creativity." The fact that Michelle augmented the reflection for the student perhaps suggests that she wanted this part of the student's essay to be reflective because she agreed with the point the student was trying to make. Had Michelle disagreed with this student's perspective we might infer that she would have been less likely to find reflection or to amplify "weak" reflection. The anti-academic appeals expressed in student papers thus earned them even more cultural capital with instructors.

Another example involves an instructor's amplifying of a student's use of the shared literacy appeal. Heather writes, "<u>To me, writing is another language, a language we all have to know in order to survive in the world.</u>" This student's words point to a joint community of literate beings. The two instructors who read her text both viewed the episode as reflection yet regarded it incomplete because the student did not offer evidence or support for the claim. Instructor Ashley remarked, "If only she had qualified it better here and throughout the paper because right now it's pretty difficult to read. I don't know what it really means to her because she didn't really express it in the paper." Although the instructor views the logical claims as weak and insufficient, she stresses the potential of the passage and marks it as reflection because of the ideological values embedded: "That is the best sentence in terms of reflection and reflective writing that I have encountered. This is where the community idea comes in—having to function in a certain type of world, in a certain community." The instructor evidently agreed with the viewpoint of this student, even though the passage is insufficiently explained. In sum, although ideological critiques did not produce instructor uptake as often as the other two elements, when ideological critiques were incorporated, instructors amplified the reflection, which led to greater instructor uptake than perhaps otherwise would have been had a different viewpoint been expressed. This finding points to some problems with the equating of reflection to ideological critiques.

Implications

The studied instructors have clear ideas as to what composition features students can incorporate into their literacy narratives to generate instructor uptake and thus meet the goal of reflection: cause-effect and evaluation; vivid, descriptive, and metaphoric language; and ideological critiques. In fact, this assignment can provide students with a wonderful opportunity to learn these highly complex rhetorical moves. Yet we must take greater care in how we structure reflection in the context of the literacy narrative. If we continue to teach the school-based literacy narrative assignment and to value reflection, we need to better articulate our goals and definitions of reflection to ourselves and to our students. We should also reveal to students how they can best meet the reflective goals instructors set by highlighting these generic elements of reflection.

In addition, we need to be more cautious in how we structure the assignment by spending more time explaining for students what exactly reflection means in practice. When we do not reveal our goals, purposes, and evaluation criteria to students, our goals for a democratic classroom may be jeopardized (see Faigley; Marinara). In fact, minority students might be further marginalized: certain privileged students might have been schooled in certain values and ideologies and thus know the payoff for invoking the victim, rebel, or hero narrative (see Alexander), while others may not understand the discourse or that instructors find such critiques worthwhile. Although the purported goal of assignments such as the literacy narrative is to be inclusive and equitable, we risk excluding students who do not share our values and thereby marginalize students who are already in such positions. Though we want to be careful not to advocate a specific formula that will lead to artificial reflective responses by students, when we reveal what we mean by reflection (and any other goals we have for writing), we provide students with concrete strategies for being successful writers. Then, our classrooms become more democratic and we ensure that all students are given the opportunity to succeed.

This study also shows that instructors need to look more carefully at how our own ideological stances might impact our reading and evaluation of student texts. Although ideological critiques were not associated with reflection as often as other elements, results do suggest that instructors equate reflection with certain values they themselves hold. In such cases, the instructors often overlooked the reflective analytical structure and instead viewed the ideological content as reflection, even amplifying the connections. While many of us share the same values favored by the teachers in this study and recognize that we bring our own opinions and experiences into the reading and evaluation of student texts, we do hope that we are fair and recognize the potential of many kinds of value appeals to indicate reflection—regardless of whether we agree with them or not. If we are truly to foster a democratic classroom, we need to further interrogate and reflect on our own privileged subject positions to ensure that we are being as impartial as possible in our responses to student texts and in our design of assignments. When we do this, we can make writing assignments more equitable and begin to defend against our own biases in the classroom.

Pedagogical Recommendations

These data underscore the need for revamping our literacy narrative pedagogies. Although this study outlines three ways that students can meet the instructor goal of reflection, the literacy narrative assignments and invention questions I have collected over the years (in textbooks, online, and from instructors in this study) rarely mention analytical moves as features of reflection. In fact, my analyses of instructor and textbook assignments find broad, somewhat vague prompts asking students to "explore and reflect on [their] experiences with language and literacy" or to "tell a story about how [they] learned to read and write." Most assignments fail to explain the specific, concrete moves students should make or what these moves might look like in practice, as I am arguing for here, nor do they include thought-provoking questions about the impact and effects of their experiences. Although some assignments do ask students to examine the "significance" of their experiences or to reflect on the event from a present perspective (prompts that are also vague for underprepared students), most assignments and the accompanying invention activities prioritize generating and culling memories rather than analyzing, evaluating, or thinking more deeply about the impact of their literacy practices and the values at work in their lives. The invention questions available on the Digital Archive of Literacy Narratives (DALN), for instance, contain three pages of memory-inducing questions but very few questions that ask students to make meaning out of these events.[12] While questions that trigger memories can be a productive exercise in leading students to remember events, such questions place too much emphasis on the literacy story itself and not enough on the critical and analytical reflection that generates the most instructor uptake. It thus seems that the design of assignments and the types of invention questions we ask may not be consistent with what instructors really value in literacy narrative assignments. We should therefore restructure the literacy narrative assignment, invention questions, and instruction leading up to the writing of this essay to make plain that when we ask students for reflection, we are looking for the composition elements outlined here. I end this essay by offering recommendations on how we can revise and expand our pedagogies on the literacy narrative assignment.

Revised literacy narrative assignments should include specific questions that lead students to consider, reflect on, and incorporate the generic elements of reflection that led to instructor uptake in this study. Assignments could explicitly ask students to include both causes *and* effects of moments in their literacy lives and to make evaluations by assessing, generalizing, and summing up. At a simple level, assignments might explicitly state, "Give both the cause and the effect of these events," or "Explore the implications of the memory/ies (e.g., why you are including this story/ies, why it matters to you, what effects it had on you, what can be learned from it)." Assignments might also encourage students to write about multiple events rather than a single event as is typical in many current assignments. Students could therefore synthesize and bring experiences together rather than view them so discretely.

In addition to revising the assignment, class instruction might also include exercises on rhetorical pattern practice or sentence combining (see Wolfe, Britt, and Alexander) that could assist students as they make decisions about the effects of these experiences or what these experiences mean to them. Instructors could even ask students to brainstorm memories and then list as many effects or outcomes of that story as possible. Another idea to assist students in reflecting on causes and effects is to ask students to create a literacy timeline or literacy map where they situate their memory/ies within a historical and cultural time period. These pedagogical activities would no doubt develop critical-thinking skills and improve rhetorical and analytical writing.

Current literacy narrative assignments already call for students to include vivid detail and description. What the instructor responses here add is that personal journey metaphors are also seen as reflection and lead to instructor uptake. Instructors might therefore engage students in discussions on metaphor, particularly journey metaphors, and how and why metaphor might function as reflection. Instructors could highlight journey metaphors in exemplary essays to demonstrate rhetorical and reflective effectiveness, or they could teach students how to tie metaphors into the logical structure of writing so that the metaphor draws even greater attention to the analytical structure and makes the essay seem even more reflective. Another idea is to ask students to find a visual image that could serve as a metaphoric anchor for the entire essay. Using figurative devices such as metaphor would lead to well-told stories that engender the desired instructor uptake and meet our reflective goals.

The assignment could be further expanded so that the types of reflective ideological critiques we value are made more evident to students. For instance, if we see it as a particular goal of literacy narratives for students to examine and reflect upon certain ideological positions, we could explicitly discuss such values and ask students to articulate how events in their literacy lives lead them to embrace, reject, or appropriate these values. This approach might help students look at their own experiences through different frameworks and, through reflection, come to greater understandings of their own literacy paths. This strategy would also benefit those students who may not understand these values, whose experiences do not align with the values, or who do not want to perform such critiques in the first place. It would also help instructors recognize that certain structures of class are being supported that we might not otherwise see. Additionally, instructors could engage the class in discussions on dominant and subdominant literacy values in our culture and invite students to use their personal literacy stories as a way to critique these values. Another strategy might be for instructors to encourage students to conduct rhetorical analyses of their audiences to determine what types of ideological critiques might be valued by these audiences and what kinds of writing might lead to uptake in the reader. Instructors could also assign literacy narratives by former students instead of, or in addition to, exemplary literacy narratives so students could concretely see and examine the ideological critiques made by the author and assess whether or not the writer was successful. These strategies are beneficial because they teach students about audience, instructor expectations, and literacy, yet they also encourage instructors to reflect on our positions in the classroom and the potential biases we might bring to our readings of student writing. If uptake is explicitly connected to memory (prior knowledge and experience), then laying bare what ideological critiques we value will better equip working-class and nontraditional students to perform the kinds of reflection we expect in this genre.

In addition to revising the assignment and expanding class instruction on the genre, we should also revise the invention activities that lead up to writing the literacy narrative. Instead of presenting students with invention prompts focused on culling memories and remembering past events, we should offer prompts and create heuristics that lead students to ponder the results and effects of their past experiences with language and to consider more critically the questions about which we would like students to respond in their essays. Few assignments I analyzed provided analytical, metacognitive questions. Most, in fact, solely focused on getting students to remember events.[13] We should, therefore, expand our invention questions to do both—(1) generate a memory (story) and (2) analyze and evaluate the effects (reflection). Instead of only asking, "Do you remember any favorite books you read at school?" we might also ask, "Why was this book your favorite? What about it was important to you at the time? What impact does it have on you now? How have the book's values impacted your views on language, reading, or writing?" Moreover, in addition to asking, "When and how did you learn to read and write?" we might also ask, "What did learning to read and write bring to you? What does it give you now? What values did the people who taught you to read and write hold? Do you share those values? How does the manner in which you learned to read and write influence you today? How might learning to read and write be compared to some other activity that you learn to do? What was at stake for your literacy sponsors?" These reflective questions encourage students not just to remember but also to critically examine and reflect on a memory's significance for their lives. Questions such as these will move students beyond mere memory to the quality reflection that the assignment is capable of producing. Ultimately, metalinguistic invention prompts and heuristics signify to students that instructors value analysis and evaluation (more than description), which might make fulfilling instructor goals more accessible for some students (see both Bruce McComiskey and Nancy DeJoy for useful heuristic models and invention strategies).

In addition to revising the questions themselves, we might also revise the way we organize invention questions. Inventions questions for these assignments are typically divided by age (preschool, elementary, junior high, etc.), a format that privileges discrete literacy event(s) rather than synthesis, connection, or comparison; this format also visually hides the connections between moments and might unintentionally prevent students from considering how literacy events work together. We could, therefore, revise our organization by grouping questions topically, thematically, or according to the values they represent. This method might encourage students during the invention stage to synthesize and blend rather than solely describe or tell. We might then ask: "Who are some of the people, institutions, or experiences in your life that have acted as literacy sponsors? How have they sponsored you? What did you/they gain? What do you think of them now?" Or, "What are your feelings about reading and writing? Where do you think your feelings came from? What in your past made you the writer/reader you are today?" We could also encourage students to consider various domains of literacy: sibling, family, religious, school, technological, social, or media literacies. This focus on a theme or domain might encourage students to make connections across ages and topics. Not only would these kinds of literacy narrative responses meet instructor uptake for reflection, but they might also provide deeper resonance for students in making sense of literacy in their lives.

These findings also emphasize potential problems with the assignment itself. If, as these findings show, instructors primarily want students to reflect in analytical and evaluative ways, then we should consider revising the parameters of the assignment so that it better signals these goals. Perhaps instead of asking for reflection, then, we could ask for cause-effect narratives, narratives structured around a metaphor, or a "literacy analysis." We could even substitute the goal of "reflection" for one of argument, reasoning, or critique. The literacy narrative might even move away from the narrative form to one that is more multimodal or thesis-driven, which might prove a more transparent and inclusive aim than reflection. Thus, instead of evaluating the experiences the student has (or has not) had, we are evaluating their ability to reason persuasively and use rhetoric effectively. Future research might examine and theorize new possibilities for the genre, perhaps evaluating how student writing or instructor uptake shifts depending on the parameters of the assignment or by creating a new assignment all together.

In conclusion, emphasizing the generic elements of reflection through assignment design and class instruction not only helps students learn how to successfully meet the goal of reflection but also gives them access to a wide range of tools that assist them in becoming successful writers. Understanding generic elements of reflection in the literacy narrative and what leads to instructor uptake can even aid students in future writing tasks and situations, no matter what the purpose for writing might be or from what educational background they might come.

Acknowledgements

This project owes a great deal of debt to many people. First, I am extremely grateful to Joanna Wolfe for her guidance and support in writing this article. I would also like to thank my interdisciplinary writing group for their insightful comments: Beth Allison Barr, Leslie Hahner, and Theresa Kennedy. The feedback I received from Laura Micciche and two anonymous reviewers was also extremely helpful in revising this essay. I also thank my husband Shane Alexander for his feedback and support. Finally, I extend special thanks to the students, instructors, and think aloud participants who helped with this project, including Tabetha Adkins, Joan D'Antoni, Jo Ann Griffin, Debra Journet, Michael Mercer, Anne-Marie Pedersen, Beth Powell, Kelli Prejean, Linda Rogers, Darci Thoune, Susan Ryan, Steve Smith, Linda Török, and Bronwyn Williams.

Notes

1. Textbooks with literacy narrative assignments include ones by Bullock; Deans; Dobrin; Lunsford, et al.; Palmquist; Ramage, Bean, and Johnson; Trimbur; and others.

2. See the Appendix for the survey.

3. The literacy myth is the idea that acquiring and developing literacy will automatically and necessarily lead to success, enlightenment and achievement (see Graff).

4. This study was approved by the IRB.

5. The essays came from five different assignments, yet the assignments were similar in that each asked students to (1) reflect (reflection was a stated goal of the assignment and the word "reflect" was used in the assignment prompt); (2) examine past experiences with literacy and reflect on the impact today; (3) write about both reading and writing experiences; and (4) be between three and five pages.

6. Although drawbacks to think alouds exist (i.e., the unnatural environment, small sample size), think-aloud research methodology is widely used in cognitive psychology and writing studies to examine reading and writing processes (e.g., Flower and Hayes; Prior).

7. While these three values are certainly not the only recurring values, they are the ones for which previous research on literacy narratives has primed us to look. Episodes could potentially contain more than one value.

8. Episodes were scored as having "no reflection" (0 points), "weak reflection" where less than half of the episode was underlined by the instructor (1 point), or "strong reflection" where more than half of the episode was underlined (2 points). This number was then divided by the total number of values to give each episode its proportional reflection score.

9. It is important to note that these generic elements can overlap: logic can be inflected with certain ideologies and class structures; metaphor has functions beyond just a heightening of style (e.g., analogy, argument, comparison); and ideology can be embedded in analytic or metaphoric appeals. It also seems difficult to isolate passages

that are descriptive, vivid, or evocative. Nonetheless, I distinguish them here because the instructors isolated them in this way in their assessments of what constituted reflection in the genre. Significantly, since these three categories emerged from the instructors' responses during the think-alouds, they may have been different if another group of instructors or student essays were used.

10. These percentages are based on the total number of times something was marked as reflection.

11. Underlining indicates moments instructors marked as reflection. All instructor and student names are pseudonyms.

12. Although the audience for the DALN is not necessarily a college composition course, instructors still use the DALN as a resource for designing assignments and creating teaching units on the genre.

13. Bullock's assignment includes questions that prompt students what to do with memories once they are generated: "How did [the experience] change or otherwise affect you? What aspects of your life now can you trace to that event? How might your life have been different if this event had not happened or had turned out differently? Why does this story matter to you?" (33).

Works Cited

Adler-Kassner, Linda. "The Shape of the Form: Working-Class Students and the Academic Essay." Linkon 85-105. Print.

Alexander, Kara Poe. "Successes, Victims, and Prodigies: 'Master' and 'Little' Cultural Narratives in the Literacy Narrative Genre." *CCC* 62.4 (2011): 608-33. Print.

Anderson, Chris. "Hearsay Evidence and Second-Class Citizenship." *College English* 50.3 (1988): 300-08. Print.

Bartholomae, David. "Inventing the University." *Journal of Basic Writing* 5.1 (1986): 4-23. Print.

Barton, David, and Mary Hamilton. *Local Literacies: Reading and Writing in One Community*. London: Routledge, 1998. Print.

Bawarshi, Anis. "Taking up Language Differences in Composition." *College English* 68.6 (2006): 652-56. Print.

Beebee, Thomas O. *The Ideology of Genre*. University Park: Pennsylvania State UP, 1994. Print.

Bizzell, Patricia, Christopher Schroeder, and Helen Fox, eds. *Alt Dis: Alternative Discourses and the Academy*. Portsmouth: Heinemann, 2002. Print.

Brodkey, Linda. "On the Subjects of Class and Gender in 'The Literacy Letters'." *College English* 51.2 (1989): 125-41. Print.

Brooks, Joanna, with Fern Cayetano. "The (Dis)location of Culture: On the Way to Literacy." Linkon 56-68. Print.

Brown, Deborah. "Promoting Reflective Thinking: Preservice Teachers' Literacy Autobiographies as a Common Text." *Journal of Adolescent & Adult Literacy* 42.5 (1999): 402-10. Print.

Bullock, Richard. *The Norton Field Guide to Writing*. 3rd ed. New York: Norton, 2013. Print.

Carpenter, William, and Bianca Falbo. "Literacy, Identity, and the 'Successful' Student Writer." *Identity Papers*. Ed. Bronwyn T. Williams. Logan: Utah State UP, 2006. 92-108. Print.

Caywood, Cynthia L., and Gilian R. Overing, eds. *Teaching Writing: Pedagogy, Gender, and Equity*. New York: SUNY P, 1987. Print.

Chandler, Sally. *New Literacy Narratives from an Urban University: Analyzing Stories about Reading, Writing, and Changing Technologies*. Cresskill: Hampton, 2013. Print.

Clark, Caroline, and Carmen Medina. "How Reading and Writing Literacy Narratives Affect Preservice Teachers' Understanding of Literacy, Pedagogy, and Multiculturalism." *Journal of Teacher Education* 51.1 (2001): 63-75. Print.

Coe, Richard, Lorelei Lingard, and Tatiana Teslenko, eds. *The Rhetoric and Ideology of Genre: Strategies for Stability and Change*. Cresskill: Hampton, 2002. Print.

Deans, Thomas. *Writing and Community Action: A Service-Learning Rhetoric with Readings*. New York: Longman, 2003. Print.

DeJoy, Nancy. *Process This: Undergraduate Writing in Composition Studies*. Logan: Utah State UP, 2004. Print.

Devitt, Amy J. *Writing Genres*. Carbondale: SIUP, 2004. Print.

Dewey, John. *How We Think: A Restatement of the Relation of Reflective Thinking to the Educative Process*. Boston: Heath, 1933. Print.

Digital Archive of Literacy Narratives. "Step 1: Compose/Tell Your Story." *Digital Archive of Literacy Narratives*. Web. 20 Nov 2014. <http://english.marion.ohiostate.edu/mccorkle/DALN/step1.html>.

Dobrin, Sidney. *Writing Situations*. New York: Longman, 2014. Print.

Eldred, Janet C., and Peter Mortensen. "Reading Literacy Narratives." *College English* 54.5 (1992): 512-39. Print.

Faigley, Lester. *Fragments of Rationality: Postmodernity and the Subject of Composition*. Pittsburgh: U of Pittsburgh P, 1992. Print.

Ferretti, Eileen. "Between Dirty Dishes and Polished Discourse: How Working-Class Moms Construct Student Identities." Linkon 69-84. Print.

Flower, Linda S., and John R. Hayes. "Problem-Solving Strategies and the Writing Process." *College English* 39.4 (1977): 449-61. Print.

Fox, Steve. "Memories of Play, Dreams of Success: Literacy Autobiographies of First Year College Students." *English in Texas* 28.1 (1997): 17-26. Print.

Franzosa, Susan Douglass. "Authoring the Educated Self: Educational Autobiography and Resistance." *Educational Theory* 42.4 (1992): 395-412. Print.

Freadman, Anne. "Uptake." Coe, Lingard, Teslenko 39-53. Print.

Gilyard, Keith. *Voices of the Self: A Study of Language Competence*. Detroit: Wayne State UP, 1991. Print.

Giroux, Henry. *Border Crossings: Cultural Workers and the Politics of Education*. New York: Routledge, 1992. Print.

Glaser, Barney G., and Anselm L. Strauss. *The Discovery of Grounded Theory: Strategies for Qualitative Research*. Chicago: Aldine, 1967. Print.

Graff, Harvey J. *The Literacy Myth: Literacy and Social Structure in the Nineteenth-Century City*. New York: Academic, 1979. Print.

Green, Ann E. "Writing the Personal: Narrative, Social Class, and Feminist Pedagogy." Linkon 15-27. Print.
Haswell, Richard H., and Janis Tedesco Haswell. "Gender Bias and Critique of Student Writing." *Assessing Writing* 3.1 (1996): 31-83. Print.
Higgins, Lorraine, Linda Flower, and Joseph Petraglia. "Planning Text Together: The Role of Critical Reflection in Student Collaboration." *Written Communication* 9.1 (1992): 48-84. Print.
Kill, Melanie. "Acknowledging the Rough Edges of Resistance: Negotiation of Identities for First-Year Composition." *CCC* 58.2 (2006): 213-35. Print.
Kutz, Eleanor. *Exploring Literacy: A Guide to Reading, Writing, and Research*. New York: Longman, 2004. Print.
Lankshear, Colin. "Frameworks and Workframes: Literacy Policies and New Orders." *Unicorn* 24.2 (1998): 43-58. Print.
Linkon, Sherry L., ed. *Teaching Working Class*. Amherst: U of Massachusetts P, 1999. Print.
Lunsford, Andrea, Lisa Ede, Beverly Moss, Carole Clark Papper, and Keith Walters. *Everyone's an Author*. New York: Norton, 2012. Print.
Marinara, Martha. "When Working Class Students Do the Academy: How We Negotiate with Alternative Literacies." *Journal of Basic Writing* 16.2 (1997): 3-16. Print.
Marshall, James D., Peter Smagorinsky, and Michael Smith. *The Language of Interpretation: Patterns of Discourse in Discussions of Literature*. Urbana: NCTE, 1995. Print.
McComiskey, Bruce. *Teaching Composition as a Social Process*. Logan: Utah State UP, 2000. Print.
Meyers, G. Daniel. "Celebrating Diversity through the Language Autobiography." *Voices in English Classrooms: Honoring Diversity and Change*. Ed. Lenora Cook and Helen C. Lodge. Urbana, IL: NCTE, 1996. 3-10. Print.
Nagle, Jane. "Social Class and School Literacy." *Radical Teacher* 44 (1993): 21–23. Print.
Palmquist, Mike. *Joining the Conversation: A Guide for Writers*. 2nd ed. Boston: Bedford/St. Martin's, 2014. Print.
Paterson, Stephanie. *Embodied Narratives: Ways of Reading Student Literacy Histories*. Diss. U of New Hampshire, 2001. Ann Arbor: UMI 3006147. Print.
Pratt, Mary Louise. "Arts of the Contact Zone." *Profession* 91: 33-40. Print.
Prior, Paul. "Tracing Process: How Texts Come into Being." *What Writing Does and How It Does It*. Ed. Charles Bazerman and Paul Prior. Mahwah: Erlbaum, 2004. 167-200. Print.
Ramage, John D., John C. Bean, and June Johnson. *The Allyn & Bacon Guide to Writing*. 6th ed. New York: Longman, 2012. Print.
Reid, Shelley. "Starting Somewhere Better: Revisiting Multiculturalism in First-Year Composition." *Pedagogy* 4.1 (2004): 65-92. Print.
Roen, Duane, Gregory R. Glau, and Barry M. Maid. *The McGraw-Hill Guide: Writing for College, Writing for Life*. 3rd ed. New York: McGraw-Hill, 2013. Print.

Rose, Mike. *Lives on the Boundary: The Struggles and Achievements of America's Underprepared.* New York: Free, 1989. Print.

Rose, Shirley K. "Reading Representative Anecdotes of Literacy Practice; or 'See Dick and Jane Read and Write!'" *Rhetoric Review* 8.2 (1990): 244-59. Print.

Rounsaville, Angela. "Selecting Genres for Transfer: The Role of Uptake in Students' Antecedent Genre Knowledge." *Composition Forum* 26 (2012): 1-14. Web. 11 April 2013. <http://compositionforum.com/issue/26/selecting-genres-uptake.php>.

Royster, Jacqueline Jones. "A View from a Bridge: Afrafeminist Ideologies and Rhetorical Studies." *Feminism and Composition: A Critical Sourcebook.* Ed. Gesa E. Kirsch, Faye Spencer Maor, Lance Massey, Lee Nickoson-Massey, and Mary P. Sheridan-Rabideau. Boston: Bedford/St. Martin's, 2003. 206-34. Print.

Ryden, Wendy A. *In the Public I: Rhetoric and Subjectivity in First-Person Writing.* Diss. CUNY, 2002. Ann Arbor: UMI 3063876. Print.

Sandman, John, and Michael Weiser. "The Writing Autobiography: How to Begin a Two-Year College Writing Course." *TETYC* 20.1 (1993): 18-22. Print.

Schön, Donald. *The Reflective Practitioner: How Professionals Think in Action.* New York: Basic, 1983. Print.

Scott, J. Blake. "The Literacy Narrative as Production Pedagogy in the Composition Classroom." *TETYC* 24.2 (1997): 108-17. Print.

Selfe, Cynthia L., and Gail E. Hawisher. *Literate Lives in the Information Age: Narratives of Literacy from the United States.* Mahwah: Erlbaum, 2004. Print.

Selfe, Cynthia L., ed. *Multimodal Composition: Resources for Teachers.* Cresskill: Hampton, 2007. Print.

Soliday, Mary. "Translating Self and Difference through Literacy Narratives." *College English* 56.5 (1994): 511-26. Print.

Trimbur, John. *The Call to Write.* 6th ed. New York: Longman, 2013. Print.

Villanueva, Victor, Jr. *Bootstraps: From an American Academic of Color.* Urbana, IL: NCTE, 1993. Print.

Wallace, Cindy. "Storytelling: Reclaiming an Age-Old Wisdom for the Composition Classroom." *TETYC* 27.4 (2000): 434-39. Print.

Webb, Patricia R. "Telling Stories In/Out of Class: Writing Narratives about Writing." *Composition Forum* 10.1 (1999): 30-53. Print.

Williams, Bronwyn T. "Heroes, Rebels, and Victims: Student Identities in Literacy Narratives." *Journal of Adolescent and Adult Literacy* 47.4 (2003/2004): 342-45. Print.

Wolfe, Joanna, Cynthia Britt, and Kara Poe Alexander. "Teaching the IMRaD Genre: Sentence Combining and Pattern Practice Revisited." *JBTC* 25.2 (2011): 119-58. Print.

Yagelski, Robert P. *Literacies and Technologies: A Reader for Contemporary Writers.* New York: Longman, 2001. Print.

Yancey, Kathleen Blake. *Reflection in the Writing Classroom.* Logan: Utah State UP, 1998. Print.

Young, Morris. *Minor Re/Visions: Asian American Literacy Narratives as a Rhetoric of Citizenship.* Carbondale: SIUP, 2004. Print.

Appendix: Instructor Survey

Part I: Demographic Information

Rank: _____ Professorial Faculty
_____ Full-time Instructor or Lecturer
_____ Part-time Instructor or Lecturer
_____ Graduate Student Teaching Assistant
_____ Other: (please describe) _____

Number of years you have taught **composition courses** at the university level. _____

<u>Definition of the literacy narrative assignment</u>: The literacy narrative assignment typically asks students to examine and consider how their past experiences with reading, writing, and schooling have shaped their current views on literacy, education, schooling, and/or identity.

Do you use or have you assigned a literacy narrative assignment in your composition courses? _____Yes _____No

If you answered "NO" to the above question, you do <u>not</u> need to complete the survey.

If you answered "YES," complete the following:
1. In which composition courses have you assigned the literacy narrative?
2. What do you hope to achieve by assigning the literacy narrative in your courses?

Part II: Criteria for evaluating literacy narratives in first-year writing courses. Listed below are criteria that composition instructors might use to evaluate literacy narratives. Please circle the answer that best corresponds to how much importance you place on each criteria when evaluating and grading literacy narratives in first-year writing courses.

Extremely Important   Very important   Important   Marginally Important   Not Important

1. Evidence that student is personally engaged in the text
2. An original and interesting thesis
3. Evidence that student has changed in some way in the writing
4. Clear overall organization around a central thesis
5. Evidence that the voice in the narrative seems authentic
6. Awareness of sociopolitical issues
7. Evidence of reflection in text

8. Movement from description of events to analysis of events
9. Grammatical correctness
10. Ability to persuade a reader
11. Paragraph-level organization
12. Student has distanced him/herself from past events, experiences, and behavior
13. Ability to separate past events from current beliefs and assumptions
14. Evidence of awareness to multicultural issues
15. Clear sentence structure and syntax
16. Ability to explore ideas that are personally meaningful to the student
17. Stories that challenge dominant notions of literacy acquisition
18. Provides critiques of schooling and educational experiences
19. Evidence of resistance
20. Evidence of critical thinking
21. Evidence the student has a broad understanding of literacy
22. Evidence that student is critically aware that literacy is a social process
23. Evidence that student sees him/herself as a writer
24. Ability for students to complicate their own notions of "self" and identity
25. Evidence of student empowerment
26. Provides critiques of dominant, sanctioned notions of literacy
27. Provides a well-told description of events
28. Explains why events were significant
29. Evidence student has denaturalized the process of acquiring literacy
30. Evidence student's consciousness has been transformed
31. Evidence of personal growth

Part III: Purposes for using the literacy narrative in first-year composition courses. To what extent do you see each of the following as a purpose of using the literacy narrative in your composition classes? Please circle the answer that best applies:

Strongly Agree   Agree   Disagree   Strongly Disagree

1. The purpose is for students to explore their own ideas.
2. The purpose is for students to be critical.
3. The purpose is for students to demonstrate their knowledge.
4. The purpose is for students to convince someone of something.
5. The purpose is for students to demonstrate reflection.
6. The purpose is for students to demonstrate the significance of something.
7. The purpose is for students to prove a point about something.

8. The purpose is for students to display critical thinking.
9. The purpose is for students to be informative.
10. The purpose is for students to investigate literacy experiences that have not been studied.
11. The purpose is for students to illustrate some "turn" or change in their beliefs
12. The purpose is for students to instruct someone about something.
13. The purpose is to for students to develop skills in description.

Part IV: Open-ended questions

1. What is your definition of reflection?
2. Do you assign exemplary, published literacy narratives in your classroom, such as those by Kingston, Gilyard, Douglass, Villanueva, or Rodriguez? ____Yes _____No
3. If yes to #2, which specific texts do you use?
4. How do you use these texts? What are your purposes for using these texts?

Part V: Think-aloud protocol follow-up

Would you be willing to participate in a think-aloud protocol and interview about literacy narratives? If yes, please write your name and email address in the space provided below.

Gloria Anzaldúa's Rhetoric of Ambiguity and Antiracist Teaching

Sarah Klotz and Carl Whithaus

This article addresses approaches to antiracist pedagogy employed in a rhetoric course at a large public research university. Drawing upon our experience teaching a diverse group of students from a common text shared across disciplines, we show how and why students resisted binary constructions of race and racism and instead formulated an emergent rhetoric of ambiguity to voice and write about their experiences with race in the twenty-first century.

The new mestiza copes by developing a tolerance for contradictions, a tolerance for ambiguity.

—*Gloria Anzaldúa*

This article reflects on our experiences teaching a writing-intensive, general education humanities course focused on issues of (in)tolerance and American culture. Our pedagogy of open-ended questions led to a method we term the "rhetoric of ambiguity," a discourse practice that privileges overlapping, intersecting, and constantly reshaping identity categories as a productive way to address racism in America today. This rhetoric emerged out of our students' reading and discussions of Gloria Anzaldúa's *Borderlands/La Frontera*; we suggest that a rhetoric of ambiguity as pedagogy extends the concept of mestiza rhetoric into viable, antiracist classroom practices. Our work builds on strands in composition studies that draw heavily from feminism, Chican@ studies, and critical pedagogy. Following the publication of Anzaldúa's *Borderlands/La Frontera*, Lisa Ede, Cheryl Glenn, and Andrea Lunsford began to advocate for Anzaldúa's mestiza rhetoric as an alternative to either/or, debate-based models of rhetoric. More recently, Adela Licona has returned to Anzaldúa to trouble our notions of writing subjects, build coalitions, and generate activist dispositions and grassroots literacies. Paula Rosinksi and Tim Peeples too have drawn our attention to the rhetorical possibilities of a Problem-Based Learning (PBL) praxis that resonates with Anzaldúa's unsettling rhetorical stance. Our turn to ambiguity expands upon these works and calls for a pedagogical role for Anzaldúa's text as a model for what it means to speak about the complexities of race and racism in a writing-focused classroom.

The term "ambiguity," emerging as it does from our students' perspectives, indexes doubt, uncertainty, and hesitation. It charts the territory of silence, discomfort, and even fear that students felt approaching the topics of race, ethnicity, and sexuality. It reminds us as instructors that these topics are not merely fertile ground for intellectual growth, but also deeply personal matters. In addition to providing a vocabulary to discuss hybridity, intersectionality, and multiplicity, ambiguity demands a return to the process whereby we came to name ourselves within predetermined categories. Ambiguity generates coalitions by bringing students and teachers to a common ground of doubt—doubt whether our existing discourse practices hold the key to antiracist activism, doubt whether storied theorists are the best models for revising our rhetorical practices. Academic spaces privilege certainty, knowing the right answer, and proving one's knowledge to those who have the power to judge—the professors. A rhetoric of ambiguity provides a corrective to this knowledge-power relationship by centering student voices and making room for transformative antiracist practices to emerge perhaps in spite of the authority of teachers and texts.

Originally our course was designed to use Beverly Daniel Tatum's work on racial identity development as the organizing perspective on race and racism. Anzaldúa's *Borderlands/La Frontera* was incorporated as an important rhetorical text, but was not the primary text for framing discussions of race. In Tatum's formulation, racial identity "refers to the process of defining for oneself the personal significance and social meaning of belonging to a particular racial group" (16). Tatum's text was also our Campus Community Book Project text and as such was part of a larger attempt to incorporate our university's Principles of Community into the daily experiences of students. Tatum's ideas seemed especially useful in a humanities course that focused on rhetoric because she aims to "make the idea of talking about race and racism less intimidating . . . to [help her audience] see the importance of dialogue about this issue" (xvii). For us, Tatum's text is all about enhancing public discourse around race, a decidedly rhetorical project. She provides a psychological perspective on how racial identity comes into being and informs behavior. Even more importantly, she provides a series of terms to generate meaningful and ideally transformative discussion—prejudice, internalized oppression, racism, and white privilege, to name a few. For all of these reasons, we decided to position Tatum's book at the center of our unit on race and rhetoric.

However, our undergraduate students pushed against Tatum's formulation of race. Her theory of *racial identity development* and her strategies for combating racism would have had a chance to resonate more powerfully in a class where students divided along white/black or white/minority lines, but the students in our course embodied multiple identity formations. They ranged from Latino/as to Asian Americans to Anglos to multiracial students; the majority insisted that their identities were complex and as informed by gender, sexuality, class, peer group, and/or neighborhood and city-of-origin as by race or ethnicity. For instance, we think of a Japanese-American student for whom the hyphen signals not a multi-generational Japanese lineage but rather a Japanese mother and an American father; a queer Vietnamese young man who was astounded and delighted to be studying pre-med on a campus with a relatively vibrant LGBTQ culture; and a student whose tribal affiliations included indigenous peoples from the Philippines and the Southwest United States. Variations on these complex identities were reflected in a significant number of the students enrolled in the course and caused them to see Tatum's work as "trying too hard" to combat racism from an exclusively dualistic perspective. While they sympathized with her antiracist stance, students resisted her arguments on how racism developed and how most effectively to combat it.

In planning class activities, we had drawn heavily on feminism (Ede, Glenn, and Lunsford), Chican@ Studies (Anzaldúa; Baca; Licona), and critical pedagogy (Giroux; hooks; Shor; Wallace) to create a collaborative classroom culture of inclusivity. The participatory structure of this writing course encouraged us to work through the perceived disjuncture between Tatum's book and students' experiences. While we wanted students to examine their resistance to Tatum's ideas (in particular how privilege informed their blindness to anti-black racism), we also wanted to honor how their lived experiences reflected encounters with racism and bigotry that did not fit neatly within Tatum's account. This tension challenged us to listen carefully to students' input and to see how they worked with other texts to critique racist discourses. As teachers aware of how dominant discourse could shut down oppositional voices, we were caught in the uncomfortable situation of wanting to defend Tatum's book from students' active critiques, while also validating the basis of those critiques. As a minority woman systematically outlining how to combat racism, Tatum's work was vital to our original vision of the course. However, as the class developed, it became clear that Tatum's limited discussion of intersectionality—the focus of a single chapter, not an approach that was integrated throughout her book—did not resonate with the students. Too strong of a defense of her book would have caused us to force students' lived experiences into a master narrative rather than allowing spaces for students' readings of how racism had, or had not, impacted their lives.

While we had been caught somewhat off guard by the students' mostly negative reactions to Tatum's book, a response to this pedagogical challenge emerged as the class worked through Anzaldúa's writing. As teachers, we found the students leading us toward a different orientation for antiracist teaching practices. During a class discussion, the students focused on Anzaldúa's development of "a tolerance for contradictions, a tolerance for ambiguity" (101) as a rhetorical approach that could foster dialogue; we ended up brainstorming and then working as a class to develop practices that shifted classroom dynamics away from the more binary antiracist approach implicit in Tatum's racial identity development theory. In her introduction to *Why Are All The Black Kids Sitting Together in the Cafeteria?* Tatum acknowledges that her book is based upon her life experiences as a black woman, university professor, and researcher of black children and families. She recognizes that "racism is a live issue for other groups as well," citing Latino/a, Asian American, American Indian, and biracial students as influences for her own expanding sense of racial identity development (xviii). However, her text does not move "Beyond Black and White," the title of part four, until chapter eight. Our students wanted to place their own experiences at the center of the emerging antiracist discourse earlier in the course to acknowledge the role of ambiguity in identity matters. Space for ambiguity emerged when we engaged Anzaldúa's work, brought Anzaldúa's and Tatum's antiracist agendas into dialogue with each other, and participated in emergent rhetorical practices such as contrasting multiple antiracist agendas to determine the specific anti-racist discourse that reflected our collective goals. Students reshaped our pedagogy and collaboratively generated a rhetorical theory that reflected their experiential knowledge about race and racism in American culture.

Our article recounts how a course designed to engage in dialogue about racial identity development and racism moved away from an overview of rhetorical theories and an officially sanctioned discussion of Tatum's book toward a more nuanced, more difficult, student-centered discussion that recognized a rhetoric of ambiguity as key to understanding how students experienced the intersections of race/ethnicity, religious backgrounds, and gender/sexual orientation. By encouraging our students to participate in knowledge production, we found that a participatory pedagogy not only put Anzaldúa's rhetoric into practice but generated new possibilities for antiracist discourse as well. While this one iteration of the course Rhetoric and Tolerance in American Society does not represent a template for antiracist teaching in all contexts, the narrative and thick description we provide suggest that productive dialogues about racism can be built by (1) understanding the history of discourses of (in)tolerance within a society; (2) exploring and questioning a model (e.g., Tatum's book) for critiquing racism/intolerance; and (3) providing students with the freedom to explore their own experiences, express ideas about those experiences (even if the initial voicing of those ideas could be seen as a form of racism or at least underdeveloped racial critique), and develop rhetorical terms (e.g., a rhetoric of ambiguity) that speak to/from those experiences.

Geographies of Ambiguity: Institution, Region, Language

We taught Rhetoric and Tolerance in American Society at the University of California, Davis a large, public research university in the western United States. The course examined how public debates about religion, race, and gender/sexual orientation have functioned over the last three hundred years in American culture. Designed to introduce students to rhetorical theories ranging from those of Aristotle to Kenneth Burke and Gloria Anzaldúa, the course also sought to foster students' abilities to engage in difficult conversations without resorting to a win-lose debate model. We integrated the study of public writing, speeches, sermons, digital videos, and literary works within historical, religious, and rhetorical frameworks. Students in the class developed critical analyses of human experiences, achievements, and conditions with an emphasis on how public debates in the U.S. have employed cultural differences to either include or exclude groups from broader communities.

Given the unexpected turn our antiracist pedagogy took, we use this article to reflect on how identity impacts classroom practices, especially in a course that asks questions about tolerance of differences. As David Wallace has argued, "personal identity is intimately bound up in the practice and pedagogy of rhetoric, even if that identity is not always immediately apparent to all involved" (4). For this reason, we want to be explicit about our multiply situated positions as teachers as well as the racial landscape of our institution and the representative body of students we worked with in our course. While our campus has a diverse student population, that diversity does not reflect the racial and ethnic makeup of our state (see Table 1). In comparison with the overall state population, Asians are overrepresented, while Latino/as, African Americans, and Native Americans are underrepresented. Whites are also underrepresented but not by as significant a margin as Latino/as, African Americans, or Native Americans. In this context, the critique of white racism toward blacks put forward in Tatum's text, officially sanctioned by our institution as the Campus Community Book, did not resonate with students. At moments, however, class discussion verged on what Tim Wise has termed "Racism 2.0, or enlightened exceptionalism" (9). In this form of racism, bigotry does not exclude the possibility of an exceptional member of an oppressed racial group from achieving success in the dominant culture, but the systemic practices of the culture foster discrimination against most of the members of subjugated racial groups. Let us be clear, our students are not bigots. Far from it! They are thoughtful, reflective individuals working through their perceptions of racism, racist discourses, and the constructs of race and ethnicity in twenty-first-century American society. These are difficult, challenging conversations; we saw the students' willingness to engage, and especially to challenge Tatum's model of racial identity development not as dismissive but as a struggle to understand racism and its impacts on their lives.

Table 1. Comparison of Ethnic Diversity at Our Institution and in the State of California

Student Ethnic Self-Identification	University Demographic (2010 Undergraduate Enrollment)	State Demographic (2010 U.S. Census)
African American	3%	7.2%
American Indian	1%	1.9%
Asian	39%	14.9%
Hispanic/ Latino@/ Chican@	15%	37.6%
Pacific Islander	--	.7%
White (Non-Hispanic)	35%	42.3%
Multiracial	--	4.8%
Other	1%	--
Unknown	4%	--
Non US	3%	--

Sources: UC Davis Office of Budget and Institutional Analysis and U.S. Census Bureau, 2010 Census.

While our students represent diverse ethnic, racial, national, and linguistic identities, we as instructors (at least physiologically) are much more easily categorized as white. Sarah Klotz is a queer female doctoral student from the southeastern U.S. of Western European descent. Carl Whithaus is a white male faculty member in his early forties; he grew up in the southeastern U.S. and in southeastern Asia. We both occupy positions of racial privilege and professional authority. An antiracist, student-centered pedagogy seeks to ameliorate these skewed power dynamics, but we also taught under the assumption that we would not be able to fully identify with the positions of our diverse student population, nor would our students fully identify with our apparent identities as privileged, white, native speakers of English.

Our apparent identities mark us as authorities within the classroom, and that authority is reinforced through the social and economic structure of grading. Yet as teachers engaged in critical pedagogy, and as researchers engaged in rhetorical study, we recall Sofia Villenas's call for writers to examine how "their subjectivities and perceptions are negotiated and changed" in relation to disenfranchised communities and through interactions with the majority culture (721-22). Villenas challenges majority-culture researchers to "confront their own multiplicities of identity and histories of complicity" and "mark the points of their own marginalization" (729). That is, teachers and researchers who appear as unified, privileged subjects often have multiple, sometimes contradictory, identities. Incorporating these into class discussions may present opportunities for building coalitions among teachers and students that could be precluded by maintaining more objective, distanced relationships.

Like Villenas, Octavio and Charise Pimentel have argued for a coalition pedagogy in which instructors openly display their political views to build common ground with minority students. They argue that instructors should make their multiple identities visible so that students who share elements of these identities will feel welcome to build relationships with the instructor. They remind us that instructors appearing to occupy positions of privilege must be careful to prevent students from assuming that they are allied with conservative viewpoints (116). When we read *Borderlands/ La Frontera* near the end of the quarter and talked through Anzaldúa's refusal to privilege a single component of her identity over any other, we could better articulate the multiplicities of our own positions. The students engaged in these conversations about the shades and complexities of identities, not because of our actions, but rather because of how Anzaldúa's text approached these issues. Our investment in participatory pedagogy made space for students to reroute discussions on identity toward a rhetoric of ambiguity instead of a rhetoric of binaries. Based on student input, we will be better equipped to practice a coalition pedagogy in future courses by making our complex positions visible in the classroom environment and therefore encourage relationships and critical conversations between students and ourselves from early on.

Yet, even as our students pushed us to alter our pedagogical approach, Racism 2.0 and what Wise would point to as white denial of racism did surface in our class discussions. In fact, denials about the extent of white racism toward blacks were voiced as frequently by Asian American or Latino/a students as by whites. Students did not deny that there was a history of slavery and discrimination, but they wanted to limit the extent to which we saw the legacy of slavery and its white supremacist ideology influencing contemporary distributions of wealth, power, and prestige. For our students, white racists were a thing of the past as were skinheads, whom students associated with movies such as *American History X*. The students readily endorsed a logic that claimed "bad people are racists." The problem with that view is, as our colleague Pat Turner put it, "to suggest that bad people were racist implies that good people were not." Turner was writing about the popular summer movie *The Help,* which portrayed the lives of African American domestic workers in the Jim Crow South. But whether this equation is generated from discussions in a course on Rhetoric and Tolerance in American Society or from many Americans' responses to a Hollywood movie, equating racism with only clearly evil individuals is a distortion of the subtle, and brutal, history of racism in America.

The trick is to look at racism, sexism, heterosexism, and religious intolerance and to recognize that they can and have been put forward not only by people you would despise but also by people you would like. This is an ambiguous and contradictory place to stand. If that moment of recognizing the ambiguities of our positions could occur for larger numbers of people, we would go a long way towards challenging enduring racist practices and behaviors. We did not come anywhere close to achieving that lofty goal in our course, but our students did help us to consider how we perceive and interact with one another when writing and talking about racism. An important aspect of that consideration was who gets to name and define the concepts we use. In the end, students insisted that Anzaldúa offers rhetorical concepts for developing antiracist ways of approaching the world that were as viable, if not more, than rhetorical concepts from Aristotle, Burke, Mikhail Bakhtin, and antiracist concepts from Tatum.

The Rhetoric of Ambiguity: Characteristics and Analyses

During class discussion of *Borderlands/ La Frontera,* we put forward a basic thesis that the text was concerned with moving beyond dualistic or binary thinking toward a mestiza rhetoric and consciousness. Our discussion posed three main questions: (1) Can we describe this text as rhetorical theory? (2) What rhetorical performances are possible in the text that would be excluded from either a classical, Aristotelian rhetoric or a modern dialogic rhetoric such as Burke's or Bakthin's? (3) And, in what ways does Anzaldúa's work encourage awareness of cultural difference? Through a close analysis of rhetorical strategies, the students concluded that yes, in fact, *Borderlands/La Frontera* is a rhetorical theory both in its implicit structures and its self-reflexive writing about identity, language, argument, and discourse.

In a whole-class discussion, we named Anzaldúa's work a rhetoric of ambiguity. This reflected a distinction between *Borderlands/La Frontera* and the other rhetorical theories we considered in class (i.e., Aristotle's, Burke's, and Bakhtin's), but it also acknowledged that Anzaldúa was doing theoretical work that could have implications for how we name and categorize each other. Anzaldúa's text, students insisted, was not just a text about Anglo racism toward Chican@s; rather, it encouraged the development of a mestiza rhetoric premised on border crossings and ambiguities. While this view emerged from the students' engagement with the text, it reflected ongoing discussions in rhetoric and composition and suggested ways of extending antiracist rhetorical approaches and pedagogies advanced by Lunsford, Wise, Villenas, and Licona. Each of these scholars sketches pedagogical approaches that engage and challenge both students and teachers. What our students underscored was the importance of ambiguity in Anzaldúa's work as a way to discuss identity and racism in collaborative groups. While Aristotle, Bakhtin, and Burke provide robust frameworks for analyzing rhetorical situations, Anzaldúa's rhetoric of ambiguity allowed the students to account for potential contradictions within speaking subjects. Naming does not have to be singular for Anzaldúa but is rather a border crossing, a double naming, just as the Rio Grande River itself is doubly named as the Rio Grande and the Rio Bravo. Our students used Anzaldúa's perspective to hold and account for different stances within the same speaking subject. Aristotle had provided a framework based on rhetorical appeals for understanding speaker, audience, and structure; Burke allowed us to analyze rhetorical performance in history and context; and Bakhtin introduced the concept of dialogue and multiple voices. But Anzaldúa allowed students to see that even within a rhetorical analysis of structure, dialogue and context, ambiguities in identity, language-use, and naming emerge as tools for a contemporary rhetor engaged in antiracist projects.

Working in small groups (four to seven people), students selected passages from *Borderlands/ La Frontera* that demonstrate key rhetorical moves of a developing rhetoric of ambiguity. Working with input from eleven student groups, as a class we chose five features of Anzaldúa's rhetoric through which to explore ambiguity and nondualistic thinking: genre, language, tejana figures, identity formation, and riverbanks as borderlands. In this section, we work through the details that emerged from student discussions to explain how the rhetoric of ambiguity engaged students to think critically about racial and ethnic identities vis-à-vis tolerance in American society. In Anzaldúa's terms, "*la mestiza* constantly has to shift out of habitual formulations; from convergent thinking, analytical reasoning that tends to use rationality to move toward a single goal (a Western mode), to divergent thinking, characterized by movement away from set patterns and goals and toward a more whole perspective, one that includes rather than excludes" (101). In this passage, Anzaldúa points to the multiple meanings of racial identity that a rhetoric of ambiguity can generate. Anzaldúa's insistence on nonexclusion allowed our students both to vocalize their own lived experiences and imagine a discourse that could tolerate differences rather than excluding, eliding, or erasing them.

Multiple Genres

The first rhetorical strategy that we identified was Anzaldúa's multiple and mixed genres, that is, her use of poetry, prose, storytelling, epigraph, and personal narrative. Students had become familiar with the term genre from our work on Bakhtin and were therefore able to recognize, identify, and analyze the different genres at work within the text. The student groups determined and presented to the class that multiple genres were necessary for Anzaldúa to make her argument about a mestiza consciousness. Students claimed that genre-switching was analogous to the linguistic code-switching in the text. For Anzaldúa to step beyond the "habitual formations" of Western thinking, she needs new generic modes (101). Thus, the reader hears the voice of a teacher scolding Anzaldúa as a child, or feels disoriented as a saying in Spanish or a poem in English breaks the flow of more traditional academic prose. Anzaldúa's rhetoric refuses to exclude nonacademic genres in much the same way that it refuses to exclude nonstandard forms of English or Spanish. Ambiguity, or in this case polyphonic writing, enhances this politics of non-exclusion and helps Anzaldúa address how she has been excluded by refusing to privilege one part of her identity over any other.

Multilingual Texts

Students confidently identified the multilingual elements of the text as another essential component of the rhetoric of ambiguity. The text mainly alternates between Spanish and English, but also includes Nahuatl (an indigenous language of Mesoamerica that traces back to Aztec roots), and nonstandard forms of English and Spanish. Students used Anzaldúa's chapter, "How to Tame a Wild Tongue," to connect linguistic and ethnic identity. Anzaldúa writes that "ethnic identity is twin skin to linguistic identity—I am my language" (81). She explores how nonstandard Englishes have been systematically attacked in the United States. Many of our students come from multilingual households and identified code-switching as a component of their own language as they move between academic and intimate contexts. Vershawn Young's term "code-meshing" might better describe the discourse of our multilingual students, which they saw mirrored in Anzaldúa. Young argues that a paradigm of code-meshing, as opposed to code-switching, "promotes linguistic democracy, as students are not called to choose but are rather allowed to blend language and identities" (Young and Martinez xxiv). Like Young, our students recognized how attacks on language are racist. Many of our students were bilingual if not multilingual; they reported having felt their ethnic identities disparaged through a commonplace attitude of the inferiority of languages other than English. Discussing this issue opened up an analysis of systemic racism in a way that had not occurred with Tatum's historicist take on antiblack racism in the United States. Students argued that "linguistic terrorism" (Anzaldúa's term) was intimately tied to racial intolerance and that a rhetoric of ambiguity would work as a corrective by exposing readers and audience members to languages outside of standard academic English.

Tejana Figures

Students pushed beyond Anzaldúa's more direct use of genre and language variation to identify the subtler rhetorical techniques of figurative and symbolic language. Teachers and students identified the Virgin of Guadalupe and Coatlicue as figurations of ambiguity. For Anzaldúa, these expressions of feminine spirituality personify inclusion and tolerance. The Virgin of Guadalupe "is the symbol of ethnic identity and of the tolerance for ambiguity that Chicanos-mexicanos, people of mixed race, people who have Indian blood, people who cross cultures, by necessity possess" (52). Coatlicue, an Aztec goddess, "depicts the contradictory. In her figure, all the symbols important to the religion of the Aztecs are integrated . . . she is a symbol of the fusion of opposites: the eagle and the serpent, heaven and the underworld, life and death, mobility and immobility, beauty and horror" (69). Anzaldúa uses these figures to show how contradictions and ambiguity are not only tolerated by but essential to rhetorical traditions indigenous to the Americas. The tejana figures of Coatlicue and the Virgin of Guadalupe were not immediately legible to students as rhetorically powerful but contributed to a larger process of thinking through Anzaldúa's text as a corrective to discourse practices based in binaries. Our communal attempt to think past dualistic rhetorics was at times a struggle, in part because our previous readings had largely drawn on a male, Western tradition. Anzaldúa's incorporation of religious and spiritual figures challenged us to think beyond the constraints of accepted academic logics. Our class's development of alternative approaches to race and racism relied on Coatlicue and the Virgin of Guadalupe as examples of internal contradiction in identity. What is racism at its core if not a system based on binary divisions that fails to fully account for the complexity of human subjectivity? Anzaldúa's use of tejana figures allowed us to move away from abstractions to a more concrete form of antiracist rhetorical theorizing.

Identity Formations

The disorientation that resulted from a rhetorical strategy privileging ambiguity led us to make connections that we might not have seen, particularly the intersections among identity categories. Anzaldúa's grappling with identities of Chicana lesbian and feminist further the rhetoric of ambiguity by revealing identity to be intersectional and incoherent. She has no homeland. She resides in a borderland because no one community fully accepts her for the "multiple and contested nature of her own identity" (Wallace 120). Anzaldúa connects identity to knowledge-building when she writes, "being a lesbian and raised Catholic, indoctrinated as straight, *I made the choice to be queer.* . . . It's an interesting path, one that continually slips in and out of the white, the Catholic, the Mexican, the indigenous, the instincts. . . . It is a path of knowledge. . . . It is a way of mitigating duality" (41). Similar thinking informs her use of languages, genres, and tejana figures, but here Anzaldúa ties knowledge to her bodily and elected identities. Her way of knowing derives from her sexuality, her gender, her religious background, her history, and her ethnicity. As we tried to find ways to talk about tolerance beyond black and white, Anzaldúa offered students an intersectional approach that connected race and ethnicity with each unit of our course (religion, gender, sexuality). But more important than the convenient tie-in to other course content was how Anzaldúa's approach helped us build coalitions across identity categories and power differentials—students and teachers worked together to generate knowledge and students crossed identity barriers to have difficult but transformative conversations about how race and racism structured their experiences and discourse practices.

Riverbanks as Borderlands

The final strategy that we explored as a class was Anzaldúa's use of borderland symbolism to move beyond dualistic/binary thinking. While much has been written on Anzaldúa's organizing symbol, the borderlands, our class found that another symbol—the Rio Grande River—best encapsulated the rhetoric of ambiguity. The students' interest in the banks of this river echoes Licona's extension of borderlands rhetoric through a focus on the Rio Grande River, or as it is called in Mexico, the Río Bravo. Licona writes:

> Borderlands rhetorics are steeped in spatialized context that began, for [her], on the U.S./Mexico border where a river serves as the dividing line. One river with two names, both true and each rhetorically produced and imposed as acts of empire. Standing on one side and looking south it is the Rio Grande. Standing on the other side and looking north it is the Río Bravo. (135)

The doubleness of naming a river becomes a means of holding onto ambiguity and exploring contradictions not only about geographic and political space but also about identities. After thinking through the genre, language, tejana figures, and the theory of identity in the text, students returned to the framing question: in what ways does *Borderlands/La Frontera* address or encourage tolerance?

Anzaldúa articulates the relationship between rhetoric and tolerance best in her metaphor of the banks of the Rio Grande:

> But it is not enough to stand on the opposite riverbank, shouting questions, challenging patriarchal, white conventions. A counterstance locks one into a duel of oppressor and oppressed; locked in mortal combat, like the cop and the criminal, both are reduced to a common denominator of violence. The counterstance refutes the dominant culture's views and beliefs, and for this, it is proudly defiant. All reaction is limited by, and dependent on, what one is reacting against. . . . At some point, on our way to a new consciousness, we will have to leave the opposite bank, the split between the two combatants somehow healed so that we are on both shores at once. (100)

In this passage, Anzaldúa shows that alternative rhetoric is not only oppositional; it is also coalitional. She demands that marginalized discourses and rhetors engage in the messiness of identity to move beyond an us versus them mentality. The students in this class embodied complex multiracial and multiethnic identities, even the students who identified as primarily Anglo, Latin@, or Asian insisted that their identities were as informed by gender, sexuality, class, peer group, and/or neighborhood and city-of-origin as by any racial or ethnic identity. The students adapted and took up Anzaldúa's move to go beyond us versus them; they participated in discussions and created written works that articulated nuanced forms of identity.

Borderlands/La Frontera makes use of multilingual discourse, genre mixing, identity-based knowledge, tejana figures, and riverbank symbolism to enact a rhetoric of ambiguity. Her alternative rhetoric allowed our students to explore race, ethnicity, other identity categories (which they may or may not inhabit), and tolerance in a nondualistic rhetorical mode. Her use of the river as metaphor makes clear that alternative rhetoric is a border-crossing activity that uses language and meaning-making to build understanding and community across lines of difference. These conclusions emerged from a student-centered classroom where instructor experience and training fell short of generating productive antiracist discourse. In the following section, we examine critical pedagogy methods as powerful means to open up rhetorical possibilities in antiracist teaching.

Developing Open Dialogue about Race through Critical Pedagogy and PBL

The pedagogical techniques we used for discussing racism and racist discourses in Rhetoric and Tolerance in American Society emerged from our readings of Paulo Freire, bell hooks, Ira Shor, David Wallace, Paula Rosinksi, and Tim Peeples. When students contribute to the knowledge production of a course, they take part in a long history of critical pedagogy. Shor's model of "empowering education" emphasizes student participation within the university classroom as a disposition that will transfer to the public sphere. Shor champions "a critical-democratic pedagogy for self and social change. It is a student-centered program for multicultural democracy in school and society. It approaches individual growth as an active, cooperative, and social process" (15). A pedagogy grounded in participation encourages students to enter the classroom as knowledge producers, not merely passive receivers of knowledge. In what follows, we describe our course and contextualize our experiences within the field of critical pedagogy to argue for a rhetorical stance of ambiguity for teachers and students engaged in antiracist practice.

Overall our syllabus was structured so that we first discussed issues of tolerance and intolerance around religion, then race and ethnicity, and finally ended with a discussion of gender and sexual orientation. The readings on race and ethnicity began with Tatum's "Part I: A Definition of Terms";" for the same class meeting, we asked students to read excerpts from Burke's *A Grammar of Motives*. The idea was to expose students to Tatum's concept of racism as a system based on privilege that is distinct from prejudice (3-13). Tatum argues that people of color can be prejudiced but not racist "because they do not systematically benefit from racism" (10). In this definition, Tatum is careful to acknowledge the power of language choice and its influence on how we perceive the world. When planning the course, we believed that this attention to language as a force for shaping perceptions would resonate with Burke's dramatistic rhetoric and his concept of the pentad. While students seemed to understand Burke's pentad, particularly in relationship to considering a rhetorical act as a stage or a performance, class discussion was more labored around the opening section of Tatum's book than we expected.

After this class meeting, the two of us discussed the session, and felt that the next set of readings, particularly Tatum's "Part IV: Beyond Black and White," would resonate more fully with the diverse students in our class. In anticipation of some student resistance, we had, in fact, arranged the schedule so that Tatum's detailed discussion of people of color in Part IV would come before our discussion of Parts II and III, which explicitly focus on the legacies of white racism toward blacks. We felt that Tatum's broader discussion of people of color and the racism they encountered would provide more points that students could identify with rather than her focused discussions about African Americans and whites found in Parts II and III of her book.

The readings for the next class included not only Tatum's text, but also selected chapters from Gloria Anzaldúa's *Borderlands/La Frontera,* Elizabeth and Stuart Ewen's *Typecasting: On the Arts and Sciences of Human Inequality*, and three versions of Sojourner Truth's "Ain't I a Woman" speech. Later readings included Farhad Manjoo's "How Black People Use Twitter" from *Slate*, Bharati Mukherjee's "Imagining Homelands," and Susan Saulny's recent *New York Times* article about college students increasingly identifying as multiracial. As we worked through these texts, students continued to resist Tatum's framework. They pushed up against the idea that they were complicit in antiblack racism, even, or especially, as members of other racial minorities. Our status as white teachers added to the fraught nature of these discussions. How could we claim to understand students' experiences of race and racism? Drawing on the practices of Tatum, a faculty member and president of an elite, private East Coast liberal arts college, did not immediately provide us with an authoritative ethos for the students enrolled in the course. Discussions were civil, but students expressed their resistance to Tatum's text in subtle ways. They responded to questions after significant prompting but the answers were superficial and politically correct, not substantive. Students were looking for the right answer rather than engaging in uncomfortable discussions about race. The wheels were spinning, but not in a good way. Think oil on the pavement.

Tatum's methods for confronting racism complement Shor's critical-democratic pedagogy in that Tatum deploys dialogue and reflection to confront racism. In addressing how whites can abandon individual racism as well as recognize and oppose institutional racism, Tatum names six stages: contact, disintegration, reintegration, pseudo-independence, immersion/emersion, and autonomy (93-113). Describing her classes and workshops, Tatum emphasizes that individuals progress through these stages when they engage in conversations that make them rethink established attitudes and behaviors. These stages require reflection and investment from individuals. Tatum's method for antiracist teaching is interactive and involves the participatory work of students. We expanded the horizon of participation in our course to allow students to question texts that did not fully account for their own experiential knowledge, even if those texts seemed, at the outset, to be essential building blocks for achieving the course's goals.

Participatory learning also resonates with insights developed by Damián Baca, Adela Licona, and Sofia Villenas. Developing antiracist teaching strategies requires openness to students' perspectives and experiences. Sometimes the most meaningful works for instructors will not speak to students, but having flexibility and allowing students to shape what concepts are valued led to more productive dialogue than following a planned curriculum. This approach shares key features with a PBL model most recently applied in the writing-classroom context by Paula Rosinski and Tim Peeples. As these scholars explain, PBL is a type of engaged pedagogy that initiates learning through an ill-structured problem around which all learning centers. PBL provides the opportunity for teachers to think critically about what types of rhetorical subjects our pedagogies invite (10). In our course, the ill-structured problem was how to talk and write about racism in American culture and how to cultivate comfort with hesitation, being wrong, and dwelling in the interstices between fixed identity categories. When Tatum's book failed to resonate with students, we let the problem itself generate the terms of the debate. Students took the lead as we negotiated new approaches and new texts to develop emergent antiracist discourses. As in Peeple's and Rosinski's model, "new content, skills, methods, et cetera [were] gathered and generated through the process of investigating and addressing this key problem," rather than being modeled or supplied by instructors or course texts alone (10). Because we wanted our students to build dispositions of openness and flexibility around highly fraught antiracist discussions, our pedagogy reflected these key traits as well. By overlapping scholarship from antiracist rhetors and teachers with the storied tradition of American critical pedagogies and PBL methods, our praxis challenged students and teachers alike to embrace ambiguity and discomfort, and to see what antiracist discourses emerged from a rhetorical stance in flux.

This approach was at odds with the physical and institutional course setup in many ways. The classroom was large with sitting capacity for ninety students; the desks were all front facing and bolted to the floor with folding desktops. Sixty-two students were enrolled. The physical set up of the room was designed to facilitate lectures and allow the instructor to display materials on a large screen and to play audio through a sophisticated sound system. The one feature of the room that facilitated student-centered learning was the wireless Internet access, which enabled students to work with the course readings or the open web during class discussions. The class met twice a week for ninety minutes. The ten-week course included three weeks on the race/ethnicity and tolerance readings; three on tolerance for religious practices; and the final three weeks on gender categories and sexual identities. While the last week of the course allowed space to actively consider how these identity categories intersected, Anzaldúa's work pushed us to look at those intersections earlier and throughout the last half of the sessions.

While the physical set up of the classroom worked against a discussion-oriented, student-centered approach, we built in numerous activities that disrupted a passive-learning, lecture-style class. Each session had at least two opportunities for small group discussion and/or the sharing of individual student writing with peers. We designed these activities so that the student groups could report or present their findings to the entire class. In this way, we were able to shape both individual ninety-minute sessions as well as the flow of the entire course to reflect concerns and responses from the group of students in the room with us. With a large lecture class we run the risk of a small set of confident students answering the majority of questions posed by instructors, but small-group work ensured that more voices would enter the conversation. Klotz also read student writing from in-class and homework assignments to make sure that issues raised in student writing became part of class discussion.

In the spirit of critical pedagogy, students generated final exam questions in small groups at the end of each of the three course units. Anzaldúa made such an impression that nearly one quarter of the multiple-choice exam questions (12 out of 50) centered on *Borderlands/La Frontera*. No other course reading received such thorough attention on that student-generated final. Students honed in particularly on Anzaldúa's claim that ethnic identity is linguistic identity (81). Two exam questions drew upon this concept of the deep connection between ethnicity and language. For our students, theories of rhetoric and race came together most coherently through language use. Multilingualism, code-meshing, and linguistic pride resonated strongly with our students' experiences with race and racism.

Students also used their exam questions to apply Anzaldúa's concepts to other course readings such as Dorothy Allison's essay "Femme," a piece about the author's alienation as a lesbian growing up working class in the South. Many exam questions took up the connection between sexuality and ethnicity. For example, one question asked, "Anzaldúa's claim that for the lesbian of color, the ultimate rebellion she can make against her native culture is through her sexual behavior shows _____." The correct answer read, "the confluence and conflicts that can appear between racial/ethnic and sexual identities." It clearly made an impression on our students that Anzaldúa refused to silence her lesbian identity to appease her Catholic or Latin@ communities. Bringing sexuality into conversation with issues of race and belonging allowed students to confront multiple axes of oppression and see how the silencing of dialogue around sexuality was parallel to the awkwardness and fear they experienced when first asked to discuss race in an academic context. To confront issues of (in)tolerance around religion, race/ethnicity, and gender/sexual orientation in an open and genuinely engaged fashion required that we honor student voices and student perspectives. We structured the course so that student views would not only shape classroom discussion but would also have an impact on what we evaluated and what counted in terms of that all important currency—grades.

The race and ethnicity unit in our course began as an opportunity to discuss Tatum's book. We hoped that students would address systemic racial intolerance in a workshop setting and develop new communication skills that might address these systemic issues. When students took the lead, we ultimately redefined how we would achieve our goals. Students participated by challenging one conception of race— systemic white privilege and systemic anti-black racism—in favor of another—an ambiguous racial identity grounded in language, region, sexuality, gender, and other categories of affiliation. Our experience speaks to the necessity of problems, trouble, and discomfort in our teaching, and the openness of a rhetoric of ambiguity to address power and identity within our classroom contexts. Incorporating antiracist teaching strategies into a writing-intensive general education course challenges a banking model of knowledge transfer where enlightened instructors transform less knowledgeable students. Our course became a space where undergraduates could explore Anzaldúa's *Borderlands/ La Frontera* as a rhetorical theory that opened discussions that had been shut down by Tatum's racial identity development theory and more traditional rhetorical theories. The work of our students helped us conceptualize a rhetoric of ambiguity as an extension of what composition studies values as a non-binary, mestiza rhetoric; the rhetoric of ambiguity developed explicitly anti-racist pedagogies and frank discussions about lived experiences of race and racism in the early twenty-first century.

Works Cited

Allison, Dorothy. "Femme." *Skin: Talking About Sex, Class And Literature*. Ithaca: Firebrand Books, 1994. 151-158. Print.

Anzaldúa, Gloria. *Borderlands/La Frontera*. San Francisco: Aunt Lute Books, 1999. Print.

Aristotle. "Aristotle's Rhetoric." Rhetoric EServer. Ed. Lee Honeycutt. EServer, 2011. Web. 20 August 2013. <http://rhetoric.eserver.org/aristotle/>.

Baca, Damián. *Mestiz@ Scripts, Digital Migrations, and the Territories of Writing*. New York: Palgrave Macmillan, 2008. Print.

Bakhtin, M.M. *Speech Genres and Other Late Essays*. Trans. Vern W. McGee. Austin: Texas UP, 1986. Print.

Burke, Kenneth. *A Grammar of Motives*. 11th ed. Berkeley: U of California P, 2000. Print.

Ede, Lisa, Cheryl Glenn, and Andrea Lunsford. "Border Crossings: Intersections of Rhetoric and Feminism." *Rhetorica: A Journal of the History of Rhetoric* 13.4 (1995): 401-41. *JSTOR*. Web. 14 May 2014.

Ewen, Elizabeth, and Stuart Ewen. *Typecasting: On the Arts and Science of Human Inequality, a History of Dominant Ideas*. New York: Seven Stories, 2008. Print.

Freire, Paulo. *Pedagogy of the Oppressed*. New York: Continuum, 1995. Print.

Giroux, Henry A. *Border Crossings: Cultural Workers and the Politics of Education*. New York: Routledge, 1992. Print.

hooks, bell. *Teaching to Transgress: Education as the Practice of Freedom.* New York: Routledge, 1994. Print.

Licona, Adela. *Zines in Third Space: Radical Cooperation and Borderlands Rhetoric.* Albany: SUNY, 2012. Print.

Lunsford, Andrea. "Toward a Mestiza Rhetoric: Gloria Anzaldúa on Composition and Postcoloniality." *JAC* 18.1 (1998): 1-29. Print.

Manjoo, Farhad. "How Black People Use Twitter." *Slate.* 10 August 2010. Web. 20 August 2013. <http://www.slate.com/articles/technology/technology/2010/08/how_black_people_use_twitter.html>.

Mukherjee, Bharati. "Imagining Homelands." *Letters of Transit: Reflections on Exile, Language, and Loss.* New York: New, 1999. 65-86. Print.

Pimentel, Charise, and Octavio Pimentel. "Coalition Pedagogy: Building Bonds between Instructors and Students of Color." *Included in English Studies: Learning Climates That Cultivate Racial and Ethnic Diversity.* Ed. Victor Villanueva and Shelli B. Fowler. Urbana: NCTE, 2002. 115-24. Print.

Rosinski, Paula, and Tim Peeples. "Forging Rhetorical Subjects: Problem-Based Learning in the Writing Classroom." *Composition Studies* 40.2 (2012): 9-32. Print.

Saulny, Susan. "Black? White? Asian? More Young Americans Choose All of the Above." *New York Times.* 29 January 2011. Web. 20 August 2013. <http://topics.nytimes.com/top/news/us/series/race_remixed/index.html?scp=1&sq=saulny&st=cse. >.

Shor, Ira. *Empowering Education: Critical Teaching for Social Change.* Chicago: Chicago UP, 1992. Print.

Tatum, Beverly Daniel. *Why Are All the Black Kids Sitting Together in the Cafeteria? And Other Conversations About Race.* New York: Basic, 1999. Print.

Truth, Sojourner. "Ain't I a Woman." *The Anti-Slavery Standard* (2 May 1863). 4 April 2011. Web. 1 June 2015. <http://www.sojournertruth.org/Library/Speeches/AintIAWoman.htm>.

---. "Ain't I a Woman." *History of Woman Suffrage.* 2nd ed. Vol.1. Ed. Elizabeth Cady Stanton, Susan B. Anthony, and Matilda Joslyn Gage. Rochester: Charles Mann, 1889. 116-17. Web. 4 April 2011. <http://www.gutenberg.org/files/28020/28020-h/28020-h.htm>.

---. "Ain't I a Woman." Women's Rights Convention, Akron, Ohio. 29 May 1851. 4 April 2011. Web. 1 June 2015. <http://www.sojournertruth.org/Library/Speeches/>.

Turner, Pat. "Dangerous White Stereotypes." *New York Times.* 28 August 2011. Web. 1 June 2015. <http://www.nytimes.com/2011/08/29/opinion/dangerous-white-stereotypes.html?_r=1>.

UC Davis. Office of Budget and Institutional Analysis (BIA). "Enrollment by Ethnicity - Fall 2007 through Fall 2014." 3 Nov. 2014. Web. 4June 2015. <http://budget.ucdavis.edu/data-reports/documents/enrollment-reports/eethnicity_fcurr.pdf>.

U.S. Census Bureau, 2010 Census. "Total Population." *2010 Census, United States Census Bureau.* United States Department of Commerce. 2010. Web. 1 May 2013. <http://factfinder.census.gov/faces/nav/jsf/pages/index.xhtml>.

Villenas, Sofia. "The Colonizer/Colonized Chicana Ethnographer: Identity, Marginalization, and Co-Optation in the Field." *Harvard Educational Review* 66.4 (1996): 711-31. Print.

Wallace, David L. *Compelled to Write: Alternative Rhetoric in Theory and Practice.* Logan: Utah State UP, 2011. Print.

Wise, Tim J. *Between Barack and a Hard Place: Racism and White Denial in the Age of Obama.* San Francisco: City Lights, 2009. Print.

Young, Vershawn Ashanti, and Aja Y. Martinez, eds. *Code-Meshing as World English: Pedagogy, Policy, Performance.* Urbana: NCTE, 2011. Print.

An Intimate Discipline? Writing Studies, Undergraduate Majors, and Relational Labor

T J Geiger II

This article takes survey and interview responses from undergraduate writing majors in two independent writing programs as points of departure for reflection on the disciplinary work of writing studies. Though scholarship about writing majors focuses on these programs as sites for the distribution of disciplinary expertise, students in this study placed significant attention on teachers' relational labor. By focusing on teachers' demonstrations of care, students invite consideration of central concerns in writing studies: the relationship of disciplinary knowledge to teaching, the value students derive from advanced writing instruction, and the labor dynamics mobilized within writing major programs. Ultimately, while sometimes appearing to mobilize gendered cultural scripts that historically marginalized writing instruction and writing instructors, student comments about relationships suggest the importance of disciplined, informed care in disciplinary work.

The faculty in the writing program understand themselves as not just research producers, but also as people working with their students.

—*Jeremiah*, senior writing major at Private Research University

Looking back on the four years that I've been here, I really have grown. . . . None of the teachers say it's going to be easy, but they do offer encouragement. They're here to help.

—*Gail*, senior writing major at Liberal Arts College

The composition student's teacher combines the two images of mother and maid.

—*Susan Miller*, Textual Carnivals: The Politics of Composition (137)

Jeremiah and Gail, participants in a study I conducted of the undergraduate writing major, describe their relationship intensive encounters with teachers whom they perceived as personally dedicated to their ongoing writing development.[1] Sharing a perception of writing faculty in his program as both experts who produce knowledge and teachers who build relationships, Jeremiah highlighted relational labor as critical to his understanding not only of their work but also of the discipline. In a similar vein, Gail valued faculty's honest assessments, "encouragement," and "help" within the community of students and faculty at her school. Taken together, these mutually informing practices cultivated an environment that promoted, over four years, an informed perspective on writing. The relational emphasis the participants name as central to the writing major is striking. It is all the more striking when placed alongside Susan Miller's comment stressing the ideological complex that genders and constructs composition and literacy teachers as service workers who respond to student needs and deficits (137). Arguments for undergraduate writing majors often link these programs to claims that champion writing studies as a discipline with a body of professional knowledge adjudicated by experts. Accounts presented by Jeremiah, Gail, and other students support that link. However, students located their rhetorical education not only in teachers' expertise, but also in the relationships teachers forged with them. In this article, I explore writing studies' disciplinarity in light of self-reports from writing majors who emphasized teachers' relationships with them, an emphasis that—while at times seems to echo Miller's summary of the composition teacher's symbolic stance, a figure dedicated to providing service-oriented "help"—raises questions about the centrality of humane connections in undergraduate disciplinary engagement.

Taking what some students value about the writing major as a point of departure, this article assesses the interplay of disciplinarity as expert knowledge *about* writing and pedagogy with the labor-intensive teaching *of* writing that entails relationships grounded in significant instructor-student contact as well as individualized response to students and their work. If the writing major is "the missing piece in the argument for the disciplinary status of writing studies" (Howard, "History" xxii), then it becomes particularly important to listen to the voices of students who inhabit this missing piece—students like Jeremiah and Gail. In an attempt to listen to these voices, I conducted a study that collected survey, interview, and textual data from writing majors in two programs in different institutional contexts. Writing majors frequently privileged the intensely relational labor instructors exerted on behalf of students' rhetorical education, and they characterized this labor in highly affective terms. While student accounts constructing writing studies as an intimate discipline might at times seem to undercut the goal of disciplinary status, I contend that writing majors' interest in relationships (1) indicates how that goal has been pursued in ways that maintain the discipline's traditional emphasis on teaching *and* (2) affirms the significance of professional knowledge about writing. In other words, pursuing forms of academic status (e.g., an undergraduate major) need not equal the subjugation of the teaching of writing or the displacement of intimate relationships. Given that undergraduate writing major programs constitute exciting sties for rhetorical education, we have much to learn about debates over teaching and disciplinarity from students in these programs. What they taught me is that both expert knowledge and humane relationships matter in disciplinary projects.

In what follows, I first explore claims that the pursuit of disciplinary status diminishes the role of pedagogy within writing studies. As a strategic move, some proponents of the writing major understandably attempt to distance it from ideological traditions that narrowly circumscribe literacy and that lay claim to first-year writing (FYW). The writing major is also understood as a site for teaching *about* writing as well as for the teaching *of* writing. Indeed, the relationship intensive teaching of writing has its own lengthy history within U.S. advanced composition courses. This history supports claims that locate intimacy at the center of writing studies. Second, I examine study participants' richly rhetorical conceptions of writing and their highly affective characterizations of teachers' labor. Students link relational labor to rhetorical notions of writing. Affirming the writing major as a vehicle for promoting disciplinarity through the dissemination of expert conceptions of literacy, many writing majors understand the discipline as involving both rhetorical constructs and affective attitudes. Third, students also position undergraduate disciplinary inculcation as necessarily bound up in caring relationships. At times, their characterizations of these relationships appeared to mobilize cultural scripts similar to those that have historically gendered and marginalized writing studies and its teachers. I conclude by discussing some implications of this research for the disciplinary work of writing studies.

Disciplinarity versus Teaching? A Question of Traditions

The writing major—which entails advanced study in writing and rhetoric—serves as a critical location for inquiry about the discipline. Scholarship about it appears with some regularity (see the Where We Are section on writing majors and programs in this issue), and writing major programs have continued to grow since the last official count in 2009 (Committee on the Major). Readers of *Composition Studies* will recall the 2007 special issue dedicated to the writing major. In 2010, Greg Giberson and Thomas Moriarty's *What We Are Becoming: Developments in Undergraduate Writing Majors* appeared, showing that these programs operate within wide-ranging structures and offer varied opportunities for students' rhetorical production and study. Also in 2010, Deborah Balzhiser and Susan McLeod demonstrated patterns in writing major curricula. Randy Brooks, Peiling Zhao, and Carmella Braniger view writing majors as participants "who might in fact change the assumptions of the field" (46). As Christian Weisser and Laurie Grobman demonstrate in their study of undergraduate alumni, the field has much to learn from students who major in writing. In particular, they examine how students' experiences and beliefs complement and extend writing studies scholarship about "professionalism" in the writing major (52-55). Dominic DelliCarpini makes a similar observation, noting how discrepancies may exist between faculty and student perceptions of a "professional writing" major ("Re-Writing the Humanities"). He also shows how students come to value discipline specific inquiry. Others have shown how writing majors' discourse can inform how the field conceptualizes undergraduate research (DelliCarpini and Crimmins) and the teaching of style (DelliCarpini and Zerbe). In this article, I attend to how writing majors can contribute to our deliberations about disciplinarity and intimacy.

Among scholars, one worry about achieving disciplinary status is that it will lead writing studies professionals to distance themselves from teaching labor. Rebecca Moore Howard opens her introduction to *Coming of Age: The Advanced Writing Curriculum*, the 2000 edited collection that was one of the first to advocate for four-year curricula in writing, by noting, "As composition studies has gained disciplinary status, it has developed an increasingly troubled relationship to its own pedagogy" ("History" xiii). Susan Miller comments in 1991 on the conflation of the desire to end composition instructors' low-level status with the goal of extricating the field's "members from the defining activity of any sort of academic practitioner—teaching" (193). In 1987, Stephen North predicted that, as the field developed, scholars would want to move away from teaching (367). It would seem that with the definitive establishment of a scholarly discipline, the relative desirability of theory rises and that of pedagogy falls. According to Bruce Horner, this dynamic within writing studies may result from an acceptance of the general hierarchies of academic labor that subordinate teaching to research. Horner describes and critiques what he perceives as a general attitude that holds (1) scholarly activity as esteemed work because of the relative ease with which it can be commodified and accrue exchange value and (2) teaching and service as necessary labor (2, 5-6). Such an attitude, Horner claims, also entails devaluing practical traditions of composition instruction, placing disciplinarity over teaching (172-73). Accepting Howard's claim that the writing major complicates distinctions between theory and pedagogy ("History" xiii), I wonder about the totalizing nature of Horner's assessment of academic professionalism. At the same time, many arguments for the writing major position it as a significant development in the establishment of writing studies' disciplinary status, and some of these proposals distance the writing major from the teaching traditions of FYW.

Indeed, some important early calls for advanced writing curricula demonstrate an interest in separation from FYW as a pre- or non-disciplinary service course, a course defined by the teaching *of* writing. The pieces that bookend *Coming of Age* exemplify this interest. In the introduction, Howard claims that advanced "curricula help to move the discipline of writing studies out of the *confines* of the first-year sequence" ("History" xxii, emphasis added). Robert J. Connors concludes the afterward on a liberatory note: "Though emerging from the *cave* of the first-year requirement will be liberating, we must also face the fear that comes with letting go of *familiar chains*" (149, emphasis added). Likewise, Miller uses language of constraint when comparing FYW to the diverse array of early twentieth-century advanced composition courses: "[W]e *cage* ourselves by identifying with the freshman enterprise" (76, emphasis added). We hear of the *confines, cave, chains, cage* of the pre-disciplinary FYW sequence, but this labeling differentiates the new and historical possibilities of advanced instruction from the limiting ideologies that perpetually call literacy crises into being. These scholars' comments certainly don't equal a marginalization of pedagogy in the service of disciplinarity; however, they do signal a compelling investment in what advanced courses provide teachers and the field.

This investment means that *scholars'* feelings matter when we consider disciplinarity. As the terms of escape and freedom above suggest, the establishment of disciplinary status, the development of a writing major, and the promotion of expertise about literacy all touch issues of affect. Some arguments for an advanced writing curriculum, like those cited above, *feel* like an affective rebellion as much as an intellectual one against hegemonic conceptions of literacy that historically shaped FYW. Tom Kerr argues that an "abundance of feeling . . . *always already* accompanies" the text-oriented enterprises occurring within English departments (and writing programs, too) and that "[t]he feeling of what happens, whether addressed directly or not, profoundly affects *what* happens" (26; see also Bizzell; Daniell; Gere; Herrington and Curtis; Jacobs and Micciche; McLeod; Micciche). Feelings are also implicated in scholars' work to build advanced curricula and to advance the field. John Trimbur claims in his *Coming of Age* piece that at least some courses acquire their "advanced character or feeling . . . because of what" they allow him as an instructor to accomplish: "namely to pay undivided attention" to intellectual concerns "without feeling guilty that [he's] not teaching students how to write" (113).[2] This differentiation between the teaching *of* writing and teaching *about* writing—or about other issues broadly connected to literacy and rhetoric—does not necessarily devalue pedagogy. It claims space for a pedagogy of professional expertise that understands knowledge about writing as a content worthy of study in its own right. This of/about distinction might, however, distance advanced courses from philosophies that place student-teacher interactions at the center of the discipline. In other words, the writing major might not only enable professionals to work against ideological traditions of FYW that constrain literacy but also allow them to separate themselves from the teaching *of* writing.

Relational labor characterized in affective terms (e.g., intimate and interpersonal) holds a complicated place in the history of advanced instruction and in various debates about writing studies' disciplinarity.[3] Thomas Newkirk draws on the history of advanced composition to claim that the central conflict facing writing studies involves "'the politics of intimacy,' the systematic devaluation of individual contact that marginalizes" composition instructors (115-16). Focusing on nineteenth-century composition teacher and scholar Barrett Wendell's English 12, a junior-level composition course at Harvard, Newkirk describes the practices he imagines at the heart of writing studies. Wendell's course involved "writing conferences, the use of student writing as the primary texts of the course, peer critiquing, analytic evaluation tools," and these practices contributed to "a stimulating relationship with individual students" (119).[4] Newkirk worries that this tradition would lose out as composition achieved academic status (128). In contrast, other scholars contend that intimate conceptions of teachers and students thrive. According to Kelly Ritter, intimacy won the day. She claims that "emphasiz[ing] the valuation of the personal (and interpersonal) in helping students acquire literacy" stems from "now-idealized goals originally articulated by process pedagogy" (390). This now prominent valuation derives from the process pedagogy movement and privileges practices that cultivate instructor-student relationships (Ritter 412-13). While Ritter critiques the privileged status of the interpersonal relationship in pedagogy, and I address this critique later, for now I note that claims about intimacy command scholars' attention. And if scholars' affective investments matter, what about the affective investments of undergraduates dedicated to the study of writing? What might we learn about issues of disciplinarity and intimacy from writing majors, and what research brought me to focus on these themes?

Methodology

As Annie Mendenhall observes, "Disciplinarity is a tricky subject in rhetoric and composition" (84). It's tricky not least of all because of methodological issues. How do we research this topic? Some have, in fact, called for us to abandon it as an inquiry. Karen Kopelson expresses a concern regarding writing studies scholars' apparent devotion to disciplinary self-reflexivity. Her argument takes on a certain urgency through a hermeneutical engagement with survey responses from rhetoric and composition doctoral students at two institutions. I certainly want to honor the voices of those graduate students. I also share with Kopelson a commitment to a "living rhetoric and composition" (775). A living field *should* continue to engage in self-reflexive inquiry, revisiting recurrent questions in light of changing conditions and expanding constituencies. Such conditions and constituencies include the growing number of writing major programs and their students. My treatment mirrors Kopelson's piece in some regards by engaging in reflexive inquiry through the discourse of students in the field at two institutions—albeit a different kind of student: undergraduate writing majors as opposed to doctoral students.

I solicited self-reports about the experiences of students in writing major programs at two institutions: Private Research University and Liberal Arts College. Both of these private, non-religious institutions in New York have independent writing programs with undergraduate majors named on the Conference on College Composition and Communication list of writing major programs. Private Research University's writing major had a curriculum focused on rhetorical theory and genre, and it also included professional writing and some creative nonfiction. Additionally, Private Research University offered a composition and rhetoric doctoral program. Liberal Arts College's writing program blended creative, nonfiction, and professional writing with some courses in rhetorical theory.

Blending quantitative and qualitative instruments, I investigated writing majors' attitudes and beliefs about their experiences through survey responses, interviews, and student work. All data were collected in order that they might be considered together and interpreted in concert. During the first phase of this study, I used a cross-sectional survey to solicit responses through mostly closed-ended questions (which also had fields for written comments). Questions in the survey were designed to gain data about students' attitudes, opinions, beliefs, and experiences as writing majors. At the end of the survey, students were offered the opportunity to volunteer for a follow-up interview and/or to submit a sample of their writing (and these writing samples are not examined in the present article). The second phase of my research involved interviewing willing participants. I employed semi-structured interviewing techniques, asking a set of questions to all participants as well as asking follow-ups when appropriate.

In using methods that solicit student-generated data, my interest centered on what the field learns when it takes as a site of inquiry the discourse of undergraduate writing majors and the vernacular terms in which they articulate their experiences. At Private Research University, the survey was distributed on the majors' listserv and was shared on class listservs by at least two upper-division instructors, resulting in thirty responses. I also visited three upper-division classes in person and distributed paper copies of the survey. This step produced twelve more results from writing majors. Of those forty-two survey respondents, I conducted interviews with seven students. At Liberal Arts College, the survey was distributed through the writing majors' listserv. Three days after that e-mail went out, forty-four students submitted responses. I conducted interviews with six students. These materials served as touchstones for my hermeneutical inquiry into writing studies disciplinarity.

Relational Labor Within the Writing Major

Students in this study often defined the writing major in connection with interpersonal interactions that supported their literacy development and that inculcated a rhetorical view of writing as a social enterprise. Following Raymond Williams' view that the most important products workers produce are themselves, Horner argues that students, through the material social processes of writing, engage in processes of subject "(re)production," both "responding to and re-creating the context of" the self and its production (247). Interactions with faculty, part of the context for writing, encourage not only writing majors' literacy acquisition, but also a sense of themselves as individuals who matter, which in turn can fuel their capacity to take rhetorical action. Students in this study echo one of the conclusions reached by Anne Herrington and Marcia Curtis: "Time gave [students] . . . [the] opportunity to revise themselves in much the same way they revised their essays" (381). As Herrington and Curtis use it, "time" isn't just the passage of days and semesters. It involves what students and teachers do with their time. And while it certainly does not equal *time with faculty*, it is inclusive of those interactions.

The mutually informing movement between an expanding sense of a student's own abilities and a specific timetable is hard to trace, but some students nevertheless claimed that their interactions within the writing major prepared them for varied rhetorical endeavors. Indeed, Mark, a Liberal Arts College junior, commented during his interview on the difficulty of articulating precisely when and where he learned something that persisted. However, he insisted that his interactions with others over time contributed to his growth as a writer:

> [W]orkshops with other talented writers (and professors, especially) have been valuable for my personal development. The degree to which I engage with every word and space in a sentence I write now is far beyond the level of thought I put into an entire plot when I was in high school. I can't tell you 'this class taught me this' or 'I got better at A when I did B,' but I'm much better at writing now than I was four years ago. (Personal interview)

While unable to recount the specific timetable of his learning, Mark felt that an interaction-rich environment encouraged his potential as a writer. Throughout his studies, he realized that potential through increasingly accomplished expressions. Workshops with Liberal Arts College instructors in particular (but also with visiting creative and nonfiction writers as well as fellow student writers) contributed to his "personal development," which functions here as synonymous with *writing development*. Constructing a developmental scheme, Mark highlighted how the increased attentiveness he brought as a college junior to "every word" exceeded what he exerted when crafting "an entire plot" in high school. The interactional scene Mark described led him to gain an increased sense of his own efficacy as a writer, affirming writing as a social practice.

From the vantage point of some writing majors, even as course design is important, the quality of the encounter between faculty and students forged for them a rhetorical paradigm of writing.[5] For example, Gail, a Liberal Arts College senior, spoke of the connections among personal interactions, individual writing growth, and the complexity of literacy:

> The [encouragement of] faculty and community [among writing majors] work with each other because you have a community of people who understand what it is to write, which is really helpful. . . . There were teachers who would give writing assignments and projects, but it was more about getting us to think than it was to just improve our writing. . . . Looking back on the four years that I've been here, I really have grown. . . . None of the teachers say it's going to be easy, but they do offer encouragement. They get you ready for what [post-graduate life is] going to be like because they know. They're here to help. (Personal interview)

Gail's understanding of writing exceeded purely instrumentalist terms and questioned notions of writing as reducible to manipulating textual features. Faculty efforts were directed toward not only the development of discrete skills (i.e., "just improve our writing") but also the promotion of critical engagement through writing (i.e., "it was more about getting us to think"). In scholarship that treats students' general assumptions about college writing, writing for school appears in overwhelmingly instrumentalist terms (Durst) and peers emerge as lacking in contrast to those culturally recognized as Authors (Horner 244-46). Contributing a different vision, Gail discussed writing and responding in relational and affectively positive terms. Her vision of writing as a socially situated activity developed over the course of several years and in the context of a teaching and learning community.

For some students, relationships became a vehicle through which the writing major questioned culturally dominant frames that figure literacy as transactional textuality and neutral skills. Jeremiah, a senior, began his interview by raising Private Research University writing program's vision statement and its explicitly articulated political commitments:

> One thing I did know about the Writing Program before I entered it—and it was [a] major factor about why I decided to enter the Writing Program—was the vision statement. . . . There was a really

> externally focused vision statement . . . [with] a focus on justice, a focus on understanding the means through which people talk about justice and achieve it. (Personal interview)

The program's website described writing as "central to a just society" (citation withheld to respect anonymity). Inspired by this vision, Jeremiah saw interactions with faculty and graduate students as providing the basis for learning. He connected this concern for justice to issues of time, which meant both the time he took to understand the program and the time he spent with writing teachers: "I feel like I definitely took the time I needed because I had such good relationships with the faculty and graduate students. I was able to ask them questions and figure out what the philosophy was" (Personal interview). As he says, *because* of these relationships, Jeremiah felt authorized to take time to reflect on his learning, further cultivate these relationships, and determine his place within the writing major at his institution. By emphasizing relationships within a particular place, and writing as connected to a programmatic concern with "justice," Jeremiah exercised the situational attentiveness of a rhetorical agent who seeks opportunities for purposeful composing.

Instructors' relational labor within the writing major involved exercising a deep regard for students in ways that encouraged their rhetorical faculties. Three excerpts from Jeremiah's interview bring into focus the affective, interactive scene of literacy learning that connects students and teachers. He detailed the difficulty he had composing the application materials needed to apply for matriculated student status. A creative nonfiction instructor created space inside and outside the classroom to support his writing:

> There was something [off-putting] about producing those documents and being evaluated. . . . But I was in a creative nonfiction class. . . . I used that opportunity to start writing my college admissions essay. It was the first time I had felt somewhat free to do so and felt somewhat empowered and felt somewhat like my voice and my ability to produce intertwined. . . . Her mentorship and the way she structured that course, in a clichéd way, it gave me a voice. (Personal interview)

Jeremiah also discussed the nature of his communications with faculty throughout the Private Research University writing program:

> I just have never e-mailed a professor within the writing program with a concern, an idea, a suggestion [. . .] and not gotten a very thoughtful, empathetic (excited, even) response from them. . . . I've met with writing professors and for the weeks that come, they'll keep

> returning to those conversations that we had. They'll think of me in the hallway, and they'll get excited about those kinds of relationships. It seems like they sought to be a professor because they thought they'd get to have those relationships. (Personal interview)

And these relations sometimes continued after a course was over:

> I have been in courses that I didn't like at the same time that I had amazingly close mentoring relationships with those faculty members. . . . They sent e-mails to me about certain opportunities that became available, and I still keep up those relationships even when I'm out of their classes. . . . The faculty in the writing program understand themselves as not just research producers, but also as people working with their students. (Personal interview)

In Jeremiah's account, writing teachers are identified as having a desire for relationships. That desire, in fact, is named as an exigency for seeking an academic career that allows teachers to employ various relational tactics. For example, by revisiting previous conversations with a student and layering them into later exchanges, teachers communicated that students' words found an audience attentive to the particular concerns—and life—of a unique person.

The affective component of faculty engagement was central to Jeremiah. From Jeremiah's perspective, exchanges with faculty that carried an idea beyond a single conversation also expressed an "empathetic" regard for—and "excited" engagement with—his projects, ideas, and *him*. Projects Jeremiah discussed at length included those connected to his self-claimed queer identity, which attempted to intervene in the politics of sexuality: "In almost all of my classes, I've incorporated LGBT work. . . . I was able to think about my own value as a queer person with a unique story that might speak to issues, that might be helpful to other people—or that might meaningfully challenge some of the ways we think about LGBT people" (Personal interview). Affectively charged relational labor helped Jeremiah undertake writing that mattered to him and that faculty saw as valuable. In this way, his teachers were "research producers," but they also operated as "people working with their students" (Jeremiah, Personal interview). Given that Jeremiah attended a research-intensive institution with a composition doctoral program as well as a writing major, his perception shows us how intimate pedagogy is not diminished because of disciplinary accomplishments, such as establishing doctoral programs and undergraduate majors.

As demonstrated in the account above, *mentorship*, an activity fundamentally grounded in relationships and in the project of human becoming, surfaces as a central theme for some writing majors. When Jeremiah described the creative nonfiction course, the instructor listened—and was present—to the anxieties Jeremiah had about composing. What he called her "mentorship" (i.e., the interaction itself and the textuality that surrounded it) became a source of encouragement, a source that made Jeremiah feel connected to a power that enabled him to produce texts. He believed that this relationship helped him connect with his "voice" and his ability to write. Mentorship supports people as well as writing processes. In their introduction to *Undergraduate Research in English Studies*, Laurie Grobman and Joyce Kinkead contend that "mentorship is crucial" to meaningful student research accomplishments (xvi). Margaret E. Whitt and Matthew Henningsen treat relationships as fundamentally interactive. Jane Greer frames the mentorship of undergraduates as labor with pedagogical, disciplinary, and institutional dimensions ("Nontraditional" 41). Joonna S. Trapp and David Elder view mentorship as affective labor: a student undertakes work "in the presence of someone who *cares* [. . .] to know and consider the values and beliefs of the student and how those are formed" and the *feeling* of the encounter is critical (10-11). This professional attention to mentorship as bound up with the relational work of students' becoming echoes writing majors' perceptions.

Even though instructor-student interactions may begin in a particular course, that mentorship contributed to students' *ongoing* development as writers. In this regard, teachers appeared to enact Carl Vandermeulen's suggestion that students of creative writing "need people they trust to tell them who they are and what they are capable of becoming" (121). Three Liberal Arts College students mentioned the importance of independent studies to their development, but Mark addressed at length how a small senior thesis seminar and an independent study helped him develop a mentorship relationship with one creative writing faculty member:

> It really comes down to having a relationship with a professor that extends outside of the classroom. Because I've worked one-on-one with [one professor], we've become comfortable talking about not only the work I bring in those days, but also fiction and writing/reading in general. . . . Since [she] and I were working on so many different things together, our meetings often became catchalls: we'd talk about the project itself, my other fiction, applying to graduate school, readings and other works of interest, etc. She helped suggest literary magazines for me to submit work to, etc. . . . On 'down' weeks, we talk about what I have, but then about other stuff.

Having the institutional sanction of an independent study afforded Mark and his teacher the freedom to determine their interactions. Regular meetings were dedicated to Mark's writing and "'down' weeks" to sharing reading materials, considering publication opportunities, and supporting his graduate school applications. Mark also noted, "It's really up to having a lovely mentor like [this instructor], as profs don't get paid for the credits they teach through independent studies. But [she's] been my biggest advocate in the department and encouraged me to keep working" (Personal interview). Again, relational labor is characterized affectively. This "lovely" mentor supported Mark's learning and other opportunities.

While Mark's account showed how mentorship is possible after a traditional course ends, it's certainly not automatically given. In her survey response, Jennifer, a Liberal Arts College junior, offered this comment regarding how often she spoke with faculty about professional or graduate school options: "I want to! They're always overwhelmed." Likewise, two other Liberal Arts College students interviewed for this study readily acknowledged their perception of the multiple demands on faculty time and labor—particularly teaching demands. Just prior to our interview, Jennifer conferred with a professor from the previous year to discuss a forthcoming public presentation. Though such encounters took place, she also reported uncertainty about how to make them a more regular occurrence—even when she had a specific concern (e.g., applying to graduate school):

> I don't know, sometimes it feels like there's this weird thing after a class ends. Maybe I'm not supposed to talk to them, and I would really like to talk to some of my professors about, for example, how I don't have any idea how to research grad schools. It's something I'm interested in, but I don't know if it's a viable goal. . . . They're all busy with the classes they have right now. (Personal interview)

Without a structured occasion for conversation, Jennifer could not quite imagine how to overcome the affective barrier (i.e., the "weird" feeling) that prevented her from contacting faculty after a course ended. Her forthcoming public presentation offered a specific rationale. Echoing Jennifer's desire, four Private Research University survey respondents indicated an interest in having more contact with faculty after a course ended. They also seemed to think more faculty interaction would be possible because, as two students wrote, "professors [are] very open to such things" and "they're approachable." This approachability must surely be viewed as a positive attribute. At this point, I want to acknowledge how students' interest in interpersonal and affective issues may act as a *complicated* affirmation of writing studies' disciplinarity, an interest that carries affordances as well as potential problems.

The (Possible) Trouble With Relationships

While writing majors valued relationships with faculty that prepared them for varied writing opportunities, it is not always clear to students how that labor intersects with discipline-specific or expert knowledge. From the perspective of students in the present study, disciplinary and professional commitments among academic faculty in general might interfere with relational labor. For example, Jeremiah understood his interactions with instructors in other disciplines as productive, but also carefully contained by the teacher-student relationship: "I've gone to office hours of people outside the writing department, and I can have a really great meeting with them, but it's really understood that that's the time we have together—that meeting" (Personal interview). In the context of a research-intensive university, faculty in general might perceive this restraint as necessary in order to balance teaching and research. Accounting for this phenomenon as he also saw it at Private Research University, Tyler, a senior, explained,

> I guess the core requirement is the best example of this. . . . It seems like a lot of the departments teach as if their classes exist in a vacuum. . . . On the one hand, the professors, they're there for that specific department, so you can't fault them for teaching what they know. At the same time, other than [introductory] writing, I really didn't see any attempt to make the lower-level classes more available to a wider audience. (Personal interview)

By "available," Tyler meant that writing courses provided both "content" (i.e., knowledge *about* writing) and practices that supported students' interests in—and goals for—writing. Given that Tyler called attention to the interrelationship of knowledge and practice, I again find myself uncertain of Trimbur's claim that the importance of the teaching *of* writing might diminish in advanced courses ("Theory" 113). Tyler found teachers within the writing major who promoted a productive negotiation of student and program goals by encouraging purposeful student composing that connected conceptual knowledge to material practices.

That kind of negotiation is why I view my present focus on largely interpersonal relationships as relevant to the theoretical dimensions of pedagogy, disciplinarity, and teacher-identity. Howard claims that arguments about obviously laudable efforts sometimes award too much influence to the work of individual instructors ("Postpedagogical"). Readers might say (1) that it seems fairly obvious to claim that substantial personal involvement with students "is surely a Good Thing that will surely result in Better Learning and Happier People" (Howard, "Postpedagogical" 225), and (2) that such a claim individualizes pedagogical efforts rather than produces systematic developments. At the same time, the actions described above are material social *practices* (e.g., *labor*)—not innate dispositions—that promote students' literacy learning.

And yet, even if this interaction-focused discourse does not equate teaching with specific personalities and even if the practices students described constitute a form of labor, might student accounts about these practices construct teaching (particularly literacy instruction) as a practical set of skills developed *without* reference to expert knowledge? When Mark named the quality possessed by his mentor that facilitated their work, he called her "lovely." Gina spoke of teachers and the feeling they produced for her as "nice." When Gail characterized teachers' efforts, she said, "They're here to help." *Lovely, nice, help*—perhaps these terms were simply readily accessible. However, these characterizations disquietingly echo cultural scripts that historically defined composition instruction in highly gendered and lay terms. Donna Strickland's historical work documents how writing instruction was viewed as practically oriented, routine, and non-intellectual labor (19-37). Susan Miller notes that teachers directed this labor toward the perceived "mundane" details of student writing (127). This construction of composition instruction as practical mundane labor also coded and devalued teaching as a feminine activity (Holbrook; Miller 121-41; Schell; Strickland 38-44).

It is in this regard that Kelly Ritter expresses concern over the valorization of teaching as interpersonal labor and critiques it as a romanticized good in literacy instruction (412). Miller places the personally involved, self-sacrificial role adopted by (and placed upon) composition instructors (14-15) within an ideological complex that figures the composition teacher as a maid/mother/disciplinarian who urges students to master the privileged vernacular and who regulates their use of it (137). According to Ritter, practitioners identify with this self-sacrificing stance, making the field "*dependent* upon it for its pedagogical imperative" (392). This dependence leads Ritter to question, for example, the idea of writing as an "enterprise between teacher and student, deserving of lavish attention to personalized, repeated response" (413) because of how it relies upon a gendered ideology of "help" that may prove "counterproductive to the discipline of composition studies as a whole" (390). The critique carries force when we consider, as Ritter does, the majority workforce staffing FYW with its labor-intensive relational teaching of writing: contingent women faculty who comment, conference, and comment again (388). Literature regarding these exploitative and politically damaging dynamics—not an assumption of intimate labor as non-disciplinary or undesirable—makes me pause when students in the writing major mobilize an affect-laden language of help in connection with teachers' labor.

Conclusions and Implications

In light of the above critiques, students' perceptions of relational labor might temper zeal for claims that the writing major serves the goal of disciplinary status. However, similar accounts from students about compassionate faculty interactions are not unique to writing studies. Nel Noddings has long been an advocate of teacher "care" for students, treating care as a dynamic of receptivity in which the teacher receives into herself the worldviews and feelings of students so as to promote their development (30-33). Longitudinal investigations of literacy learning throughout college demonstrate an interest among students in faculty's disciplined care (i.e., knowledgeable and humane engagement). Herrington and Curtis note that the four students in their study "reported learning most from instructors who gave them positive recognition as thinking persons behind and within their prose" (361). This finding was true of faculty in gender studies, sociology, and psychology. In psychology, one student, Rachel, placed value on "understanding," which Herrington and Curtis took as the psychology faculty member's understanding "of the subject matter itself" and the student's "own personal connection with her subject matter" (363).

As we consider the writing major, particularly in independent writing programs of the sort studied here, perhaps we have an opportunity to imagine care and relational labor distributed equitably within an academic unit such that all faculty promote among undergraduates professional expertise and affective attitudes that encourage a rhetorical vision of literacy. In this regard, writing studies and its undergraduate majors might help shape the future of literacy politics in progressive ways. Perhaps that sounds a bit too idealistic, too Rhetopian (as Wayne Booth put it in *The Rhetoric of Rhetoric*), but we can dream. Of course, we work and care and do caring work in a world with particular labor conditions and histories that differentially privilege and constrain faculty. For example, the 2006 Modern Language Association (MLA)'s "Still Standing: The Associate Professor Survey" reported the additional time it often takes women members of the MLA, across institution types, to achieve promotion from associate to full professor. The work differences contributing to this outcome seemed not about tremendous differences in professional labor time: "Overall the differences reported between men and women in the amount of time devoted to" various work responsibilities "are small—an hour or less a week" (11). These differences included women reporting that they devote two hours less each week to research than men and over two hours more each week to various teaching-related activities. The report concludes, "Cumulatively, these microdifferences over time may result in a major inequity, such as we see in the substantial difference in time between women and men in attaining the rank of professor. . . . What may be slight differences when taken singly may, when taken together, cascade to produce major inequities" (21). While I studied independent writing programs and did not collect data on questions about tenure and promotion timelines, I recall Miller's searing insight from 1991 that writing studies and writing programs frequently create hierarchies similar to those within literary studies and English departments. Consequently, while caring faculty involvement seems important to undergraduate disciplinary involvement—and should be celebrated—we need to keep a critical focus on how relational labor is distributed within a program and a writing major.

Given both the potential value and problems of extensive relational labor, I conclude by highlighting the implications of my study for our disciplinary work.

- *Relationships and expertise*: Students did not view relational investment *alone* as enough to achieve their learning goals. For example, Mark valued his mentor's wide knowledge base and access to her library; Jennifer wanted to understand and pursue graduate school options; Jeremiah appreciated mentorship within a program that promoted a critical awareness of writing as political. In short, it was important that teachers *cared*, but students recognized the need for *informed care*.
- *Writing as rhetorical*: Through their comments about the relational labor involved with literacy learning, writing majors articulated a capacious vision of writing that challenges popular instrumentalist notions of writing as primarily a set of discrete skills. Within a spacious curriculum filled with rich interactions between faculty and students, writing majors valued not only demonstrable abilities, but also an object of study: writing. While some students' emphases may sound similar to arguments that construct FYW as a non-disciplinary service course, what they described was not simply a service major nor were their teachers seen as personalities more than professionals. Students often viewed writing in rhetorical terms: situated, not context-free; social, not solely personal; collaborative, not entirely individual; and (though less often) explicitly politically implicated, not neutral.
- *Writing majors—programs and persons*: Scholarly treatments tend to focus on writing majors as programs. The title of Giberson and Moriarty's important collection functions as a kind of synecdoche for this trend; the focus is on "*what* we are becoming" in terms of curriculum, programs, and disciplinary emphases. Writing majors are often imagined as synonymous with official curricula: they become who we want them to become. Some notable works do examine writing majors from the standpoint of student experience (DelliCarpini; DelliCarpini and

Crimmins; DelliCarpini and Zerbe; Weisser and Grobman). But the recurrent themes of *mentorship, time,* and *human becoming* in the context of instructor-student relationships highlight the need to remember in scholarly treatments of the writing major (i.e., programs) not only *what*, but also *who*, writing majors (i.e., students) are becoming. And we can learn a great deal about that from students themselves.

The relational labor many students value operate in tandem with the professional expertise of teachers, not as a negation of that expertise. This generally affective, relational framing of instructor labor—along with students' rhetorical conceptions of writing—may suggest that increasing disciplinary status does not diminish the field's teaching emphasis, that expertise *about* writing is as important as the teaching *of* writing. Such a hopeful conclusion should not be taken as naïve optimism or obliviousness to the labor involved. Rather, it is an invitation for us to continue self-reflexive inquiry in ways that acknowledge the complicated role of intimacy in undergraduate disciplinary involvement and that match the field's own promising claims about the writing major as well as our own confidence that expert knowledge about writing matters. Ultimately, disciplinary work seems as much about care (toward students and toward faculty) as expertise.

Acknowledgements

Whatever remains unclear or incomplete in this article, the responsibility rests with me. Whatever is done well is thanks to many people. Laura Micciche, Doug Downs, and an anonymous reviewer at *Composition Studies* provided insightful comments. Rebecca Moore Howard, Eileen Schell, and Lois Agnew shepherded this project in its early forms. Many thanks to my redoubtable writing group friends: Jacob Babb, Annie Mendenhall, Erika Strandjord, and Julia Voss. All these colleagues demonstrated disciplined care for my work. And thanks also to the students who participated in this research.

Notes

1. Study participants' names and institutions' names are pseudonyms.
2. In some ways, this notion of advanced instruction perpetuates what Spencer Schaffner critiques in his discussion of the writing major: a binary between writing as content and writing as practice (55).
3. A discourse of intimacy likewise surfaces in discussions of disciplinary undergraduate research. In Jane Greer's introduction to the tenth anniversary volume of *Young Scholars in Writing* (*YSW*), she claims, "A calculus of intimacy . . . would allow us, then, to account more adequately for the ways in which *YSW* has fostered new relationships, destabilized hierarchies, and expanded possibilities for learning" (1).

4. There are additional rich descriptions of English 12 and student responses to the course in Katherine H. Adams' *A History* (47-53). Adams demonstrates that issues of student writing development and instructor-student relationships run throughout the history of general advanced literacy courses (*A History*; *A Group*). Newkirk and Adams offer a revision to the standard account that depicts late nineteenth-century Harvard faculty, including Wendell, as primarily concerned with current-traditional values and practices.

5. In terms of course design, at Liberal Arts College, Mark noted the productive nature of the workshop model and Jennifer called attention to courses that involved theoretical readings. At Private Research University, Tyler privileged the freedom to choose the subject of his writing and valued the diverse genres in which he was asked to write for many rhetorical purposes.

Works Cited

Adams, Katherine H. *A Group of Their Own: College Writing Courses and American Women Writers, 1880-1940*. Albany: SUNY P, 2001. Print.

---. *A History of Professional Writing Instruction in American Colleges*. Dallas: Southern Methodist UP, 1993. Print.

Balzhiser, Deborah, and Susan McLeod. "The Undergraduate Writing Major: What Is It? What Should It Be?" *CCC* 61.3 (2010): 415-33. Print.

Bizzell, Patricia. "Feminist Methods of Research in the History of Rhetoric: What Difference Do They Make?" *Rhetoric Society Quarterly* 30 (2000): 5-17. Print.

Booth, Wayne C. *The Rhetoric of Rhetoric: The Quest for Effective Communication*. Malden: Blackwell, 2004. Print.

Brooks, Randy, Peiling Zhao, and Carmella Braniger. "Redefining the Undergraduate English Writing Major: An Integrated Approach at a Small Comprehensive University." Giberson and Moriarty 32-49.

Committee on the Major in Rhetoric and Composition. "Writing Majors at a Glance." *CCC*. NCTE, 2009. Web. 30 Dec. 2009. <http://www.ncte.org/library/NCTEFiles/Groups/CCCC/Committees/Writing_Majors_Final.pdf>.

Committee on the Status of Women in the Profession. "Still Standing: The Associate Professor Survey." *Modern Language Association*. MLA, 2009. Web. 25 Mar. 2014. <http://www.mla.org/pdf/cswp_final042909.pdf>.

Connors, Robert J. "Afterword." Shamoon, Howard, Jamieson, and Schwegler 143-50.

Daniell, Beth. *A Communion of Friendship: Literacy, Spiritual Practice, and Women in Recovery*. Carbondale: SIUP, 2003. Print.

DeJoy, Nancy. *Process This: Undergraduate Writing in Composition Studies*. Logan: Utah State UP, 2004. Print.

DelliCarpini, Dominic. "Re-Writing the Humanities: The Writing Major's Effect upon Undergraduate Studies in English Departments." *Composition Studies* 35.1 (2007): 15-36. Print.

DelliCarpini, Dominic, and Cynthia Crimmins. "The Writing Center as a Space for Undergraduate Research." Grobman and Kinkead 191-211.

DelliCarpini, Dominic, and Michael J. Zerbe. "Remembering the Canons' Middle Sister: Style, Memory, and the Return of the Progymnasmata in the Liberal Arts Writing Major." Giberson and Moriarty 177-203.

Durst, Russel. *Collision Course: Conflict, Negotiation, and Learning in College Composition.* Urbana: NCTE, 1999. Print.

Gail. Personal interview. 31 Mar. 2012

Gere, Anne Ruggles. *Intimate Practices: Literacy and Cultural Work in U.S. Women's Clubs, 1880-1920.* Urbana: U of Illinois P, 1997. Print.

Giberson, Greg A., and Thomas A. Moriarty, eds. *What We Are Becoming: Developments in Undergraduate Writing Majors.* Logan: Utah State UP, 2010. Print.

Gina. Personal interview. 8 Aug. 2011

Greer, Jane. "Editor's Introduction." *Young Scholars in Writing* 10 (2013): 1-4. Print.

---. "Nontraditional Students as Undergraduate Researchers: Expanding Horizons for Adult Learners and Their Mentors." Grobman and Kinkead 30-48.

Grobman, Laurie, and Joyce Kinkead, eds. *Undergraduate Research in English Studies.* Urbana: NCTE, 2010. Print.

Herrington, Anne, and Marcia Curtis. *Persons in Process: Four Stories of Writing and Personal Development in College.* Urbana: NCTE, 2000. Print.

Holbrook, Sue Ellen. "Women's Work: The Feminizing of Composition." *Rhetoric Review* 9 (1991): 201-29. Print.

Horner, Bruce. *Terms of Work for Composition: A Materialist Critique.* Albany: SUNY P, 2000. Print.

Howard, Rebecca Moore. "History, Politics, Pedagogy, and Advanced Writing." Shamoon, Howard, Jamieson, and Schwegler xiii-xxii.

---. "Postpedagogical Reflections on Plagiarism and Capital." *Beyond Postprocess.* Ed. Sidney I. Dobrin, J.A. Rice, and Michael Vastola. Logan: Utah State UP, 2011. 219-31. Print.

Jacobs, Dale, and Laura R. Micciche, eds. *A Way to Move: Rhetorics of Emotion and Composition Studies.* Portsmouth: Boynton/Cook, 2003. Print.

Jeremiah. Personal interview. 5 Apr. 2012.

Kerr, Tom. "The Feeling of What Happens in Departments of English." Jacobs and Micciche 23-32.

Kopelson, Karen. "Sp(l)itting Images; or, Back to the Future of (Rhetoric and?) Composition." *CCC* 59.4 (2008): 750-80. Print.

Mark. Personal interview. 4 Apr. 2012.

McLeod, Susan. *Notes on the Heart: Affective Issues in the Writing Classroom.* Carbondale: SIUP, 1996. Print.

Mendenhall, Annie. "The Historical Problem of Vertical Coherence: Writing, Research, and Legitimacy in Early 20th Century Rhetoric and Composition." *Composition Studies* 41.1 (2013): 84-100. Print.

Micciche, Laura R. *Doing Emotion: Rhetoric, Writing, Teaching.* Portsmouth: Boynton/Cook, 2007. Print.

Miller, Susan. *Textual Carnivals: The Politics of Composition.* Carbondale: SIUP, 1991. Print.

Newkirk, Thomas. "The Politics of Intimacy: The Defeat of Barrett Wendell at Harvard." *Taking Stock: The Writing Process Movement in the '90s*. Ed. Lad Tobin and Thomas Newkirk. Portsmouth: Boynton/Cook, 1994. 115-32. Print.

Noddings, Nel. *Caring: A Feminine Approach to Ethics and Moral Education*. Berkeley: U of California P, 1984. Print.

North, Stephen. *The Making of Knowledge in Composition: Portrait of an Emerging Field*. Upper Montclair: Boynton/Cook, 1987. Print.

Ritter, Kelly. "'Ladies Who Don't Know Us Correct Our Papers': Postwar Lay Reader Programs and Twenty-First Century Contingent Labor in First-Year Writing." *CCC* 63.3 (2012): 387–419. Print.

Schaffner, Spencer. "Grounding the Writing Major in the Socio-Graphemic Approach." *Composition Studies* 35.1 (2007): 55-56. Print.

Schell, Eileen E. *Gypsy Academics and Mother-Teachers: Gender, Contingent Labor, and Writing Instruction*. Portsmouth: Boynton/Cook, 1998. Print.

Shamoon, Linda K., Rebecca Moore Howard, Sandra Jamieson, and Robert A. Schwegler, eds. *Coming of Age: The Advanced Writing Curriculum*. Portsmouth: Heinemann Boynton/Cook, 2000. Print.

Strickland, Donna. *The Managerial Unconsciousness*. Carbondale: SIUP, 2011. Print.

Trapp, Joonna Smithermann, and David Elder. "Mentor as Method: Faculty Mentor Roles and Undergraduate Scholarship." Grobman and Kinkead 3-12.

Trimbur, John. "Theory of Visual Design." Shamoon, Howard, Jamieson, and Schwegler 106-14.

Tyler. Personal interview. 11 May 2011.

Vandermeulen, Carl. *Negotiating the Personal in Creative Writing*. Bristol: Multilingual Matters, 2011. Print.

Weisser, Christian, and Laurie Grobman. "Undergraduate Writing Majors and the Rhetoric of Professionalism." *Composition Studies* 40.1 (2012): 39-59. Print.

Whitt, Margaret E., and Matthew Henningsen. "Partners in Scholarship: The Making of an Anthology." Grobman and Kinkead 13-29.

Writing the Personal in an Outcomes-Based World

Elizabeth Kimball, Emily Schnee, and Liesl Schwabe

This essay explores the influence of the discourse and practices of the learning outcomes assessment (LOA) movement on three composition instructors' assignments and assessments. While outcomes assessment by itself can be a useful tool, it cannot be separated from the exigency that compels it, in which educational practices must be defended against a skeptical, product-oriented public. We contend that LOA has come to be interpreted at the local level as a stricture against writing the personal into the academic. Presenting our approaches one by one, we show how we engage personal writing within academic genres with differing student populations and institutional contexts—a selective liberal arts college, an urban community college, and a private religious university. We argue that the carefully planned use of personal narrative must have a role in composition precisely because it most effectively engages students in the writing process, fosters critical thinking skills, and moves students toward the true ends of a college education and the very learning goals that national LOA initiatives have articulated.

Introduction

The practice of assessment around learning outcomes seems so sound and obvious that one wonders why it has not been a part of higher education much longer than it has. Whether at the course, program, or college level, learning outcomes are meant to articulate clear objectives around which planning and teaching should revolve. Because they are clear and articulated ahead of time, the idea is that they are therefore measurable: We said we were going to do X; have we in fact done X? We know that we must do this kind of planning in order to help our students learn and to develop as teachers.

But there is a difference between this local assessment and the broader learning outcomes assessment (LOA) movement, and in this article we take a cautious and skeptical view of LOA and its impact on our work as writing teachers. We contend that the learning outcomes movement is part of a "huge and complex body of changes that have been introduced in our education system in recent years" precisely because these changes are "essential to the commodification of learning and hence to the desire to audit and monitor the performance of those involved" (Gallagher 231). LOA is part and parcel of the last decade's push towards accountability in higher education and has turned the development and assessment of learning outcomes from a local practice into a national movement with a growing infrastructure of research enterprises, professional meetings, and organizations. This movement includes the Association of American Colleges & Universities' (AAC&U) Liberal Education and America's Promise (LEAP) project in 2005, and the development of the Valid Assessment of Learning in Undergraduate Education (VALUE) rubrics in 2009. Richard Arum and Josipa Roksa's late-2010 condemnation of learning in higher education, *Academically Adrift: Limited Learning on College Campuses* (based on the results of a standardized test called the Collegiate Learning Assessment), was followed by Lumina Foundation's Degree Qualifications Profile (DQP) and "The Completion Agenda: A Call to Action" by the American Association of Community Colleges in 2011. During this period, both the George W. Bush and Obama administrations have promoted the idea that higher education is in a state of crisis and must be called to accountability.[1] Under the guise of promoting student learning, LOA scrutinizes the work of college teachers and students, and attempts to hold it accountable to external stakeholders—accreditors, policy makers, parents, students, and the general public.

One manifestation of this movement can be seen in the work the AAC&U has done to promote "the national dialogue on assessment of college student learning" through the widespread dissemination of the VALUE rubrics (AAC&U). We have used these rubrics ourselves to perform many kinds of work, from designing whole curricula to grading student papers; one of us was even an early reviewer of the rubrics when they were being developed. Though they are useful starting places and part of a national dialogue, we question the exigency from which these rubrics emerge—to hold colleges accountable to a verifiable end product—and how they are interpreted and utilized as a measurement of educational success.

Like many in composition, we see an understanding of the writing process, and the student learning that emerges through this process, getting lost amidst calls for quantifiable outcomes. We argue that as writing teachers committed to the inherent role of the personal in writing and in crafting knowledge, we must recognize the danger of the broader LOA movement to our work, particularly its insistence on end goals as a means of defending our work to external skeptics and regulators. In "The Trouble with Outcomes," Chris Gallagher writes, "if we work within the OA [Outcomes Assessment] model, it is important to consider carefully (and perhaps reconsider) how we frame and use educational ends in our profession, departments, programs, and classrooms" (43). Starting with the end goal is a problem, as John Dewey sees it, because learning along the way becomes "a mere unavoidable means to something else" (qtd. in Gallagher 45). The discourses and practices of LOA, because of their use for accountability purposes and orientation towards final products, are quite distinct from the ordinary planning and reflecting that are part of the healthy formative assessment in which all good writing teachers engage.[2]

We are further troubled by the ways in which the rubrics of the LOA movement tend to edge out personal writing and delegitimize narrative genres, which we consider essential to student learning and the development of critical thinking. For example, in the preface to the VALUE written communication rubric, at the very end of a long list of possible genres students might engage in to prove fluency in written communication, personal essays get a cursory mention. And, on the actual assessment rubric, which colleges and universities throughout the United States are being encouraged to adopt and adapt, nowhere do the words "narrative," "self," or "personal" appear. Though the preface acknowledges that "the best writing assessments are locally determined and sensitive to local context and mission," the absence of narrative is glaring (AAC&U).

Similarly, in the DQP promoted by the Lumina Foundation for Education, learning outcomes for writing are delineated as part of "communication fluency." Though "narrative" is mentioned, once again the emphasis is on "error-free" construction of a "coherent argument" (Lumina Foundation). The imposition of correctness—largely a product of class and community—at the exclusion of more personally meaningful genres of writing is troubling. As Bob Broad, an expert in local, context-driven assessment argues, "The strength of [the] hundreds of rubrics... lies in what they include; their greatest weakness is what they leave out" (*Really Value* 2).

Our goal in this essay is to show how we have witnessed and resisted the discourses of LOA in our own composition assignments and assessments, specifically in student writing that makes space for the personal. Our commitment to the personal in student and academic writing comes out of our own work to reach students and help them produce writing that is meaningful. It is also supported by the work of thinkers like Lev Vygostky, John Dewey, and Kenneth Bruffee, and is implicit in Donald Murray's axiom that "All Writing is Autobiography." Composition has by and large accepted a radical subjectivity not only as the exclusive means by which we can know but also as the means by which we can pursue justice. Consider any number of foundational pieces such as Jacqueline Jones Royster's "When the First Voice You Hear Is Not Your Own," or Mina Shaughnessy's early work to put student cognition and intention at the center of her research. Compositionists' research has long wrestled with our personal connections to our subjects.[3] And of course, we recognize our place in the long-running dialogue in the field between expressivists and constructionists, especially as Peter Elbow and David Bartholomae have grappled with this debate, and as Candace Spigelman explored in *Personally Speaking: Experience as Evidence in Academic Discourse*.[4] We embrace the "blurred genres" that Bartholomae describes (68), and the dialogic writing that is encouraged in Gerald Graff and Cathy Birkenstein's *They Say/I Say*. Writing that uses "I," we contend, encourages students to tell their own stories and develop reasoning from personal experience. This same writing can count as academic, meet course goals, and involve the most serious forms of analysis and critique.[5]

While personal forms of writing seem natural to us and well understood by theorists in our field, we assert their importance here because we see that the LOA movement, with its orientation towards products, makes personal writing ever more uncertain and misunderstood by the many stakeholders within composition: administrators, teachers, and students. The teaching and writing we describe and advocate for in this article maintains course goals for academic writing while making space for students to explore the subjectivity that shapes their own critical thinking. More significantly, the assignments and teaching models we present challenge the subtle distinctions between internal, formative assessment and the external, standardizing discourses of LOA.

Learning Outcomes in/and Composition

Debate over learning outcomes has been a part of the field of composition for some time. Before the most recent push for accountability in higher education, the Council of Writing Program Administrators (WPA) adopted the "Outcomes Statement for First-Year Composition" in 2000, which identifies "the common knowledge, skills, and attitudes sought by first year composition programs in American post-secondary education" (Harrington et al. 24). However, members of the self-named Outcomes Collective worried about the potential misuse of such a document and were quite concerned that the outcomes could be "put to uses detrimental to the spirit within which they were deliberated, drafted, and publicly advocated" (Harrington et al. 24). Elbow, in his "friendly challenge" to the framers of the Outcomes Statement, expressed concern that an "unconscious preoccupation with rhetorical awareness" may have pushed the writers away from what he considers a "foundational ability... to explore a topic for yourself, on your own, because *you* are interested" (qtd. in Harrington et al. 181; emphasis in original). In *The WPA Outcomes Statement: A Decade Later*, a companion volume to *The Outcomes Book*, published in 2013, the pervasive influence of the LOA movement is implicit in the contributors' adaptations of the WPA Outcomes Statement to satisfy both internal programmatic needs and external demands for accountability. The words "personal," "self," and "narrative" are nowhere to be found in these pages.

The omission of personal genres, even in the field's own outcomes statements, illustrates the inherent contradiction between LOA and the messy, emergent process of becoming a writer. Broad, quoting Marcia B. Baxter Magolda, points out that

> The key academic principle that helps students move toward self-authorship is, according to Marcia B. Baxter Magolda, '*that knowledge is complex, ambiguous, and socially constructed in a context*' [Magolda's emphasis]. However, rubrics, the most visible and ubiquitous tool of writing assessment . . . teach our students an exactly opposite view of knowledge, judgment, and value. At the heart of our educational and rhetorical project, rubrics are working against us. (*Really Value* 4)

Once students have a checklist in mind—whether for a specific assignment rubric or with LOA as underpinning for a course—writing and whatever knowledge it engenders becomes less a process of discovery or understanding and more a search for a perceived "right answer."

Paying close attention to the unintended consequences of learning outcomes assessment is one way to confront the bureaucratization of a tenuous human endeavor, such as writing, which demands freedom and creativity. Trevor Hussey and Patrick Smith help us see that learning outcomes are both "intended and emergent…with a continuum between the two." Outcomes can also be understood as "predicted and unpredicted" as well as defined "according to who the various constituencies may be: students, teachers, managers, the community and so on" ("Conceptual Analysis" 108). In other words, a simple statement declaring what shall be accomplished in a course (or a lesson plan or a degree) is not so simple. They write,

> The emphasis on planned learning outcomes ignores, and may even squeeze out, the emergent learning outcomes that can be so rewarding (Megginson, 1994, 1996). Indeed, it may be argued that the most fruitful and valuable feature of higher education is the emergence of ideas, skills and connections, which were unforeseen, even by the teacher. ("The Trouble" 228–29)

For us, these unforeseen connections that emerge in the exchange between classroom assignments and our students' personal experiences lie at the core of what we aspire to do in teaching composition. It is these emergent and unpredictable outcomes—which we find are most often entwined with creative and personal writing—that we explore through the lens of teaching first-year writing.

In this article, we take a critical perspective on LOA as a frame for examining our efforts to engage students' stories in academic writing courses. We argue that the carefully planned use of personal narrative involves students in the writing process and the wider aims of education, develops appreciation of diversity and difference, and most of all fosters the very critical thinking skills that nearly all writing programs promote as their central goal. We make these arguments to counter local resistance to personal writing and to contest the pervasiveness of product-oriented LOA discourses that circulate in everyday talk about writing assignments and assessments.

Negotiating Space for Personal Genres: Local Contexts

First, an explanation of how this paper came to be and what shapes our perspectives. Two of us, Elizabeth and Emily, first met as faculty in English at a new two-year college where we previously worked, whose goal was to welcome traditionally excluded young people into the joys of an integrated, inviting curriculum, one that would combine the best of the liberal arts tradition with a specific focus on graduating students with two-year degrees keyed to high demand vocations, or to move into bachelors' programs successfully. Our task as faculty was to develop the curriculum, especially to integrate developmental writing and composition courses with credit-bearing study in mathematics and interdisciplinary work.

The design of this new college, based on extensive research of successful community college models, aspired to avoid the steep learning curve and slow engagement with program assessment practices that have characterized preexisting two-year institutions. We were to plan backwards, starting with an elaborate set of degree outcomes drawn from the Lumina Foundation's DQP, and the AAC&U's VALUE rubrics. Each layer of the institution would draw down from these broad pre-determined goals to create more focused program outcomes: from graduates' broad competencies to those of specific degree programs or majors; from degree programs to the first-year general education outcomes; from general education to the outcomes of each specific course module. We were tasked with drawing up elaborate charts for each step along the way. The national and local contexts we describe above—with their singular focus on end goals—were emphasized every day, in every decision. This relentless focus on outcomes assessment speaks to Dewey's warning, as recalled by Gallagher, that the "separation of ends and means . . . leads to fixity and rigidity" (Gallagher 45). It also reveals a worrisome direction in which institutions of higher education may be headed—of their own accord or as a result of external pressures—towards a tyranny of rubrics and an obsession with measurable outcomes rather than concern for the messy, inchoate, creative process and products of real learning and writing, all of which stem inexorably from the self.

We complicate this critique of LOA by telling three stories, from the three very different institutional contexts in which we currently teach, of how we have created and preserved space for narrative in the composition classroom. The first two sections are composed by Elizabeth and Emily, and section three is written by Liesl, who had no connection to the new two-year college, but who, over the course of many conversations with Emily and Elizabeth, expressed similar challenges in teaching personal writing at her home institution. What inspired this article was the commonality across our experiences, despite the very different make-ups of our student populations and present institutions—a selective liberal arts college (Elizabeth), an urban community college (Emily), and a private religious university (Liesl). This convergence suggests that LOA discourses have made their way into a range of educational settings, and that it is therefore important for scholar-teachers of writing to investigate how they are deployed within and across varying contexts.

Context I: Small Liberal Arts College (Elizabeth)

After my time at the community college, I moved on to my current position at a small liberal arts college, which also has a graduate school, in the metropolitan New York area. With high tuition and a tree-filled campus in a wealthy suburb, one might expect a mostly white, affluent student population from well-funded high schools. However, while we are more selective than many public institutions, our students represent a wide range of cultural and economic backgrounds as well as college preparedness skills. At the time of the experience I describe here, I was interim co-director of College Writing, a first-year composition program aimed at developing academic literacies. Our program is mostly staffed by adjuncts, some of who are students in our humanities graduate programs. We drifted into this staffing model for a variety of economic reasons, which have in turn influenced the structure of the program: teachers can choose their own thematic readings and tailor writing prompts, but all assign the same assignment sequence (writing with a source, synthesis, argument, and extended argument with sources essays). We have regular teaching circles scheduled around the common assignment calendar and focused on assessing writing. At the end of the semester, students in all sections prepare a writing portfolio; our teaching faculty then meet for final portfolio assessment.

We also share a common rubric that revolves around evidence-based writing, with assessment categories focused on quality of idea, organization, evidence, context and writing situation, and mechanics. In our most recent revision of the rubric, we turned to the VALUE rubrics on writing and critical thinking for reference, building from there to create our own locally constructed document, which would be used for grading rather than for program assessment. In our planning stages, we recognized the value of the national conversation on assessment because it gave us something to start with. We have used our rubric and the assessment work around it to encourage consistency in grading across sections and to keep student writing at the center of our discussions about teaching. The rubric helps to orient new instructors to our expectations. Even with its flaws, the rubric structures conversation. However, as valuable as conversation is, discussing learning outcomes is always fraught with the competing interests and status positions of those present; the larger discourse of LOA exacerbates these differences. As noted above, our concern is that the product-oriented exigencies of LOA do not surface from external stakeholders exclusively. In fact, LOA discourses can easily be taken up and replicated in the everyday work of teaching because these discourses filter down directly to grading student work. Moreover, this everyday work of grade assignment becomes even more delicate and contestable when we are part-time or contingent writing instructors, or when we are the directors of programs staffed mostly by contingent instructors.

My concerns about how LOA influences local decision-making can be illustrated in the story of how one of my own student essays was received in our portfolio assessment meeting. In the accelerated first-year composition course, students write extended argument papers that require students to locate and engage sources. Students in my section were reading about the meaning of the liberal arts and were to develop their own topics within the theme of "issues in higher education." I worked hard at helping students understand the structure of arguments and develop strong claims of their own, which in my mind is the most challenging part of a research assignment. But I also emphasized the intensely personal nature of research. Students go through multiple stages to write their project proposals, and I insist that they find a way into the assignment that is theirs alone. One of my strongest students had shared her paper draft in a class-wide workshop. She had chosen to research students with learning disabilities in higher education. Her paper began with a one-page narrative about her younger sister and the challenges she had experienced in school to be considered intelligent and capable, even as she struggled with a learning disability. In my mind, this student was exemplifying what I wanted for all students: she had worked to create her own topic and research question within a teacher-selected theme not of her own choosing. And after her personal introduction, she developed a sophisticated argument about how learning disabilities can be a lens through which we rethink learning for everybody. I felt her paper deserved an A.

Yet when I submitted her portfolio to the teaching circle for grading at the end of the semester, her narrative did not play very well at all. The readers of the portfolio were concerned that the lengthy personal narrative had no place in a college paper. When I explained that I had wanted students to find their own way into a general assignment, and that the narrative had been well received in the student workshop, readers responded that the narrative itself was not the problem, but rather that the writer had not made an explicit enough connection to the claim. In other words, if the personal could ever play any part in academic writing, it would have to be subsumed within evidence-based argument genres. Mike Rose, who draws on personal experiences to make subtle and important claims, provides one admirable example of a writer who does use personal experience as primary research, and I had tried to show my students how they could do similar work. But my co-readers did not seem to recognize the flexibility the genre offered to draw on the personal for making evidence-based claims, and demanded a rhetorical linkage that I did not see as missing. The rubric, interestingly, did not explicitly mention that the writing had to conform to a depersonalized academic style or manner of argument. It was as if the readers assumed that it did, that concepts like "coherence" and "attention to the rhetorical situation" meant "nothing personal" and "sound disinterested." Whatever the finished product, it should look academic; it should display "college-level" writing. The response to this student paper bore out exactly Elbow's point that the emphasis on outcomes could crowd out writing done for the sake of personal exploration (Harrington et al. 181).

I could see where my fellow graders were coming from; there was a part of me that would not want to share this piece with my own more senior colleagues who teach across the disciplines, knowing the sorts of criticisms often leveled at the work we do in first-year writing. Given these imbalances of power, it's possible that the part-time instructors felt the same way about me; they needed to appear rigorous, outcomes-oriented teachers in the eyes of the boss—even if the boss had a different idea. In this way, the contingent nature of our work, which makes us answerable to others in more powerful places, can affect what we value in ways we may not have intended or desired.

In the end, there is no one genre we can teach that will be useful throughout students' entire lives, and so we ought to aim for students' acquiring the ability to take a broader view, and to interrogate their own ways of knowing and making rhetorical choices over time. What if we saw personal writing as a metacognitive skill that builds on learning or that increases facility with genre conventions? I value students' ability to engage with abstract, seemingly distant topics by thinking through the construction of their selves in relation to those topics. Is that personal connection not what drives any researcher to pursue the questions she does, no matter how far from everyday experience?

Accepting the role of the personal in metacognitive development is a risky move to make, because it means genres can fall apart in the interim. As students do this more open-ended, exploratory kind of thinking and writing, their writing will reach the day of deadline without looking like what academic genres supposedly look like. Consequently, instructors and program leaders will have to make choices about our assessment of their writing in process. If we are bound by rubrics that have emerged out of LOA-influenced movements, those rubrics may well obscure and devalue the very thinking that is in fact more complex and more desirable for the long term growth of our students. Moreover, we may not even realize that these rubrics are having this effect; their eminently reasonable frameworks mask the product-oriented ideologies of education that lie beneath them. More dangerous still, a contingent instructor is particularly compelled to show that she has coached her students to produce documents that meet the outcomes ostensibly required by a rubric. As we answer to program administrators, the institution itself, and the broader expectations of external stakeholders to produce writers who can create flawless final products, we should take care to discern our own values as writers and writing teachers, and to talk back to the rubrics and the discourses from which they come.

Context II: Large Urban Community College (Emily)

More than 15,000 students from over one hundred different countries attend the open admissions community college where I teach. Given the diversity of the student population, immigration is often the theme I choose for my composition classes. As part of our semester-long exploration of immigration, the first drafted essay assignment is to write a profile of an immigrant in the United States. We begin this assignment by working in small groups to brainstorm a set of questions students will use to interview the immigrants they will write about. This is an interesting exercise as it reveals a lot about students' prior knowledge of, interest in, and assumptions around the controversial topic of immigration. As small groups report back and we create a collective list of questions and begin to prioritize them, the first real dialogue around immigrants and immigration emerges and is spearheaded by the students themselves: Should we ask if someone is in the U.S. legally? How should we talk about immigrants who are here without documentation? Through this generative activity, critical inquiry around immigration begins even before students have conducted the first interview or read any published texts.

Given the students' backgrounds, the vast majority of them choose to interview a family member, close friend, or coworker whose immigration story they barely know. Because I suggest that they consider doing some outside research on the interviewee's country of origin, students are amazed to discover how the Duvalier dictatorship and the *Tontons Macoutes'* reign of terror led to their own mother's fleeing Haiti or how the dissolution of the Soviet Union, in the year of their birth, led their family to leave Azerbaijan for Brooklyn. This deceptively simple narrative assignment leads students directly into critical inquiry as they begin to situate the experience of one individual within the political, economic, and social trends that motivated their immigration. Peer review becomes not just an opportunity to give and receive feedback on a piece of writing to be revised, but also a way to think about the social, economic, and political forces acting upon the immigrants they are writing about. In a sense, the immigrant profiles become the foundational course texts as they raise many of the essential questions that guide our exploration throughout the semester. Of course, I cannot precisely predict the results of this assignment; as with any "emergent outcome," each classroom full of students generates its own rich and distinctive version of the immigrant experience. Inevitably though, the profiles serve to quietly disrupt some of the dominant discourse around immigration and raise questions we circle back to over the course of the semester as students read published texts and also write reading- and research-based essays.

The immigrant profile, as the very first assignment of the semester, serves another critical function in that it allows me to get to know aspects of my students' lives that might otherwise remain hidden under the homogenizing influence of urban youth culture. On the first day of class when we do a cocktail-party style icebreaker with questions related to nationality, multilingualism, and immigration, most students seem quite invested in presenting themselves as "American" as possible. Scant weeks later, through the immigrant profiles, unseen aspects of students' identities emerge. I get to know Monique's dad's waist-long dreads, his still strong Trinidadian accent, and his love for Soca music. I discover that Alex's mom survived on the streets of Guayaquil, Ecuador at the age of eight when her own mother abandoned her to forge a life in the U.S. I hear the sadness in Ahmed's story of his parents' arranged marriage in Egypt and their subsequent, acrimonious, U.S.-style divorce. Marisol, a struggling writer, begins her profile, "Run, jump, hide, be quiet!" taking readers straight into her Guatemalan mother's terrifying experience of being smuggled across the desert into the U.S. by a *coyote*. These histories are integral to my students' identities and help me to know who is in my classroom. They also validate my students' part in a larger, complex, and often contradictory immigrant narrative that would remain invisible had the personal been barred from my classroom.

Despite the fact that LOA is most prevalent at community colleges and other non-elite institutions, I am fortunate to teach in a department that, until recently, has mostly encouraged but not required collaborative portfolio assessment in our composition courses. When we began this form of collaborative assessment, a self-selected group of faculty from our composition program met to develop criteria (that is, the learning outcomes we expected students to have met) for the assessment of student portfolios. Influenced by Bob Broad's work on Dynamic Criteria Mapping, our meeting was a lively event: we filled pages of newsprint with our ideas and ambitions for our students. No one consulted the established, institutional learning outcomes for Composition I; they were not even mentioned, as far as I recall. Instead we relied on our collective decades, perhaps centuries, of experience teaching composition to develop a wish list of the kinds of writing we hoped our students would produce by the end of a fruitful semester. As in any homegrown, bottom-up project, our brainstorming led to a diversity of criteria that was broad, deep, and aspirational. It included the obvious "basic mechanical correctness" and "well-developed, focused paragraphs" but also asked students to "provide a sense of 'so what' for the reader," not "play it safe," and do "extensive revision." "Creativity, originality, and complexity" ranked high on our list right behind the more conventional "essential competencies" we hoped all student essays would demonstrate. Several semesters of implementation later we recognized the unwieldiness of such a vast range of assessment criteria, reorganized some of it to indicate what is essential and what is not, and realized that we have to make understanding the criteria part of what we teach our students (whose ability to grasp what we desire for them as writers is evidenced in a required self-assessment essay that accompanies every portfolio). For those of us who were part of the crew that developed the portfolio assessment process, the criteria remain alive and—in the spirit of the democratic, collective, and voluntary process that birthed them—are emphasized differently in each faculty member's classrooms, assignments, and assessments.

However, several semesters ago our composition program directors determined that the collaborative portfolio assessment process could provide a vital professional development opportunity for brand new full-time faculty and adjuncts. In an effort to inculcate them into the practices and values of the department, these instructors are now *required* to participate in portfolio assessment in their first semester. This simple move—from voluntary to obligatory participation—mirrors the broader national and international impulses of LOA as a movement, and has turned what seemed an ideal paradigm for the creation and implementation of learning outcomes into a hoop to jump through. To many of these brand new instructors, the criteria seem alien and overwhelming, a burden rather than a support, something to accommodate and resist rather than embrace. What was initiated and implemented by faculty to improve our teaching and our students' learning is now perceived as a top-down directive mandated by program administrators for evaluative purposes. Like the exigency of LOA itself, compulsory participation in portfolio assessment has forced these instructors into a defensive posture. Since beginning this practice, every single new faculty member has opted out of portfolio assessment after the obligatory first semester, confirming that the imposition of even locally generated learning outcomes can undermine the collaborative and democratic processes that engendered them, rendering them meaningless as a professional and program development tool.

Despite this development in the way collaborative portfolio assessment is currently implemented in my department, I have stuck with it for many semesters because, for me, the benefits of this process still outweigh the alternatives. I believe students gain from having their work assessed by someone other than their instructor and that they grow through the meta-cognitive task of selecting and presenting the pieces of their writing that demonstrate a semester's worth of learning. Not surprisingly, the immigrant profile is often an essay that students choose to include in their final portfolios. What is puzzling is that after many semesters of reading students' portfolios, I have yet to encounter another personal narrative among the essays my colleagues assign. I occasionally see hybrid genres in which students are encouraged to reflect on a text in the context of their own life experience. But the absence of overt narratives compared with the sheer number of text- and research-based essays in which personal experience is secondary to the authority of the text—if present at all—is truly disconcerting. Like Elizabeth's story, this avoidance of narrative seems like another example of internalized anxiety around what constitutes legitimate academic discourse and a narrowing of the genres that are taught in first-year composition. It also appears that even in what began as a grassroots, collective process of naming and identifying learning outcomes has unintentionally edged the creative, the personal, the narrative aside. I have not yet seen the presence of personal narratives in my students' portfolios prove disadvantageous to them in terms of pass rates. But, it increasingly feels somewhat nostalgic, subversive even, to insist on teaching narrative in composition as the universe of higher education marches inexorably in the direction of quantifiable outcomes and a valuing of more overtly "academic" genres.

Context III: Private Religious University (Liesl)

The undergraduate institution where I teach houses both a business school and a more traditional liberal arts college. Recently, some students from the business school posted a video to YouTube in which a business student appears, wearing a suit, and asks the liberal arts student, looking scruffy and mispronouncing words, what he'll have to show for his education. As the business student flips through the *Wall Street Journal*, the liberal arts student becomes increasingly distraught, even embarrassed. By the end of the one minute clip, the liberal arts student is exhausted, having stayed up all night to write a paper or do a lab, at which the business student scoffs, implying that the liberal arts are not only useless but unnecessarily demanding.

As I'm sure is the case across the country, conversations in my First Year Writing (FYW) class frequently reflect a similar either/or understanding—that college is meant to be *either* vocational *or* personally meaningful. As students become more vocal in their concerns about both the value and the expense of higher education, success seems less measured by intellectual engagement or forging humane future selves, and more by the hard evidence—usually grades, jobs, and money—students imagine will retroactively justify the time and money spent in college.

In reflecting on the development and consequences of LOA within the writing classroom, I have been particularly curious about the disconnect between how I, as faculty, conceive of LOA as the *means* toward a rigorous, relevant FYW classroom, compared to how my students think of assessment, which tends to be as an *end*—a grade, or something else that stops the conversation rather than begins it. As our wider culture puts more and more emphasis on success, inferring it is a commodity rather than a life-long, ever-evolving process, I am concerned about how students' expectations for their own educational encounters have been affected.

In many ways, my institution represents a model example of how LOA can spark important discussions among faculty members and result in worthwhile changes in the shape of an undergraduate program. Several years ago, in the midst of an extensive curriculum review, our faculty relied on both the WPA Outcomes Statement and the AAC&U guidelines as we identified, articulated, and agreed upon sixteen curricular outcomes. Simultaneously, we developed eight categories of courses that, together, comprise our core curriculum. The faculty as a whole subsequently decided which categories were "responsible" for which outcomes. For instance, every requirement, from First Year Writing to the Natural World to Cultures Over Time, *should* in some way encourage "openness to new ways of thinking" and "a lifetime love of learning and self-reflection" (Outcomes #1 and #16). Although it was last on the list, I have been proud that "self-reflection" was indeed a collectively recognized priority. As Bob Broad and others have championed, we generated *local* goals, which felt productive precisely in that they established common ground while simultaneously empowering faculty to realize the outcomes in individual ways (*Organic Writing* 1).

Frequently, however, like when confronting that YouTube video, I have to ask myself if any of it matters—if all the well-intended, thoughtful faculty rubrics, outcomes, and discussions in the world add up to anything if students are not part of the conversation. In my experience, especially early on in their first semester on campus, students are often concerned that the personal narratives and other "I"-driven arguments they write in my FYW class are too subjective or idiosyncratic or weird. Inevitably, they cite high school English teachers for whom "I" was a forbidden word. I am repeatedly asked if they can Google a topic for "proofs" instead of describing their own opinions and emotions, as I have asked. Again and again, I say, write from your experience and again and again, students ask, "Are we allowed to write about ourselves?" These are not normal jitters but deep-seated fears that their views are inconsequential and that there is no apparent connection between their lives and the "stuff" they're meant to learn at school.

In the classroom, our early discussions around these assignments are often when the long-standing tensions between the academic and vocational goals of higher education come into especially high relief. Particularly for students leery of a time-consuming and not overtly vocational liberal arts requirement, such as FYW—which is regularly perceived as a roadblock rather than a gateway to their "real" education—writing about themselves can seem to crystallize everything they have already been told (or been warned by YouTube) *not* to do in college. The assumption is that writing is hard work and probably useless.

These narrative assignments can become even more unnerving once students see their grades, as in, "How could I get a C+ when I was writing about my grandpa?" Student buy-in, at least initially, can prove just as sticky as administrative and departmental support when it comes to the investigation of personal writing, not least of all because I know they will be evaluating me, too. As a non-tenure track lecturer, I am especially aware of the importance of student opinion.

Significantly, at my institution, FYW is one of the few courses required by both the business school and the liberal arts college. This overlap has come to be one of the things I most enjoy, and find productive, about the class. In fact, over the last several years, aware of the very different expectations with which my students were pursuing their degrees, I have recalibrated the course to tackle the "crisis" of higher education head on. As we familiarize ourselves with the issues, students are eventually required to take a stand on their own educations in order to situate themselves within these debates.

For instance, reading the 2011 Pew Research Study, in which college presidents themselves disagree on the primary mission of college—"Half say it is to help them mature and grow intellectually, while 48% say it is to provide skills, knowledge and training to help them succeed in the working world" ("Worth It")—students often laugh out loud; if college presidents cannot agree, no wonder we cannot, either. When they read that Professor Mark Edmundson claims his students "usually lack the confidence to acknowledge what would be their most precious asset for learning: their ignorance" (47), we spend a lot of time thinking, discussing, and writing about what he might mean.

Ultimately, students write two graded, formal argument essays on current questions of the future of higher education. In both, they must "use themselves as an example," not only to relay their own individual experiences but also to reframe those experiences in a way that brings the national conversation to light. In one essay, they summarize some of the dominant attitudes concerning the "purpose" of college before exploring how these "expert" opinions have impacted, contrasted, or informed their own, as Graff and Birkenstein model. Students are encouraged to write "from the trenches"— about the difficulties they have had in their transitions to college, what their evolving goals include, and what preconceived notions they've come to challenge. Secondly, as a way to hone in on the process of writing specifically, the final essay for the course asks students to argue whether or not FYW should be required of all incoming students.

Time and again in these papers, students from both the business school and the college become the voices championing the importance of discussion, informal writing, and small group work, when at the start of the year most of them would have likely avoided the class altogether, had they been able to. As far as I see it, these are the very emergent outcomes we are arguing for—the subtle but powerful moments of self-discovery that come precisely through reflection on the significance of their own experiences.

As students concurrently explore the role of college in society and the value of an undergraduate degree for them personally, they realize some unexpected potential of both. In writing about themselves, they often find new insight and a deeper sense of responsibility for the choices they are making in the classroom and on the page. Confronting their assumptions, doubts, and fears through personal writing means there is no prefabricated language to hide behind, no detachment or distance from which to formulate abstract conclusions. Arguably, writing about themselves becomes some of the hardest work they have ever done.

Simultaneously, as Emily emphasizes, I find personal writing just as indispensable to my teaching as to my students' learning. To any outsider, the students at my all-male, Jewish college would appear to be different versions of the same nineteen-year-old, each wearing a yarmulke. Through their writing, however, I read about their families, their childhoods, and all the other entirely typical and yet completely unique circumstances of their lives. Sharing their stories with me and with one another contributes to the idea that these stories matter and that, by extension, I care about them as individuals.

For incoming college students feeling enormous pressure to succeed, these are rare moments when the focus shifts from everything they do not know to, in these assignments, what they do know and where they come from. In the process, I learn about their vulnerabilities, their hometowns, and their senses of humor, all of which reminds me, every semester, of just how *personal* any effective writing class must be—not a set series of exercises or lectures, but an organic, shared exchange. In order to create a safe, trusting environment where students can develop and reveal ideas, they have to first believe that they belong, an effort aided enormously by finding meaning in their own stories.

Concluding Thoughts

What we hope our students develop through personal writing in our composition courses is both a deeper sense of self-awareness and a broader understanding of the larger cultural moment they inhabit. A common misperception about personal narrative—and one of the primary reasons we believe it has been marginalized as a result of the pervasive influence of LOA—is that it encourages navel gazing, is insufficiently product oriented, and lies too far from the quantifiable outcomes our students are all supposed to demonstrate. Yet, we would argue that actually the opposite is true: that through writing the personal, students begin to recognize and articulate their connections to the world around them, and to work towards goals supported in all the higher education rubrics such as critical thinking and engaged citizenship. We focus our assignments on moments of intersection, where the wider world impacts private perspectives, choices, and experiences. Ideally, this exploration fosters a belief that writing is reflexive and that students also have the opportunity to influence the world around them, even if it's just to think critically about their own learning and growth, or to conceptualize their family history in a new and different light.

We hope that these three tales communicate the subtle ways that learning outcomes, and more specifically the LOA movement, can subvert their own end goals in the long run. Because of learning outcomes' elevated status as texts produced by and belonging to the institution, they serve the purpose of ironing out the wrinkles that characterize any kind of personal writing, and any kind of truly personal learning. Teaching a student not to do personal writing in a college paper because it is not valued in academic writing is not an education in genre: it is a schooling in the denial of the self. Additionally, we want to honor the impulse of both students and contingent faculty, who recognize and pursue the potential of personal writing with or without larger institutional support.

Gallagher points out that the "pragmatic" response to LOA is not to shrug one's shoulders and accept it as reality, but rather to hearken back to the original meaning of pragmatic: "Pragmatists ask what practical difference ideas and courses of action make, and to whom" (43). We are convinced, through our experiences teaching in varied settings with distinct student populations, that personal writing must have a role in composition precisely because it moves students toward all the ends of college education: critical engagement with ideas, with each other, and with the values and experiences that shape who we are; practice with language as craft and as means to truth; the use of evidence and logic. Only through that engagement will students develop the sensitivity to audience, language, and purpose that college graduates are supposed to exhibit and that remains a lifelong process for all writers. Though difficult to measure and chart on an assessment rubric, we argue that writing one's story and self into a larger cultural, historical, or political narrative lives at the heart of liberal education. Moreover, as we tell these intensely local stories of teaching the personal in academic writing, we do so out of concern to preserve them as narratives of our own lived journeys with our students, not—as the ever-more-present LOA discourse would have us believe—as tickets to the place called success.

Notes

1. One central repository of LOA work in the U.S. is the National Institute for Learning Outcomes Assessment; one telling article, which places LOA within an international context, is "The State of Learning Outcomes Assessment in the United States," by George D. Kuh and Peter T. Ewell. For discussion on the use of outcomes on campuses, see the collection edited by Peggy L. Maki.

2. For a discussion of neoliberalism's role in higher education, see Chris Gallagher's succinct overview of the new managed university, in which all activity is directed towards a teleological end called "success."

3. An excellent and recent overview may be found in Lee Nickoson and Mary Sheridan.

4. See Molly Flaspohler for an interesting critique of Spigelman from a librarian's perspective.

5. We recognize that there are a host of other concerns in personal writing, such as the ethics of self-disclosure and the destabilizing of the Enlightenment-era self; we set them aside for now.

Works Cited

American Association of Colleges & Universities. "VALUE: Valid Assessment of Learning in Undergraduate Education." *Association of American Colleges & Universities*. Assoc. of Amer. Coll. and U, n.d. Web. 8 Apr. 2014. <http://www.aacu.org/value/index.cfm>.

Bartholomae, David. "Writing with Teachers: A Conversation with Peter Elbow." *CCC* 46.1 (1995): 62–71. Print.

Behm, Nicholas N., Gregory R. Glau, Deborah H. Holdstein, Duane Roen, and Edward M. White, eds. *The WPA Outcomes Statement: A Decade Later*. Anderson: Parlor P, 2013. Print.

Broad, Bob. *What We Really Value: Beyond Rubrics in Teaching and Assessing Writing*. Logan: Utah State UP, 2003. Print.

Broad, Bob, et al. *Organic Writing Assessment: Dynamic Criteria Mapping in Action*. Logan: Utah State UP, 2009. Print.

Council of Writing Program Administrators. "WPA Outcomes Statement for First Year Composition." Ver. 1.0. WPA Council, Apr. 2000. PDF file. 13 June 2013. <wpacouncil.org/positions/outcomes.html.>

Dewey, John. *Democracy and Education*. Radford: Wilder Publications, 2008. Print.

Edmundson, Mark. "On The Uses of a Liberal Education: As Lite Entertainment For Bored College Students." *Harper's Magazine* 295.1768 (1997): 39.

Flaspohler, Molly R. "A View from the Academic Library." *Pedagogy* 7.2 (2007): 295-301. Print.

Gallagher, Chris W. "The Trouble with Outcomes: Pragmatic Inquiry and Educational Aims." *College English* 75.1 (2012): 42-60. Print.

Graff, Gerald, and Cathy Birkenstein. *They Say / I Say: The Moves That Matter in Academic Writing*. 2nd ed. New York: Norton, 2010. Print.

Harrington, Susanmarie, Keith Rhodes, Ruth Overman Fischer, and Rita Malencyk, eds. *The Outcomes Book: Debate and Consensus after the WPA Outcomes Statement*. Logan: Utah State UP, 2005. Print.

---. "Learning Outcomes: A Conceptual Analysis." *Teaching in Higher Education* 13.1 (2008): 107-15. Print.

Hussey, Trevor, and Patrick Smith. "The Trouble with Learning Outcomes." *Learning in Higher Education* 3.3 (2002): 220-33. Print.

"Is College Worth It?" *Pew Research Center's Social and Demographic Trends Project*. Pew Research Center, 15 May 2011. Web. 24 June 2014. <http://www.pewsocialtrends.org/2011/05/15/is-college-worth-it/>.

Kuh, George D., and Peter T. Ewell. "The State of Learning Outcomes Assessment in the United States." *Higher Education Management and Policy* 22.1 (2010): 9-28. Print.

Lumina Foundation. The Degree Qualifications Profile. Lumina Foundation for Educ., Jan. 2011. PDF file. 8 Apr. 2014. <http://www.luminafoundation.org/publications/The_Degree_Qualifications_Profile.pdf>.

Maki, Peggy L., ed. *Coming to Terms with Student Outcomes Assessment: Faculty and Administrators' Journeys to Integrating Assessment in Their Work and Institutional Culture*. Sterling: Stylus, 2010. Print.

Murray, Donald M. "All Writing Is Autobiography." *CCC* 42.1 (1991): 66-74. Print.

National Institute for Learning Outcomes Assessment. Home page. Natl. Inst. for Learning Outcomes Assessment, 2012. Web. 18 Dec. 2013. <http://www.learningoutcomeassessment.org/index.html>.

Nickoson, Lee, and Mary P. Sheridan, eds. *Writing Studies Research in Practice: Methods and Methodologies*. Carbondale: SIUP, 2012. Print.

Royster, Jacqueline Jones. "When the First Voice You Hear Is Not Your Own." *The Norton Book of Composition Studies*. Ed. Susan Miller. New York: Norton, 2009. 1117-27. Print.

Shaughnessy, Mina P. *Errors and Expectations: A Guide for the Teacher of Basic Writing*. New York: Oxford UP, 1977. Print.

Spigelman, Candace. *Personally Speaking: Experience as Evidence in Academic Discourse*. Carbondale: SIUP, 2004. Print.

Course Design

Collaborative Course Design in Scientific Writing: Experimentation and Productive Failure

D. Shane Combs, Erin A. Frost, and Michelle F. Eble

Course Description

English 3820: Scientific Writing, a writing-intensive (WI) course offered by the Department of English at East Carolina University (ECU), serves primarily science majors. According to the course catalog, it provides students with "practice in assimilation and written presentation of scientific information." The course asks students to consider the situated nature of scientific writing and also to produce scientific writing for various audiences. Throughout the course, students examine theories, methodologies, and ideologies that undergird scientific writing with an eye to perfecting both critique and imitation of scientific styles.

Institutional Context

East Carolina University, a doctoral/research institution with about 27,000 students, serves a largely rural population. Approximately 60% of enrolled students are female, 20% are minorities, and 12% are from outside North Carolina. The scientific writing course has been taught through the Department of English since at least 1967. As of 2014, it was listed as a 3000-level course option for students majoring in biology, chemistry, geography, and sociology and as an elective for students pursuing English majors and minors as well as the undergraduate certificate in business and technical communication, also offered through the Department of English. Further, all ECU students are required to take two writing foundations courses (one at the 1000 level and one at the 2000 level) and two WI courses (one of which must be within the major), which means that English 3820 primarily fulfills a WI requirement for students in the sciences. Anecdotally, the course is populated with mainly biology and chemistry students; among students graduating with biology and chemistry degrees, about half are male and the other half female and about one-third identify as minority. The Department of English has offered two to three sections of scientific writing each semester for at least the last 10 years. In that time, the course has been taught primarily by full-time teaching instructors and occasionally by tenure-track/tenured faculty in technical and professional communication (TPC).

The recent introduction of ECU's Quality Enhancement Plan (QEP), part of the university's reaccreditation process, has significantly altered the nature of composition instruction as well as WI courses (like scientific writing) across the university. The QEP is a "multi-faceted, multi-year project to integrate, align, and reinforce writing instruction for students from the day that they begin their first classes at ECU to the day that they complete their degrees and transition into the workplace or advanced study" (Academic Affairs).[1] Given this university-wide emphasis on writing, faculty from rhetoric, composition, and TPC have been central to formulating collaborative efforts with partners, especially with colleagues from biology, chemistry, and business.

One of the QEP initiatives includes the Writing Mentors program, first implemented in the 2013–14 academic year, which embeds mentors into individual WI courses to provide "additional, targeted writing support" (Ballard, Weismiller, and Sharer 42). Although the QEP provides most of the funding for this program, individual departments with graduate assistants may also support a writing mentor for a class in their department, with the Writing Center providing training and support. This was the case with this experiment in English 3820; the graduate program in the Department of English funded Shane Combs as a mentor in one of the two sections of English 3820 that we report on in this article. Graduate students often work for a semester in a writing center context before becoming a peer mentor, and they always have at least a four-hour professional development session to prepare them for the task; Shane had both experiences as a precursor to his work as a writing mentor in English 3820.[2]

Spring 2014 provided TPC faculty Erin and Michelle the opportunity to collaborate on this specialized WI course and to incorporate a writing mentor within one of the sections.[3] Neither of us had taught the course before, and we were excited to incorporate our disciplinary knowledge related to health, medical, and science rhetorics in helping students communicate within their disciplines and to public or lay audiences.

In addition to specific student learning outcomes developed for the course, English 3820 incorporated the following QEP learning outcomes, which have been adopted by all WI courses:

1. Use writing to investigate complex, relevant topics and address significant questions through engagement with and effective use of credible sources.
2. Produce writing that reflects an awareness of context, purpose, and audience, particularly within the written genres (including genres that integrate writing with visuals, audio or other multi-modal components) of their major disciplines and/or career fields.

3. Demonstrate that they understand writing as a process that can be made more effective through drafting and revision.
4. Proofread and edit their own writing, avoiding grammatical and mechanical errors.
5. Assess and explain the major choices that they make in their writing. (Ballard, Weismiller, and Sharer 42)

The assignments developed for the course helped students meet these course outcomes, and both classes used peer review. Students in both sections contributed to the university writing portfolio pilot during the Spring 2014 semester by uploading a piece of writing from the course and answering a series of metacognitive questions related to it. We also asked students to assess each of their major projects and discuss the rhetorical choices they made.

Theoretical Rationale

A specialized course like scientific writing can help teachers of composition to expand our knowledge of pedagogical possibilities. More specifically, we speak to the value of a scientific writing course for primarily science majors taught out of an English department, and we demonstrate how this course design both reflects and builds upon the value of transdisciplinary writing courses. Further, we explore the value of some specific tactics—collaborative course design, the use of writing mentor programs, and cross-class collaboration—in this specific set of circumstances.

Our version of English 3820 asked students to "consider the situated nature of scientific writing and also to produce scientific writing for various purposes." The design of this course focuses on moving students into a rhetorical space where they can explore the socially constructed nature of science, scientific rhetoric, and scientific traditions (Haraway; Harding; Wilson). Like Sarah Perrault, we wanted students "to see science as a sociocultural phenomenon, to see how it shapes and is shaped by the larger culture of which it is a part" and to "recognize the discursive nature of science-related texts, and to be able to identify and critique the rhetorical moves in those texts in terms of how those moves construct popular understandings of science" (116). To that end, we took a critical approach to the theories, methodologies, and ideologies that undergird scientific writing and asked students to work on both critique and imitation of scientific styles; critical pedagogies allowed for a productive combination of reflection on and immersion in these scientific styles. For example, Erin approached the class from an "apparent feminist" perspective (Frost), while Michelle took a critical gender studies approach (Butler; Halberstam; hooks). In both cases, students knew at the outset that we would be critiquing the notion of scientific objectivity and that their professors were purposefully making their own biases explicit in an effort to facilitate intellectual discussion about scientific debate and communication. In short, we were—and are—seeking to develop "a pedagogical approach that is inclusive to all racial/ethnic and gender groups" without being "exclusive to other cultural traditions" (Perryman-Clark 116-17).

As part of our effort to achieve both inclusivity and student investment, we created a series of three assignments that allowed students to engage deeply with a particular scientific topic of their choosing. They began with a field research assignment in which they researched a broad area of interest (e.g., genetics, conservation, planetary geography) and became familiar with journals that publish work in that area. For their second major project, they chose a more focused topic and produced a complete scientific article for one of the journal venues they had previously identified. Finally, they turned that scientific article into an article suitable for publication on CNN.com, a major news site directed at a general audience.

Students approached this final paper from a place of deep investment in their scientific topic and, as such, the task of reducing complexity while maintaining relevance was extremely challenging. This assignment was intended to produce cognitive dissonance (Festinger). These student authors were deeply disciplined to believe that everything in the science articles they had produced was vital; further, their investment in time, energy, and revisions made it hard to let go of anything deemed important for a scientific audience. However, the lay article required them to prioritize: They had to let go of many pieces of information in order to communicate effectively to nonscientific audiences. Thus, this assignment required that students believe that their own scientific article was so relevant and important that reducing its complexity was unethical while also believing (or at least appearing to believe) that communicating scientific topics to the public and lay audiences can be done effectively and in responsible ways. For advanced undergraduate students already steeped in the disciplinary values of their chosen fields, this was a difficult challenge; however, this rhetorical work resulted in the learning necessary to communicate to multiple audiences and also increased students' understandings of the relevance of their scientific work for various audiences.

Shane's presence as writing mentor in Erin's class undoubtedly influenced the writing of these articles, which we will discuss in more detail in the Critical Reflection. Our theoretical approach to incorporating a writing mentor into one of these classes followed much of the existing work on writing mentor programs. The benefits of writing mentor programs (also often called writing fellow programs) are well-established; at least thirty-five other universities have developed writing mentor or writing fellows programs (LaFrance). We were especially interested in promoting thinking about affect and critical self-reflection, a skill that Jim Henry, Holly Huff Bruland, and Jennifer Sano-Franchini found was associated with course-embedded mentoring (9). Critical self-reflection proved an important part of the aforementioned series of assignments. The lay article assignment required students to participate in cross-class peer review; Michelle's class read projects written by students in Erin's class and vice versa. In offering feedback, students had to think about how to best communicate their own credibility as reviewers while also offering the sort of critique necessary to strengthen their peers' papers. In receiving feedback, they had to deal with the affective repercussions of receiving critique on a project in which they already had invested significant time and struggle; they also had to move through that affective response to make decisions about which feedback was valuable and how best to respond productively to it. This sort of distanced or disembodied peer review has a way of creating space for students to intervene in situations they feel are unjust in ways that in-class peer review sometimes does not (Frost 111). Students undertook numerous conversations about morality—which led to productive discussions of culture and science—during this project.

This course also required students to participate in scientific debate with others via class participation and a scripted oral debate completed in small groups near the end of the semester. This compelled them to think deeply about belief systems, diversity, and the value of multiple perspectives. It also encouraged them to navigate the tension between social justice and cultural relativism. In addition to these collaborative, outward-focused assignments, students kept a personal process journal throughout the semester in which they recorded their weekly reflections on the course. This work was intended to provide a space for students to draft projects, hone their writing processes, think through their biases in approaches to science, and reflect on class discussions. In this way, our assignment structure provided a variety of opportunities for students to speak back to class discussions and course materials, and they were able to choose their method of expression based on what they judged most rhetorically appropriate given their particular contexts.

James Wilson believes that students "need to be aware that 'the discursive context is a political arena,' in the words of [Linda] Alcoff. This is especially true of scientific and medical discourse, given the enormous power, authority, and resources of medical science" (160). We, too, ascribe to this notion. Our design of this scientific writing course purposefully led students into cognitive dissonance and required them to engage in intellectual discussions of scientific topics using critical theories of embodiment, including gender, sex, sexuality, ethnicity, and race. Our incorporation of a writing mentor in one section of the course allowed us to see how this additional audience affected students' writing, and our incorporation of cross-class peer review was a useful lesson in considering the effects of disembodied critique patterns. While we do not consider these courses successful in every way, we think our findings—and failures—may prove helpful to other instructors of composition. In our Critical Reflection, we attempt to offer insights into how we will continue this experiment and how others might benefit from and build upon this work.

Critical Reflection

We have written the final section of this article in a way that allows for both joint discussion of and individual reflection on our experiences. This format reflects our belief in the value of embodied knowledges and our different positionalities and perspectives in working with students in these two sections. Because we were deeply invested in learning from each other and from the students in our classes, we want to represent that mutuality here. As we discussed what worked in the course and what we might revise moving forward, we concluded that *collaborative course design* along with *cross-class collaboration* through peer review and the *presence of a writing mentor* gives students powerful writing experiences, especially in a specialized writing course like this one.

Collaborative course design proved to be an important foundational step in this experiment. This was both Erin and Michelle's first time teaching this specific course, and Erin was also new to the institution. Working with another instructor helped us to be aware of students' learning styles and needs. For example, Michelle noted, "Erin reminded me that some students might not feel comfortable participating in a large class discussion, so I started having them discuss and work in small groups before coming together as a class." Likewise, Michelle helped Erin understand the backgrounds and aspirations of many students in this institutional context.

Further, Erin and Michelle were able to compare notes when class did not go as planned. For example, in reflecting on the *cross-class peer review*, Erin and Michelle determined that Erin's background as a journalist and Michelle's background as an Institutional Review Board member likely influenced the ways they talked about writing for the public during class discussions; it was very clear that students produced different sorts of writing for this project based on their instructor. Students in Michelle's class were at first resistant to thinking about communicating to audiences that may not have specialized scientific knowledge. This was evidenced in one of the first class meetings when a student announced that she would have to "dumb down" the topics so others could understand. Getting students to think about other audiences without thinking of them as "dumb" took some discussion about literacies (medical, health, legal, science, etc.). Conversely, students in Erin's class were so persistent about keeping complexity in their lay articles that they ultimately persuaded her to increase their maximum allowed length for the assignment—a change she allowed at least in part because of her own investment in their work at that point in the semester.

Despite this commitment to complexity, students in Erin's class found the papers from Michelle's class to be too scientific, too full of jargon, too complex—basically, inaccessible to people without scientific educations. Students in Erin's class felt that Michelle's students did not try to simplify the language for another audience. This prevented them from giving students in Michelle's class the kind of feedback they expected. Students in Michelle's class, on the other hand, thought Erin's students had produced articles that were too simple. Students in Michelle's class were invested in keeping the specialized language and knowledge in their lay articles even after peer review. Further, they felt that students in Erin's class did not take the necessary time to work on their essay drafts. Thus, even though students were presented with the exact same assignment prompt, they received different messages about their intended audiences. For all three of us with instructor/mentor roles, it was telling—and, at times, frustrating—to see how each class approached the project differently despite receiving the exact same written project description. Michelle later wrote:

> *So why the difference in the lay science article? Yes, the teachers were different but even then, we thought we were emphasizing similar things, and that students would produce similar projects across classes. But there was one other difference that I neglected to account for. Erin's class had a writing mentor, Shane, so the students had a real public audience that could respond to their work. I think this helped them envision a public audience in more concrete ways.*

While any seasoned instructor knows that the differences in class personalities can vary widely, we do think Shane's presence as a writing mentor was a significant factor for Erin's class. As Erin reflected later:

> *Students understood Shane as an audience, and they did their writing knowing (in the back of their minds or explicitly) the sort of feedback he'd give them. Some students worked with him directly on this project; others had worked with him on other projects; and still others knew him only from their time together in class. However, ALL students in this class could at least imagine Shane as an audience, and this helped to guide their writing for non-scientist readers.*

The presence of a writing mentor in Erin's class undoubtedly influenced the way that multiple parts of the design of the course played out in practice. Students met with Shane in the first few weeks of class, and he explained his role as a writing mentor and asked them about what they perceived to be their strengths and weaknesses as writers going into this course. Many, it seemed, could list a paragraph's worth of failures in writing, from grammar to clarity to the forming of an actual paragraph, yet most struggled to name one thing they considered a writing strength. Many of these juniors and seniors hadn't taken a WI course since their freshman year, and as Shane reflected later:

> *It was in their perceived lack of knowledge about writing that I revealed my lack of knowledge of scientific material. I now believe it was this space of sharing our perceived 'lacks' that made us strong as a community and made me a mentor for their writing but a learning audience for their content.*

Ultimately, we believe the presence of a nonscientific outside reader—one with authority but who was not assessing their assignments—helped students to make determinations about the benefits for and effects on a non-scientific audience. His one-on-one conferences with students were essential to the success of many members of Erin's class. Shane writes:

> *One memory that will stay with me was in my second-to-final meeting with a student named Janet, who met regularly with me throughout the semester. She worked retail and came to me with limited time (often wearing her uniform so she could go straight to work). In the aforementioned meeting, I read the first sentence and she heard an obvious error—a word left out of a simple sentence—and she snatched the paper from me, saying she was going to do better. She said we both deserved better. I offered to keep the session going, but she insisted on leaving, saying we would meet again. She came back a week later with a completely reworked paper, and I am convinced had it not been for a semester of community building we would not have had that moment of awareness and courage on her part, where she lived up to her own developing expectations of herself as a writer through the vehicle of having a writing mentor embedded in that class.*

In addition to his important role as a first reader/audience, Shane identified with students so deeply that he was able to create a productive feedback loop that allowed us to make revisions to course design. In fact, Shane's reflections will be one of the largest drivers in our decisions to make changes or keep portions of the course design in the upcoming semester. Consider the following example, written from Shane's perspective:

> *An insightful glimpse into the cross-collaboration peer review came in my work with a student named Staci. Staci e-mailed me with a draft*

of her lay paper before the cross-class collaboration, but her message was different than most of the previous e-mails from students sending papers. Whereas most e-mails sought the quickest turnaround possible on what they considered finalized versions of their papers, Staci noted that her draft may "change a bit" because of the coming cross-class collaboration. When Staci turned in the post-collaboration draft, however, her statement of a "bit" of change turned to a warning that she had changed the draft "drastically." She had been swayed by Michelle's class, which was more scientifically directed even in their lay audience paper, and she had sought to make her paper more detailed. It worried me that Staci seemed more confident after her first draft than after the cross-class collaboration. Yet, in retrospect, what she would tell me (shared below) illustrates cognitive dissonance, a successful break from a single-form draft-writing and in-class peer review, and demonstrates critical thinking about what a lay audience is beyond the work of an assignment.

When I asked Staci about the differences between in-class peer review and cross-class collaboration, she said:

"I think [everyone in my class] had the same understanding of what the paper was supposed to be and then we got the [cross-class peer review] and it was different than all of ours, because we were all in a 'general-public' kind of [mindset] and when we got theirs, it was totally different."

I asked if she was more or less confused after the cross-class collaboration and she said:

"It's weird because I would say more, but I was happier after I got my [cross-class] peer review and after I finished my final paper. I was happier with my actual article. Maybe it wasn't exactly a lay audience, but I did feel I explained things better and kind of made up for my scientific paper."

It is helpful to see that a second peer review didn't simply replace the first. Instead, students had the opportunity to not just write but be writers, to make difficult choices about content, style, word choice, and to realize there are often spaces in writing not filled by right-and-wrong choices, but by creating drafts, receiving feedback, and ultimately making the decision to go in a chosen direction. This is particularly useful, as students from this class spoke to me about their worries in making content-and-style-based decisions when it comes to seeking scholarships and writing graduate school statements of purpose.

Based in large part on this (and similar) feedback, we have elected to keep the cross-class peer review in our upcoming courses. Shane's perspective helped Erin and Michelle to understand the wide variety of feedback we got from students about this project in a different way. What felt like a failure to us at the time actually produced valuable learning for students. We are exploring options for organizing the cross-class review differently in order to ensure more uniformity in the quality and quantity of feedback. For example, students in Erin's class received so much feedback that they were forced to prioritize, which we believe was an effective activity for developing revision skills. Michelle's students received much less feedback because Erin had instructed reviewers in her class to compile their notes, and this was not as useful.

Erin's major frustration with the course centered on the scientific article. In short, this assignment was too much. We knew this and designed the course that way intentionally, but we were not fully prepared for the difficulty of assessing a project that had purposefully put students in over their heads. Likewise, Michelle was disappointed in the products of the lay science article. We did not account for the depth of students' investment in the content of their work. While this challenge was productive, we also want to ensure the course has time to achieve all its learning outcomes. Thus, we have discussed several possibilities for revisions of the course to emphasize both scientific writing within the disciplines and communicating science to public audiences.

In our upcoming courses, we plan to change the science article requirement to a white paper or research review article for a scientific audience. This allows us more control over the length and depth of the project; rather than ask students to produce work for a wide variety of journals, they will all be writing white papers of similar length and depth for a specialist audience. We also plan to have them repurpose a published science article for a general audience before we require them to do the same to their own writing. In so doing, students will develop the skills required for repurposing before they have to deal with the affective impact of repurposing their own writing. Finally, we plan to change the process journal assignment to a required social media account dedicated to science writing. This will ensure that students are having public conversations about the content of the class throughout the semester, and also will give them agency in determining how they represent themselves as scientists and writers.

Notes

1. Many writing mentor programs started in the early 1990s, and such programs tend to be small because of the expense associated with them. For example, even with significant financial support from the QEP, the Writing Mentor program at ECU reaches only a small percentage of courses; the program will place 15 mentors in 13 courses in Fall 2014, while approximately 500 courses listed as WI are scheduled to be offered across the university, according to Writing Center Director Nicole Caswell.

2. We extend our heartfelt thanks to ECU University Writing Center Director Dr. Nicole Caswell, who provided significant context about the workings of the QEP, the Writing Mentor Program, and the disciplinary and national contexts of such initiatives.

3. The research reported in this article was approved by the University and Medical Center Institutional Review Board #14-001165.

Works Cited

Academic Affairs. "Quality Enhancement Plan." East Carolina U, 1 June 2014. Web. 5 June 2014. <http://www.ecu.edu/qep/>.

Alcoff, Linda. "The Problem of Speaking for Others." *Cultural Critique* 20 (1991-92): 5-32. Print.

Ballard, Steven, David Weismiller, and Wendy Sharer. *"Write Where You Belong": Quality Enhancement Plan*. Greenville: East Carolina U, 2013. Web. 5 June 2014. <http://www.ecu.edu/cs-acad//qep/upload/ECU-QEP-Revised-Final-8-21.pdf>.

Butler, Judith. *Gender Trouble: Feminism and the Subversion of Identity*. New York: Routledge, 1990. Print.

Caswell, Nicole. Personal interview. 5 June 2014.

Festinger, Leon. *A Theory of Cognitive Dissonance*. Stanford: Stanford UP, 1957. Print.

Frost, Erin A. "Apparent Feminist Pedagogies: Interrogating Technical Rhetorics at Illinois State University." *Programmatic Perspectives* 6.1 (2014): 110-31. Web. 12 June 2014. <http://www.cptsc.org/pp/vol6-1/frost.pdf>.

Halberstam, Judith. *In a Queer Time and Place: Transgender Bodies, Subcultural Lives*. New York: New York UP, 2005. Print.

Haraway, Donna J. *Simians, Cyborgs, and Women: The Reinvention of Nature*. New York: Routledge, 1991. Print.

Harding, Sandra. *Whose Science? Whose Knowledge?* Ithaca: Cornell UP, 1991. Print.

Henry, Jim, Holly Huff Bruland, and Jennifer Sano-Franchini. "Course-Embedded Mentoring for First-Year Students: Melding Academic Subject Support with Role Modeling, Psycho-social Support, and Goal Setting." *International Journal for the Scholarship on Teaching and Learning* 5.2 (2011): 1-22. Web. 21 May 2014. <http://digitalcommons.georgiasouthern.edu/ij-sotl/vol5/iss2/16/>.

hooks, bell. *Teaching to Transgress: Education as the Practice of Freedom*. New York: Routledge, 1994. Print.

LaFrance, Michelle. "Writing Fellows Programs." *The WAC Clearinghouse*. Colorado State U, 2014. Web. 05 June 2014. <http://wac.colostate.edu/fellows/>.

Perrault, Sarah. "UWP 011: Popular Science & Technology Writing." *Composition Studies* 40.2 (2012): 112-33. Web. 10 May 2014. <http://www.uc.edu/content/dam/uc/journals/composition-studies/docs/coursedesign/Perrault.pdf>.

Perryman-Clark, Staci. "Writing, Rhetoric, and American Cultures (WRA) 125—Writing: The Ethnic and Racial Experience." *Composition Studies* 37.2 (2009): 115-34. Web. 10 May 2014. <http://www.uc.edu/content/dam/uc/journals/compositionstudies/docs /coursedesign/Perrault.pdf>.

Wilson, James C. "Making Disability Visible: How Disability Studies Might Transform the Medical and Science Writing Classroom." *Technical Communication Quarterly* 9.2 (2000): 149-61. Print.

Syllabus

ENGL 3820: Scientific Writing

Introduction to and Goals of the Course

This course asks students to consider the situated nature of particular contexts of scientific writing and also to produce scientific writing for various purposes. We will examine theories, methodologies, and ideologies that undergird scientific writing with an eye to perfecting both critique and imitation of scientific styles. In order to accomplish this work, you will be expected to do a substantial amount of reading, produce several different kinds of work, analyze the products you create, and be an active participant in our learning community. This means working in a variety of individual and group activities. Further, you are expected to come to class having thoroughly prepared the readings. Notice this does not say you must have read every word on every page. Rather, you should read for content and themes, taking main ideas and significant occurrences from the texts we cover and critically examining them. You should always be prepared to offer notes, questions, and ideas about the readings.

Materials

Cargill, M., & O'Connor, P. (2013). *Writing scientific research articles: Strategies and steps* (2nd ed.). New York: John Wiley & Sons. ISBN: 9781118570708

Penrose, A. M., & Katz, S. B. (2010). *Writing in the sciences: Exploring conventions of scientific discourse* (3rd ed.). New York: Pearson Longman. ISBN: 9780205616718

Internet access, including access to our course site on Blackboard.

Ability to read additional readings provided as PDF and Microsoft Word documents.

Word-processing and digital storage capabilities.

Assignments

The following components of the class will contribute to student grades:

- *Participation – 10 points*

This class uses discussion as a basis for collaborative learning, and engaged participation makes for a more enriching and productive learning environment for the entire class. Participation may mean speaking in class—and you should plan to do so at least once each class period—but it is also evidenced by nonverbal engagement such as paying attention, nodding, making eye contact, and so on. In order to fully participate, it is essential that you adequately prepare readings and other homework assignments. Preparing readings and homework means coming to class with the work completed and with a list of relevant questions and/or notes. Preliminary participation grades will be released before the midpoint of the semester; in addition, students may request an informal evaluation of their participation at any time.

- *Process journal – 15 points*

Throughout this course, keep track of trending science and health topics as well as your reflections on our discussions in class. Include at least one detailed (though not necessarily polished) entry each week. (Detailed means in the 300-word range at a minimum.) In addition to your weekly entries, you should include an assessment entry for each of the three major assignments (field research, science article, lay science article) that discusses why you made the rhetorical choices you did in each assignment. You may do this work in a blog, notebook, or any other format that will allow you to turn the process journal in at various unannounced points during the semester. (Note that if you choose to do this work hardcopy, being able to turn it in at an unannounced time will mean you need to bring it with you every day.)

- *Field Research – 15 points*

Complete an investigation focusing on the communications and research practices of a field within the natural sciences. This assignment should be submitted as a formal report that must include (1) a brief summary of the field chosen, (2) a list of journals relevant to the field and detailed annotations of those journals, (3) a list of research topics relevant to the field chosen, and (4) a general analysis of communication in the chosen field. This assignment should be a minimum of 1500 words. Save your final document as Name_3820_FieldResearch and turn in by emailing to FrostE@ecu.edu.

This assignment is worth 15 points out of the total 100 points in the course. Those 15 points will be allocated approximately as follows, assuming that basic requirements like proper formatting and clear (meaning, in this case, understandable and situationally appropriate) writing are already met.

Part of Report	Requirements	Points Possible
Section 1	Student provides a summary of a sufficiently narrow field (for example, don't summarize *biology*; summarize a particular area of biology). This summary should be appropriate for a lay audience (like an English instructor, for example!). (Suggested length: minimum 300 words)	3
Section 2	Student provides a list of at least five journals relevant to the field. List includes detailed annotations that discuss the area, audience, purpose, and types of articles typically published in these journals. It may also be helpful to list any affiliated organizations/publishers. (Suggested length: minimum 500 words)	5
Section 3	Student provides a list of at least three research topics relevant to the field chosen as well as reflections on how each topic might work out if chosen for future projects in this course (namely, the Science Article and Lay Science Article). Each topic should include a sentence that suggests which of the journals from Section 2 might be the most appropriate venue for an article on said topic. (Suggested length: minimum 300 words)	3
Section 4	Student provides a general analysis of communication in the chosen field. This analysis should answer questions about the style, purpose, and conventions of articles typical of this field and should draw on examples. (Suggested length: minimum 400 words)	4

- *Science Article – 20 points*

Choose one of the journals you listed in your Field Research assignment and write an article for that venue. The exact requirements of this assignment will vary depending on the journal you choose, so be aware of submission guidelines at the outset and make sure that you include those submission guidelines with your final document. Save your final document as Name_3820_ ScienceArticle and turn in by emailing to FrostE@ecu.edu.

This assignment is worth 20 points out of the total 100 points in the course. Those 20 points will be allocated approximately as follows, assuming that basic requirements are already met.

Article	Requirements	Points possible
	Note that the goal of this project is to practice writing a paper for a scholarly publication. Since you will each be choosing your own publication/journal to target—and since different journals have different guidelines—the requirements for this project will vary to a significant degree. You should use the information below to guide your work, but you should also understand that some criteria might be more or less important to your work given the journal you choose.	
	Submission includes a cover letter to the editor of the journal that synthesizes the article, explains its relevance to this venue, and confirms that you have fulfilled all requirements the journal requires.	2
	Paper articulates a narrowly defined research topic/question in the introduction. Paper also includes a concise abstract if required by the target journal.	3
	Paper demonstrates appropriate research/knowledge related to prior applicable research by synthesizing and citing important research.	5
	Paper follows submission guidelines as stated by target journal in terms of length and style. (Any exceptions should be noted in a submission memo.)	3
	Paper utilizes an appropriate organizational format based on the type of article written (research article or review article).	3
	Paper incorporates common scientific conventions as surmised through journal article analysis. For example, headings, voice, tables, etc.	4

- *Lay Science Article – 20 points*

Write a short article on the same topic as your Science Article, but this time appropriate for a nonscientific audience. This assignment should total 600-1200 words, plus a cover letter to the publication you've chosen explaining your work and its relevance. Save your final document as Name_3820_Lay-Article and turn in by emailing to FrostE@ecu.edu.

This assignment is worth 20 points out of the total 100 points in the course. Those 20 points will be allocated approximately as follows, assuming that basic requirements are already met.

Requirements	Points possible
Submission includes a cover letter to the editor of your chosen section of CNN.com that synthesizes the article and explains its relevance to this venue.	2
Submission utilizes an appropriate style / demonstrates an understanding of audience.	6
Submission appropriately explains the topic in understandable terms and cites prior research/knowledge	6
Student participated fully in cross-class peer review (including providing feedback in class on Wednesday, April 2)	6

- *Oral Debate – 20 points*

Working in groups, identify a specific popular scientific question that currently has two strong sides and prepare a debate to be presented to the class in which each side of the issue is presented. For example, in a group of four students, two group members will defend the affirmative side of the question, while two group members defend the negative side of the question. The rest of the class will be allowed to ask questions, so while most of the information can be planned out ahead, individuals will need to be prepared to answer questions. Rather than this being an actual debate in which the "yes" side would not know what the "no" side might say, both sides should work together prior to the presentation to lend the debate coherence. Students will prepare written notes for themselves for use during the debate, but only an annotated bibliography of sources will be turned in. This bibliography, which should be turned in on behalf of the entire group in hard-copy on the day of the debate, should include a minimum of ten sources.

This assignment is worth 20 points out of the total 100 points in the course. Those 20 points will be allocated approximately as follows, assuming that basic requirements are met.

Requirements	Points possible
Group submits an annotated bibliography with ten relevant sources by the end of class on Monday, May 5.	5
Group presents an approximately five-minute rhetorically aware and well-prepared debate in class on Monday, May 5.	5

Group is able to respond to questions posed by class members during the five-minute Q&A in class on Monday, May 5.	5
Individual student poses at least one question to another group of debaters during class on Monday, May 5.	3
Individual student turns in one short analysis (using stasis theory) of one of the debates given during class on Monday, May 5.	2

Course calendar

Week	Activities and Preparation
Week 1	Day One: Read the syllabus, procure the textbooks, and familiarize yourself with the course. Read: Bowdon. Day Two: Define scientific writing. Discuss Bowdon. Read: Sidler.
Week 2	Discuss Sidler. Read Chapters 1 and 2 in Penrose and Katz.
Week 3	Day One: Discuss science as a social construct. Read Chapter 3 in Penrose and Katz. Day Two: Discuss ethics. Read Chapter 13 in Penrose and Katz.
Week 4	Day One: Homework is to bring at least three articles from different scientific journals on a topic you're interested in. Day Two: Read Sections 1 and 2 in Cargill and O'Connor.
Week 5	Day One: Read Chapter 4 in Penrose and Katz. Day Two: Read Chapter 5 in Penrose and Katz.
Week 6	Day One: Peer review of field research. Day Two: *Field Research due* Read Section 3 in Cargill and O'Connor.
Week 7	Day One: Read Section 4 in Cargill and O'Connor. Day Two: Reading TBA depending on class needs.
Week 8	This week devoted to analysis of articles, beginning with examples in Cargill and O'Connor together and moving to analysis of found articles individually.
Week 9	Happy Spring Break!
Week 10	Day One: Peer review of science article. Day Two: Science Article due. Read Chapter 8 in Penrose and Katz.
Week 11	Day One: Reading TBA depending on class needs. Day Two: Homework is to work on Lay Science Article.
Week 12	Day One: Drafts for class exchange due by end of class today. Day Two: Provide feedback to partner class for cross-class peer review.
Week 13	Day One: Provide feedback to partner class for cross-class peer review. Receive feedback from partner class. Day Two: Lay Science Article due.

Week 14	Day One: Assignment of groups and topics for oral debates. Day Two: Flex Day / Group work to prepare for oral debates.
Week 15	Day One: Group work to prepare for oral debates. Day Two: Group work to prepare for oral debates.
Week 16 / Final	Oral debates during Finals Period. Process journal due.

Working with Disciplinary Artifacts: An Introductory Writing Studies Course for Writing Majors

Lori Ostergaard

Course Description

WRT 329: Introduction to Writing Studies is a course in Oakland University's (OU) Writing and Rhetoric major program that provides students with a survey of composition studies as an academic discipline. It includes an examination of the history, theories, research, curricula, and pedagogies associated with composition studies in the university. I developed WRT 329 as a gateway course for our major's writing studies track, which prepares our students for eventual graduate study in the field. In proposing and developing this course for our undergraduates, I have found myself engaged in some of the "hard time thinking" about the writing major that Robert J. Connors recommended in his afterword to *Coming of Age: The Advanced Writing Curriculum* (148). While I believe this course provides our majors with a vital introduction to the field, as I discuss in the conclusion of this course description, I believe this course raises some important questions about the very focus and foundation of our writing major at OU and about the growth of the writing major nationally.

I developed this introductory writing studies course to replace our original gateway course for the writing studies track. While the original course, Peer Tutoring in Composition, provided students with some background in writing center pedagogy as well as the theories and research that inform writing center best practices, our department recognized that majors in the academic track needed a more thorough introduction to the field as a whole. I envisioned the gateway course as a "locus for defining our discipline" for our students and our program (Tweedie, Courtney, and Wolff 260).

While our major is now seven years old, the Writing Studies course was proposed and approved as the gateway course for the academic track of the major in 2010. I have taught the course twice since it was developed.

Description of the Institutional Context

OU is located in Rochester, Michigan, twenty-five miles north of Detroit. This Carnegie-ranked Doctoral/Research University was endowed by Matilda Dodge Wilson in 1957, and was originally affiliated with Michigan State University (MSU). The university gained autonomy from MSU in 1970 and went on to experience tremendous growth in its student population and program offerings. Today OU claims over 20,000 students, including 16,935 undergraduates ("Student Profile"). The creation of a Writing and Rhetoric major and the institution of a separate department of Writing and Rhetoric in 2008 are just two small examples of the university's growth, with the most current example being the development of a medical school in 2012. Our undergraduates are predominantly local, most are commuters, and most work a minimum of 17 hours a week, "more hours than both our peer group comparison and national norms," while carrying a 12-16 credit course load each term (Office of Institutional Research and Assessment).

The Writing and Rhetoric Major is comprised of three individual tracks: professional writing, writing for digital media, and writing studies. Our professional writing and digital media tracks provide undergraduates with the theories and practices they will need to pursue careers in writing, editing, and new media design. Our graduates from these two tracks have had some success acquiring jobs in local industries.

The writing studies (or academic) track of the major was designed to prepare our undergraduates for graduate programs in composition studies. This track provides a typically small cohort of majors with a selection of courses in subjects ranging from peer tutoring to global rhetorics, from a general study of research methods in the field to a course focused on ethnography. As the gateway course for the academic track, Introduction to Writing Studies, while not a prerequisite for any other courses in this track, was designed to provide our students with a broad, but thorough, introduction to the field.

The writing studies track provides students with coursework and experiences designed to prepare them for graduate study in the field and eventually for careers as instructors or professors of composition. Since our program was established in 2008, we have graduated 49 majors. Only 10 of those majors have been in the writing studies track, and of those, 8 have gone on to study in MA programs around the country, including programs at Michigan State University, Miami University of Ohio, North Carolina State University, and the University of South Florida. While the department offers a handful of graduate classes, we do not have an MA or PhD program. The writing studies track, then, was not developed with an eye towards feeding our own graduate program, but preparing our majors who wish to pursue graduate study elsewhere.

Theoretical Rationale

WRT 329, Introduction to Writing Studies, helps our majors become conversant in the discipline of composition and rhetoric by asking them to:

- Survey disciplinary history and analyze how this history has influenced present-day composition theory, research, practice, and status in the university;
- Study the theories, research, and practices that inform the discipline;
- Examine the ways institutional contexts shape degree programs and course offerings; and
- Explore current trends in composition studies scholarship and practice.

In my proposal for the course, I argued that it should provide our writing studies majors with an introduction to composition studies as an academic field of study and a discourse community. The Writing Studies course aims to develop disciplinary insiders by moving beyond simply providing our majors with enough disciplinary knowledge to distinguish between the theories of David Bartholomae and Peter Elbow; instead, the course aims to help them construct a vision of the "'future tense' of their lives as rhetoric and composition professionals" (Miller et al. 397). The course also seeks to connect disciplinary knowledge to local contexts, to provide students with an understanding of "how profoundly local educational practices and possibilities are shaped by local constraints" (Miller 8). Finally, I envision this course helping our majors understand that the field's apparatuses, methods, and knowledges are not inevitable or pre-ordained, but rather constructed, flexible, and even fallible.

Course assignments include two major research projects, a portfolio with a reflective introduction, two short presentations, and in class as well as online activities. The two major projects in the class require that students conduct both current and historical studies of the field: a "Composition Job Market/Career Research Project" and an "Archival Research Project."

The Composition Job Market/Career Research Project requires that students research and analyze the current composition job market, narrowing the focus of their research to a single subfield within the discipline and exploring the jobs that are available to those professionals, as well as the education and degrees expected of people in that subfield, the courses they might teach, research they might engage in, and service they might provide to their academic communities.

The Archival Research Project asks that students research and analyze the discipline of composition through its historical archives. Students examine historical artifacts (local, regional, and national), placing those artifacts within both a historical context and within the context of current conversations in the field.

In the subsections that follow, I describe my first attempt to teach this course in winter 2012 and my subsequent revision for the winter 2013 semester.

In the first iteration of the course, I relied primarily on scholarly sources to introduce our majors to the discipline. In the second, more successful version, I required that students engage with a variety of primary documents, disciplinary ephemera, and historical artifacts to construct their own understanding of the field. While I will continue to revise and refine this course over the next few years, I use the opportunity afforded me by the Critical Reflection section of this Course Design to address some concerns I have about the undergraduate major as a gateway to graduate study and the profession, concerns that have shaped my design of and approach to teaching this course.

Take One: Listening to the Experts

In my initial design for this course, I began by weighing a number of questions about the course content:

- What do our majors need to know to be successful and to engage successfully in our academic track?
- How much should undergraduates reasonably be expected to know about their academic discipline?
- And since this is only a 300-level course, how and how much should this course differ from a graduate-level introductory composition course?

To a certain extent, each of these questions spoke to the content of the course, content that could easily be rendered too complex, esoteric, or idiosyncratic for undergraduate majors. And, indeed, the first time I taught Writing Studies, I believe course content ranged from too simplistic to be interesting to too difficult to be instructive. Because I focused on what I thought students should know of the field, I did not spend enough time thinking about how they should arrive at that knowledge. Thus, the first time I taught the course, I relied primarily on secondary sources to instruct students in the history, theory, practices, and research methods of their new discipline. Because these secondary works were not written for undergraduate readers, I previewed each reading assignment with a brief contextual frame and then followed up the reading assignment with a short introductory lecture and a frequently unsuccessful discussion about the material.

At the same time my students were studying published historical and theoretical works about the field, they were also accessing the university's archives for their own history projects. I assigned the history project first, assuming that it would provide us with a foundation to build upon throughout the semester, but this assignment proved to be the more difficult one for my students. Because they began these projects early in the semester, my students entered the archives with little understanding of the field and little experience working with disciplinary artifacts. As a result, I believe many of my students struggled to understand and contextualize the primary sources they found in the archives. What's more, when my contextualization of the reading assignments did not offer students enough information to aid them in their archival research or when the reading assignment was too long or, more often, too difficult for my students to get through, most simply chose not to read. This practice—one I might have adopted as an undergraduate in a similar situation—meant that most of the class was unable to synthesize information from multiple secondary sources and apply that information to the things they were discovering with their own history projects. While student evaluations suggested my students were happy with this course design overall, I knew I could do a much better job initiating our majors to the discipline.

Take Two: Constructing the Field Through Artifacts

My second time teaching the course I shifted focus from what to teach to how to teach the material. Recognizing the difficulty students in my first section of the course had both with understanding the secondary sources and with interpreting disciplinary artifacts from our university's archives and from the web, I greatly reduced the course's dependence on secondary research to focus the class more on primary sources. In this second iteration of the course, students began working with disciplinary artifacts on day one, and I added in secondary sources only as needed to help them interpret and critically analyze whatever artifacts they were dealing with at the time.

Thus, students began the semester by reading a *Forbes* article (Adams), and the comments about that article, about the workload of college faculty. Class time was spent examining, first in a very general way, the composition job market, using job descriptions posted on the Academic Jobs Wiki ("Rhetoric/Composition"). At the same time, students read Robert J. Connors' historical examination of working conditions ("Overwork, Underpaid"), and they reviewed the results of a recent survey I had administered to our part-time faculty about their paper response workload. The discussions that emerged from this preliminary research explored what it meant to pursue the job market and have an academic job in composition studies, leading to students' first major project, a prolonged analysis of jobs within one area of the field. Students researched professional/technical writing, new media, composition generalist, and community college positions for this first major project. This major assignment required that they build on their first week's research into the composition job market, and so class time was spent examining MA and PhD programs that would prepare applicants for each job, as well as journals, professional organizations, conference proceedings, and individual university department websites associated with the area of the field they were researching. Finally, I required that each student conduct an interview with a faculty member who holds an academic job in their area of research.

When their first projects were completed, we began a more thorough examination of research and scholarship in the field. While students read works by Maureen Daly Goggin ("Composing a Discipline") and Connors ("Journals in Composition Studies"), we used class time to do some journal mapping, with small groups analyzing the tables of contents (and some article abstracts) from the first ten years of *College Composition and Communication* (*CCC*). Homework assignments required that students put this historical analysis into conversation with contemporary research by first examining a single, recent two-year period of *CCC* issues and then comparing the research and scholarly focus of *CCC*s first ten years with those of the present day. While this analysis of *CCC* occupied only a few face-to-face and online classes at the beginning of the semester, students' end of the semester reflections suggested this work had helped them to understand composition as a field in flux. For example, in a final reflection, one student[1] observed that:

> Because work published in professional journals often offers a sound representation of an academic field at a particular point in time, *College Composition and Communication* provided me with a clear illustration of the trends in the field of composition over the past half century. It was especially helpful because I was able to see how the field evolved over the years by examining the previously published journals in chronological order. Analyzing *College Composition and Communication*'s publications over the course of many decades ultimately allowed me to become familiar with the field's values, where the discipline was, where it is currently, and where it is headed. (Marentette)

Each time we engaged with a new set of artifacts—journals, textbooks, course descriptions, the "Writing Majors at a Glance" database, etc. (CCCC Committee on the Major)—I reassured the class that we had done this type of document analysis before. The first time I taught this course, secondary sources like Maxine Hairston's "Winds of Change" and Goggin's "Composing a Discipline" were received with a combination of confusion and frustration. As a result, these theoretical and historical readings remained isolated from the research my students were doing. The second time I taught the course, the more challenging secondary sources students read were viewed as a way of theorizing the changes they were witnessing first hand in their study of the field's artifacts.

In preparation for their second major project, students researched histories of the field, as both genres to be modeled and as research methods to employ. They did rhetorical analyses of the 2012 CCCC conference proposals for the history area and of Lisa Mastrangelo's "Learning from the Past." From these analyses, my students speculated about what historians in the field valued, and they began to get a feel for how to research and organize their own history papers.

Before visiting our university's archives, I had the class work with some historical artifacts that I had collected from different institutions and publications from the early nineteenth and twentieth centuries. In working with these primary sources, I asked the class to make only casual notes about the artifacts they read. Then we spent the next class making connections between their individual notes and the notes their classmates had made. For example, students who examined early composition textbooks connected their observations to those made by a group who had examined published textbook reviews. Other students connected early faculty bios and obituaries to descriptions of MA theses by those same faculty. They discussed and attempted to historically contextualize letters from a university president to a female student interested in attending his university, college and high school newspaper articles, college and high school club and publication descriptions from yearbooks, as well as course catalogs, journal articles, and conference proceedings. Because they had already been exposed to a number of current disciplinary artifacts, students in this second iteration of the course were able to illustrate some facility with using historical ephemera to construct a story of the field.

Working with these artifacts helped my students see what types of documents they might encounter in our own university archives and how they might follow a research lead and code information across a variety of documents: a catalog description for a university writing course that mentions a textbook, the textbook itself, a review of that textbook in a professional journal, a summary of a conference presentation by the textbook author, and the author's MA thesis, for example.

When the class visited the university's archives, the archive librarian arranged for us to look through old university newspapers, a few bound volumes of class papers, a thesis on early student publications at the university, and various independent student publications. I gave students no instructions for dealing with these artifacts beyond, "pick something up, read through it, make a note of or take a picture of anything interesting, and then move on to something else."

For these history projects, students in my first section of this class had genuinely struggled to make connections between current conditions and past history, between secondary sources and their primary artifacts, and between the archival documents they were analyzing and current theories and practices in the field. For many students in this first class, the history projects remained disconnected from the field, presenting only an interesting narrative about some isolated or idiosyncratic local approach, study, or individual. Thus, my students struggled to locate their projects within the larger field through "generalities, hypotheses, overarching observations, and speculations" that might have made it possible for their work with our local archives to speak to larger disciplinary and social contexts (Miller 17). But then this disconnect with the wider discipline, its values, theories, practices, and assumptions, makes sense given that for students working in my first section of this class, their only real introduction to reading disciplinary artifacts occurred during their first and only class trip to the archives at the beginning of the semester.

Students in my second section of the course were already adept at critically analyzing a range of disciplinary artifacts before they ever set foot in our archives. Students in this second section also made seemingly easy connections in their first drafts between their own primary sources and the secondary sources they had read, between historical approaches to the teaching of writing and contemporary ones, and between composition theories and the documents they encountered. While the content we covered was essentially the same, I believe students in the second class learned more about the discipline and gained a greater facility and confidence with making connections between classroom practices, theories, research, conferences, articles, job descriptions, course descriptions, and programs.

When it works—and it doesn't always—I believe the Writing Studies course at Oakland University can provide our majors with:

- A firmer grasp of the way the field has evolved over the last century and of some of the social, theoretical, pedagogical, and scholarly influences that have shaped that evolution;
- A survey of our disciplinary geography—courses, degrees, jobs, conferences, journals, professional statements, debates, and influential figures; and
- An opportunity to synthesize their own research about the field with the research of other composition studies scholars.

In their portfolio introductions, students in the second class suggested that their work with disciplinary artifacts was an entirely new research activity, and most appreciated the approach because, as one student observed, "instead of simply digesting someone else's opinions, by working more with artifacts students are able to form and test their own theses and hypotheses" (Marentette). Another student noted that the class introduced her to "some research forums and pathways that I would have never considered in the past" (Mockford). She also suggested that she "liked working with the direct materials. I loved looking through all those old books! It was quite a lot of fun looking at old pictures and documents that were very important to people in the past. It was effective and got the point across on how far back the debates of composition had been going on for" (Mockford). And a third student observed that this type of work had helped her to feel

> more involved with the field. Rather than relying predominately on secondary texts, by pursuing old journals, looking through the job market, etc. I feel that I received a better experience of the field itself. This approach worked because it made us, as students, work a bit harder for the information rather than having it simply handed to us. In addition, by looking at these artifacts from the field, it became clear what the field valued at different points in time. Seeing these different values and how they were expressed was far more beneficial than reading a secondary text which spelled out what the field believes to be important. (Romlein)

Rather than encounter only other people's interpretations of the field, the artifact approach allowed my students to produce their own critical evaluations. Rather than rely on secondary sources to tell the full story of composition, I believe students in the second iteration of this course began to view published scholars less as experts and more as collaborators who could aid these new researchers in developing their own stories of the field.

Critical Reflection

For our final week of class, I asked my students to examine our own Writing and Rhetoric major, not as something static or inevitable, but as a flexible and fallible course set constructed by faculty within the writing and rhetoric department. As they analyzed our major, these students identified what they saw as gaps or silences in the curriculum, and their discussions of those gaps led to their imagining new courses for our major core and suggesting new faculty specializations to meet those course needs. Their suggestions revealed a considerable amount of knowledge of the field and reflected the amount of study they had already conducted examining our disciplinary values. But their analyses also revealed that they may have gained an understanding of what our major provided and what it lacked. In their discussions of the major, as with their discussions of the artifacts preserved in the archives, students noted the significance of omissions and silences, of what was privileged, and what may have been marginalized within their own undergraduate program.

This final week of classes represented a kind of milestone for this group. When they enrolled in Writing Studies, most of my students were unaware that the writing major marked a new stage in our disciplinary evolution. Over the course of the semester, though, many came to recognize the place the major would assume in the history of the discipline, and to see themselves as pioneers exploring a new academic territory. In their discussions about our writing major at Oakland University, I was reminded of Connors' advice more than a decade ago, that the field of composition should "spend some hard time thinking about exactly what the undergraduate writing major that is currently falling into our laps should look like" ("Afterword" 148). And I was heartened by the ways students in this second section of the class seemed both able and eager to do some of that reflective work by semester's end.

Our field has already engaged in some critical reflection on the major: through the publication of a special issue of this journal, in the publication of Greg Giberson and Thomas Moriarty's *What We Are Becoming*, in a few dozen journal articles and conference presentations, in the creation and subsequent work of the CCCC Committee on the Major and Committee on Undergraduate Research, and in every new proposal for a writing major. But fifteen years after Connors's call, I cannot help but wonder if we are in danger of being swept away by the momentum of this new phase in our disciplinary development or beguiled by the possibilities for "disciplinary expansion and redefinition" that our undergraduate degrees promise (Estrem 12). Seven years after developing a writing and rhetoric major, my own department has only now gained the critical distance we need to rethink some of our early decisions and to assess what skills and knowledges our majors should reasonably be expected to possess upon graduation.

In the same volume where Connors recommended critical reflection on the major and speculated about how a major might help composition studies to "finally grow up as a discipline and take our natural place in the undergraduate curriculum" ("Afterword" 149), Richard Bullock worried that the field might adopt the kinds of "disquieting and morally suspect" practices that have led to the overproduction of literature MAs and PhDs (21). In his chapter for *Coming of Age*, Bullock wonders if composition studies will repeat the sins of other disciplines in our rush to embrace this new era for the field (21). He observes that

> The literature programs from which many of us earned our degrees acted irresponsibly, urging undergraduate students to begin graduate study with the lure of assistantships, packing their classrooms with full-time enrollments (FTEs)—generating graduate students, and providing senior professors with ego-stroking advisees. . . . I think we

need to ask ourselves how much we want to expand our disciplines, not necessarily as a way of improving the education of students but as a way of gaining access to the same perquisites enjoyed by our parents and siblings. (22)

Bullock's is a chilling warning to a field only newly engaged in the work of undergraduate program development, and it conjures up Stephen North's critique of English graduate programs where curricula were constructed to meet the intellectual desires of faculty, rather than the educational needs of graduates who "contributed to the corporate economy as students, enrolling for coursework, providing employment for the graduate faculty, and (one way or another) paying tuition" (24). North suggests that the presence of these students provided graduate literature faculty with "a kind of corporate bonus," permitting them to teach their specialization in an environment that demanded little reciprocity: "the professor could afford to be the specialist whose duty began and ended with him[/her]self" (27).

While the majority of writing majors across the country train students for work as professional writers, work those majors may undertake with a bachelor's degree, a handful of programs, like the one I helped to design at Oakland University, provide an alternative track for students wishing to pursue graduate study in the field. In offering a gateway to graduate study, departments like mine must be careful not to contribute to the systematic overproduction of graduate students that has made the exploitation of a professional workforce in composition studies inevitable.

In designing WRT 329 for the writing studies track of our major, I have striven to keep these dire warnings for our field in mind by creating a course that should serve, at least in part, as a wake-up call to undergraduates who might otherwise be "lured [to academic work] by the promise of academic freedom and the unbounded pleasures of the mind" (Miller 209). I worry that this course and our writing studies track may serve only to exacerbate the "syndrome of enticement and abandonment, bait and switch" that Bullock and others suggest characterized graduate programs in English (22). As we continue to develop and revise our own major at OU, I hope we will heed the warnings of Bullock and others about unchecked, unreflective disciplinary growth.

Even as I attend to these warnings and even as my department continues the conversation about our major and its responsibilities to undergraduates that we began anew last fall, I have to admit that I find it nearly impossible to deny the appeal of working with undergraduate writing majors. I am also beguiled by the promise of a generation of composition studies students who, unlike their peers earning degrees in other areas of English studies, will enter composition graduate programs with a more thorough and nuanced understanding of writing studies, rhetoric, and literacy education (Lauer viii). In addition to providing students with this foundational disciplinary knowledge, however, I believe I have a responsibility to ensure that our majors at OU enter the field with their eyes wide open, fully aware of both the promises and the perils of academic study.

My hope for our undergraduate programs is that we continue with this new phase of our discipline's development with our eyes open, questioning any assumption that the writing major is a natural, earned, or preordained (rather than constructed) next step for the field and engaging in the kinds of collaborative and critical "hard time thinking" that Connors recommended at the turn of this century ("Afterword" 148).

Notes

1. Student participants have provided informed consent, agreeing to have their work cited here (IRB 622663-1).

Works Cited

Adams, Susan. "The Least Stressful Jobs Of 2013." *Forbes*. Web. 15 December 2013. <http://www.forbes.com/sites/susanadams/2013/01/03/the-least-stressful-jobs-of-2013/>.

Bullock, Richard. "Feathering Our Nest? A Critical View from Within Our Discipline." Shamoon et al. 19–24. Print.

CCCC Committee on the Major in Rhetoric and Composition. "Writing Majors at a Glance." *Conf. on Coll. Composition and Communication*, NCTE, 9 January 2009. Web. 17 December 2012. <http://www.ncte.org/library/NCTEFiles/Groups/CCCC/Committees/Writing_Majors_Final.pdf>.

Connors, Robert J. "Afterword: 'Advanced Composition' and Advanced Writing." Shamoon et al. 143–49. Print.

---. "Journals in Composition Studies." *College English* 46.4 (1984): 348–65. Print.

---. "Overwork/Underpay: Labor and Status of Composition Teachers since 1880." *Rhetoric Review* 9.1 (1990): 108–26. Print.

Estrem, Heidi. "Growing Pains: The New Major in Composition and Rhetoric." *Composition Studies* 35.1 (2007): 11–14. Print.

Giberson, Greg, and Thomas Moriarty, eds. *What We Are Becoming: Developments in Undergraduate Writing Majors*. Logan: Utah State UP, 2010. Print.

Goggin, Maureen Daly. "Composing a Discipline: The Role of Scholarly Journals in the Disciplinary Emergence of Rhetoric and Composition Since 1950." *Rhetoric Review* 15 (1997): 322–48. Print.

Hairston, Maxine. "The Winds of Change: Thomas Kuhn and the Revolution in the Teaching of Writing." *CCC* 33.1 (1982): 76–88. Print.

Lauer, Janice. "Foreword." Giberson and Moriarty vii–viii.

Marentette, Spencer C. "Personal Statement." 17 April 2013. TS. Oakland University E-portfolio, Rochester, MI.

Mastrangelo, Lisa. "Learning from the Past: Rhetoric, Composition, and Debate at Mount Holyoke College." *Rhetoric Review* 18.1 (1999): 46–64. Print.

Miller, Richard E. *As If Learning Mattered: Reforming Higher Education*. Ithaca: Cornell UP, 1998. Print.

Miller, Scott L., Brenda Jo Brueggemann, Bennis Blue, and Deneen M. Shepherd. "Present Perfect and Future Imperfect: Results of a National Survey of Graduate Students in Rhetoric and Composition Programs." *CCC* 48.3 (1997): 392–409. Print.

Mockford, Emma. "Personal Statement." 17 April 2013. TS. Oakland University E-portfolio, Rochester, MI.

North, Stephen M. *Refiguring the Ph.D. in English Studies: Writing, Doctoral Education and the Fusion-Based Curriculum*. Urbana: NCTE, 2000. Print.

Office of Institutional Research and Assessment. *Spotlight on OU: NSSE Data Suggests Mixed Relationship between First Year Retention Rates and the Number of Hours that Students Work*. December 2009. Web. 12 April 2014. https://www.oakland.edu/upload/docs/OIRA/Spotlight%2017%20Student%20Retention%20and%20Off%20Campus%20Working%20Hours.pdf

"Rhetoric/Composition 2013." *Academic Jobs Wiki*. Web. 12 July 2015.

Romlein, Jeanne. "Personal Statement." 17 April 2013. TS. Oakland University E-portfolio, Rochester, MI.

Shamoon, Linda K., Rebecca Moore Howard, Sandra Jamieson, and Robert A. Schwegler, eds. *Coming of Age: The Advanced Writing Curriculum*. Portsmouth: Boynton, 2000. Print.

"Student Profile: Fall 2014." *Student Information and Enrollment History*. Office of Institutional Research and Assessment, Oakland University, 8 October 2014 Web. 28 June 2015. <http://wwwp.oakland.edu/Assets/upload/docs/OIRA/Info_2014.xlsx >.

Tweedie, Sanford, Jennifer Courtney, and William I. Wolff. "What Exactly is This Major? Creating Disciplinary Identity Through an Introductory Course." Giberson and Moriarty 260–76.

WRT 329, Introduction to Writing Studies, 4 credits

Catalog Description: a survey of composition-rhetoric as an academic discipline, including an examination of the history, theory, research, curricula, and practices associated with composition-rhetoric in the university. Prerequisite: completion of the university writing foundation requirement.

Extended Description: WRT 329, Introduction to Writing Studies, is the gateway course for the Writing Studies or academic track in the Writing and Rhetoric Major. As such, it provides a survey of the history, theory, research, curricula, and practices in the field of composition–rhetoric (writing and rhetoric studies). Your work in this class will require that you engage with the discipline of composition-rhetoric as it is shaped and informed by institutional and historical contexts, and to research the careers available to composition specialists in a variety of academic institutions.

Course Objectives

Students in WRT 329, Writing Studies, will become conversant in the discipline of composition-rhetoric by

- Surveying disciplinary history and analyzing how this history has influenced present-day composition theory, research, practice, and status in the university;
- Studying the theories, research, and practices that inform the discipline;
- Examining the ways institutional contexts shape degree programs and course offerings;
- Exploring current trends in composition-rhetoric scholarship and practice.

Our work this semester will focus on the field of composition studies from both historical and current perspectives. For the first third of the semester we will examine works addressing academic labor and the composition job market. During the second third of the semester we will study various theoretical and intellectual approaches to research and teaching in the field. Finally, we will conclude the semester by reading foundational and local histories of the field and by conducting some of our own archival research.

Required Texts

Articles available through JSTOR or online; book chapters uploaded to Moodle

Adams, Susan. "The Least Stressful Jobs Of 2013." *Forbes*. Web. 15 December 2013. < http://www.forbes.com/sites/susanadams/2013/01/03/the-least-stressful-jobs-of-2013/>.

Balzhiser, Deborah, and Susan McLeod. "The Undergraduate Writing Major: What is it? What Should it Be?" *CCC* 61.3 (2010): 415–33. Print.

Berlin, James A. "Contemporary Composition: The Major Pedagogical Theories." *College English* 44.8 (1982): 765–77. Print.

CCCC Committee on the Major in Rhetoric and Composition. "Writing Majors at a Glance." *Conf. on Coll. Composition and Communication*, NCTE, 9 January 2009. Web. 17 December 2012. <http://www.ncte.org/library/NCTEFiles/Groups/CCCC/Committees/Writing_Majors_Final.pdf>.

Connors, Robert J. "Journals in Composition Studies." *College English* 46.4 (1984): 348–65. Print.

---. "Overwork/Underpay: Labor and Status of Composition Teachers Since 1880." *Rhetoric Review* 9.1 (1990): 108–26. Print.

George, Diana, and John Trimbur. "The 'Communication Battle,' or Whatever Happened to the 4th C?" *CCC* 50.4 (1999): 682–98. Print.

Giberson, Greg, and Thomas Moriarty, eds. "Introduction: Forging Connections Among Undergraduate Writing Majors." *What We Are Becoming: Developments in Undergraduate Writing Majors*. Logan: Utah State UP, 2010. 1–10. Print.

Goggin, Maureen Daly. "Composing a Discipline: The Role of Scholarly Journals in the Disciplinary Emergence of Rhetoric and Composition Since 1950." *Rhetoric Review* 15 (1997): 322–48. Print.

Hairston, Maxine. "The Winds of Change: Thomas Kuhn and the Revolution in the Teaching of Writing." *CCC* 33.1 (1982): 76–88. Print.

Knoblauch, C.H. "Rhetorical Constructions: Dialogue and Commitment." *College English* 50.2 (1988): 125–40. Print.

L'Eplattenier, Barbara E. "Opinion: An Argument for Archival Research Methods: Thinking Beyond Methodology." *College English* 72.1 (2009): 67–79. Print.

Mastrangelo, Lisa. "Learning from the Past: Rhetoric, Composition, and Debate at Mount Holyoke College." *Rhetoric Review* 18.1 (1999): 46–64. Print.

North, Stephen. "Chapter One." *Making of Knowledge in Composition: Portrait of an Emerging Discipline*. Upper Montclair: Boynton, 1987. Print.

Ostergaard, Lori. "Open to the Possibilities: Seven Tales of Serendipity in the Archives." *Working in the Archives: Practical Research Methods for Rhetoric and Composition*. Ed. Alexis Ramsey, Wendy Sharer, Barbara L'Eplattenier, and Lisa Mastrangelo. Carbondale: SIUP, 2010. 40–50. Print.

Ritter, Kelly. "Archival Research in Composition Studies: Re-Imagining the Historian's Role." *Rhetoric Review* 31.4 (2012): 461–78. Print.

Major Figures Articles for Individual Presentations

Bartholomae, David. "Inventing the University." *Journal of Basic Writing* 5.1 (1986): 4–23. Print.

Bartholomae, David, and Peter Elbow. "Responses to Bartholomae and Elbow." *CCC* 46.1 (1995): 84–92. Print.

Berlin, James. "Rhetoric and Ideology in the Writing Class." *College English* 50.5 (1988): 477–94. Print.

Berthoff, Ann E. "Is Teaching Still Possible? Writing, Meaning, and Higher Order Reasoning." *College English* 46.8 (1984): 743–55. Print.

Bruffee, Kenneth A. "Collaborative Learning and the 'Conversation of Mankind.'" *College English* 46.7 (1984): 635–52. Print.

Crowley, Sharon. "Composition is Not Rhetoric." *Enculturation* 5.1 (2003): n.pag. Web. 15 December 2012. < http://enculturation.camden.rutgers.edu/5_1/pdf/crowley.pdf >.

Elbow, Peter. "Closing My Eyes as I Speak: An Argument for Ignoring Audience." *College English* 49.1 (1987): 50–69. Print.

Flower, Linda, and John R. Hayes. "The Cognition of Discovery: Defining a Rhetorical Problem." *CCC* 31.1 (1980): 21–32. Print.

Flynn, Elizabeth A. "Composing as a Woman." *CCC* 39.4 (1988): 423–35. Print.

Gilyard, Keith. "African American Contributions to Composition Studies." *CCC* 50.4 (1999): 626–44. Print.

Royster, Jacqueline Jones, and Jean C. Williams. "History in the Spaces Left: African American Presence and Narratives of Composition Studies." *CCC* 50.4 (1999): 563–84. Print.

Shaughnessy, Mina P. "Introduction." *Errors and Expectations: A Guide for the Teacher of Basic Writing*. New York: Oxford UP, 1977. Print.

Assignments

- Composition Job Market/Career Research 20%
- Archival Research Project 20%
- Final Portfolio 20%

- In-Class and Online Participation, Presentations (2), and Discussions 40%

Job Market/Career Research (20%): Your first project of the semester will involve you in an analysis of the 2012–2013 composition job search. You will begin by examining the job postings on the Academic Jobs Wiki for composition-rhetoric ("Rhetoric/Composition"). You will also research various academic positions open to compositionists who hold MAs or PhDs in the field (community colleges, liberal arts colleges, writing centers, WAC programs, English departments, separate departments of writing). You will read research related to academic jobs in composition (both historical works and contemporary ones). Finally, you will write a 4-6 page paper analyzing the job market and career prospects for compositionists specializing in one area of the field.

Your Job Market/Career Research Project will be assessed for the following:

1. The quality of your research into the academic training and career prospects for faculty focusing on your chosen area of the field. This will also include the research you conduct online into graduate programs in this area and the interview you conduct with a faculty member working in that area.
2. Your ability to synthesize both the primary research you have gathered—researching graduate programs and the MLA job list, and interviewing someone within that area—with some of the secondary sources we've read in class and others you have collected as part of your research into the teaching, scholarship, and service of faculty working in that area.
3. The quality of your written presentation of this research and the value of your research as an introduction to that area within the field.

Archival Research Project 20%: Our final research project for the semester will require that you begin a study of the archives of composition by examining some historical artifacts within the context of our ongoing discussions about the field. The artifacts you choose to collect and analyze may be textbooks, journals, conference programs and/or proceedings, dissertation or theses topics, or primary source materials from a single institutional site of instruction. Your artifacts should span a significant five- to ten-year period in composition history, and your analysis will explain how these artifacts conform to, support, complicate, or confound what we know about composition theory, research, and/or practices during this time. You should write your analysis with an eye towards developing this paper into a conference presentation, Writing Excellence Award essay, or a writing sample for graduate school.

Your Archival Research Project will be assessed for the following:

1. The quality of your research into an archive within the field of composition, including your ability to describe your research methods, identify the limitations of the archive and your study of it, and contextualize your reading of the primary artifacts within existing historical research within the field.
2. Your ability to synthesize both your interpretation of the historical artifacts you have gathered with some of the secondary sources we have read in class.
3. The quality of your written presentation of this research and the value of your research to students of composition history.

Final Portfolio 20%: As the gateway course for the academic track, WRT 329 will prepare you for future studies here at OU and beyond by helping you to create your academic portfolio. This portfolio will contain a personal statement by you that introduces both the work you did in this class and how that work shapes your understanding of the field, its career and research possibilities. Your portfolio will also contain both of the major projects you completed in this class and any other work you believe illustrates your understanding of composition as an academic discipline.

Your Personal Statement will be assessed for the following:

- Your ability to reflect upon what you have learned of the field of composition throughout the semester.
- Your ability to express your understanding of the field, its history, and its career and research possibilities.
- Your understanding of how a study of the field's artifacts may reveal its values, biases, theories, and assumptions.

Your Portfolio will be assessed for the following:

1. The inclusion of all required drafts.
2. The inclusion of additional materials that illustrate your engagement with the field.
3. The quality of the short summaries you provide for these materials.

In-Class and Online Class Work 40%: Your class participation and productive engagement in class discussions and projects is something that I expect to be able to take for granted this semester. I expect that everyone in this class will illustrate a high level of professionalism, attend classes regularly, and arrive prepared to participate. This class will introduce you to various, and sometimes complex, aspects of the academic discipline of composition, so I expect informed and lively discussions; compelling classroom presentations; and thoroughly researched, well-reasoned, and well-written projects and presentations. Participation in face-to-face and online classes accounts for 40% of your grade. Failure to attend either face-to-face or online classes will result in both an absence for the course and 0s on any in-class or online assignments.

Your In-Class and Online Work will be assessed for the following:

1. The quality of your responses during in-class or online discussions, as demonstrated through your understanding of the course material and engagement with the questions under consideration for those discussions.
2. The quality of your responses to your peers' major projects.
3. Your active and engaged participation in class activities, group projects, presentations, and short writing assignments.

Extra Credit: Extra credit will be offered in the form of 4.0s to replace the lowest grades you have received on your weekly forum posts in Moodle. You cannot replace a 0 with a 4.0, but if you complete any of the extra credit activities below, I will replace your lowest forum grade above a 0 with a 4.0. You may complete as many of the extra credit assignments below as you are able.

- One 4.0 will be given to anyone who writes and submits a proposal (individual or panel) to present their research at a local/regional/state academic (undergraduate or otherwise) conference.
- This semester the Department of Writing and Rhetoric will be interviewing job candidates for a tenure-line position in Professional Writing. We will bring four candidates to campus for daylong interviews, and during their interviews, each candidate will give a presentation ("job talk") discussing their research (in most cases, research they have conducted for their dissertations). You will receive extra credit for attending any/all of these presentations and writing up a short (250-word) summary of what you learned at the talk (up to four 4.0s to replace your low forum post grades).

Schedule

Part 1: Academic Labor—Scholar in the Ivory Tower or Mad Woman in the Basement	
Week 1	Assigned Read course syllabus and complete the first week online Friday forum. Read Stephen North, Chapter One from *Making of Knowledge in Composition*
Week 2	Begin researching the Academic Jobs Wiki Assigned Read Susan Adams, "The Least Stressful Jobs Of 2013" Read Robert J. Connors, "Overwork/Underpay" Begin Working on Project 1, Job Market/Career Research
Part 2: The Development of a Discipline	
Week 3	Begin researching journals in composition Assigned Read Robert J. Connors, "Journals in Composition Studies" Read Maureen Daly Goggin, "Composing a Discipline"
Week 4	Continue researching journals in composition Assigned Read Diana George and John Trimbur, "The 'Communication Battle,' or Whatever Happened to the 4th C?"
Week 5	Begin research of professional conferences; draft questions for interview with a faculty member who works in your project 1 research field. Read Maxine Hairston, "The Winds of Change" Peer review of Project 1
Week 6	Project 1 due Assigned Read Deborah Balzhiser and Susan McLeod, "The Undergraduate Writing Major: What is it? What Should it Be?" Begin working on Project 2, Archival Research Project
Week 7	Begin study of writing majors, MA programs, and PhDs. Assigned Read Greg Giberson and Thomas Moriarty, "Introduction" Study "Writing Majors at a Glance"

Part 3: Theories and Research in the Field	
Week 8	Begin researching major figures in the field of composition. Assigned Read C.H. Knoblauch, "Rhetorical Constructions" Read James Berlin, "Contemporary Composition" Begin preparing an individual presentation on a major figure in the field. Read the assigned work by your major figure and find at least one other work by that figure to read and analyze: Berthoff, Ann E., "Is Teaching Still Possible?" Bartholomae, David, "Inventing the University" Bartholomae, David, and Peter Elbow, "Responses to Bartholomae and Elbow" Berlin, James, "Rhetoric and Ideology in the Writing Class" Bruffee, Kenneth A., "Collaborative Learning and the 'Conversation of Mankind'" Crowley, Sharon, "Composition is Not Rhetoric" Elbow, Peter, "Closing My Eyes as I Speak" Flower, Linda, and John R. Hayes, "The Cognition of Discovery" Flynn, Elizabeth A, "Composing as a Woman" Gilyard, Keith, "African American Contributions to Composition Studies" Royster, Jacqueline Jones, "History in the Spaces Left" Shaughnessy, Mina P., "Introduction" to *Errors and Expectations*
Week 9	Working with archival material in class and taking a trip to the archives Assigned Read and rhetorically analyze Lisa Mastrangelo, "Learning from the Past" Read and rhetorically analyze at least two CCCC 2012 history proposals.
Week 10	Individual presentations due on major figures in the field. Assigned Read Lori Ostergaard, "Open to the Possibilities" Begin working on group presentations on issues in the field
Week 11	Coding archival sources and drafting the discussion section. Assigned Read Kelly Ritter, "Archival Research in Composition Studies"

Week 12	Read collected histories of our university; listen to oral histories; continue researching, coding, and drafting in class.
Week 13	Group presentations on issues in the field

Assigned
Read Barbara E. L'Eplattenier, "Opinion: An Argument for Archival Research Methods" |
| Week 14 | Drafting/refining the introduction and methods sections for Project 2.

Peer review of Project 2 partial drafts

Assigned
Begin preparing your Portfolio and Personal Statements |
| **Part 4: Reflecting on What You've Learned** ||
| Week 15 | Peer reviews of Project 2 (full drafts) and Personal Statements, attend an in-class/office hour conference for paper 2 |
| Week 16: Exam Week | 1. Present a summary of your Project 2 to the class
2. Submit final drafts of Project 2 and Portfolio |

Where We Are: Undergraduate Writing Majors & Concentrations

"Where We Are" highlights where we are as a field on matters current and compelling. In this installment of co-written essays, faculty and undergraduate students address the current state of undergraduate writing majors and concentrations. —*Editor's Note*

Coauthoring the Curriculum: Student Voices and the Writing Major

Erin Bradley, Melissa Davis, Michelle Dierlof, Keith Dmochowski, John Gangi, Laurie Grobman, Kristy Offenback, and Melissa Wilk, Penn State University, Berks

According to the call for submissions for this special issue, "Student voices and experiences are a necessary, but so far under-represented, component in how we account for the progress of undergraduate writing majors and concentrations." After reading several articles on the writing major, including four from *Composition Studies*, in our professional writing major capstone class, we recognized a noteworthy dissonance among undergraduate writing majors, marked by their curricular differences. As a group of seven senior professional writing majors guided by one professor, we reached an understanding of the major issues currently facing writing programs, especially in regard to specific areas of study. The seven students also discovered that each of us holds a unique enthusiasm for one particular curricular element. Below we offer seven curricular recommendations for the undergraduate writing major; these components we explore are not an exhaustive list of essential coursework but instead represent our individual writing passions.

A Gateway to Writing Studies' Complexities: Keith

Let me take you back to a moment that illustrates the central importance of a gateway course to a writing major. In Dr. Christian Weisser's Introduction to Writing Studies, I was assigned a project that required an examination of my individual composition process through video. I had always been far more comfortable behind a keyboard than a camera, and so the thought of recording and watching myself was both terrifying and exciting, catapulting me from my comfort zone into the unknown. It forced me to examine my creative thought patterns and to introspect externally by physically representing, through video, something I had never before considered. I learned much more than how to write: I learned how *I* write.

The video literacy narrative was one among many assignments that offered a mashup of technique and theory, through which students "examine writing not only as a skill one must master, but also as a complex object of study" (Weisser and Grobman 44). Indeed, the gateway course should expose students to influential theories, like John Swales' discourse communities and James E. Porter's intertextuality. To actualize critical and composition skills, writing students need to apply multifaceted understandings of writing to our own experiences and to culture and society, such as when I discovered that Swales' characteristics of discourse engender a massive exchange of information in the bodybuilding community, knowledge which facilitates its communal evolution. Overall, the gateway experience allowed me to appreciate the integral role complex rhetorical concepts and techniques play in shaping individuals and communities.

Multiple Genres, Multiple Audiences: Erin

Taking courses in various genres such as technical writing, business writing, journalism, and public relations can nourish students' abilities to think about what their writing is trying to accomplish and teach them to tailor their writing for different audiences, genres and purposes. In a study, Weisser and Laurie Grobman analyzed alumni of their professional writing program and found that "among the most important traits of our alumni respondents is their rhetorical proficiency. As expected, most of these graduates state the importance of understanding audience and purpose in creating documents and in marketing themselves" (50). When I interned for a hockey magazine called the *Pink Puck*, I continually thought about my audience and their expectations. One issue I had to consider was terminology: knowledgeable hockey fans would expect me to use common hockey terms such as "checking," "icing," and "hooking." However, hockey newcomers would require more explanation. Therefore, I had to find a balance between keeping experienced readers interested and newcomers informed. My solution was adding context clues. For instance, instead of saying a player was caught hooking, I would say that the player received a penalty for hooking. Having written across various genres in my coursework, I was able to meet the challenges posed by the *Pink Puck*'s complex rhetorical situation by paying attention to the details and understanding my audiences.

Belles-Lettres? Oh Dear!: John

Literature has an important role to play in a writing major. However, Deborah Balzhiser and Susan H. McLeod are "particularly fascinated by the required courses in Chaucer, Shakespeare, and Milton" in certain writing majors because they do not understand the "rationale" or desired outcomes for these courses (422). In my experience, instruction on Chaucer's work can teach the importance of voice, agency, and discourse in a distinctly profound way. For instance, after "The Prologue" has constructed its social hierarchy and the Knight has narrated his lofty epic, the Miller seizes the kairotic moment and disrupts the "natural" flow of the narratives. He demonstrates *the essential tool* of an effective rhetor—the courage to stand and speak, to be heard. Further, the Wife of Bath is a self-actualized female protagonist who operates an international textile business and has had *her* choice of husbands—five of them to be exact. As another example, The Clerk advocates equality as the source of marital harmony, while the Wife of Bath argues that harmony comes from the husband's deference of power to his wife, not to mention the bitter Merchant who rejects the possibility of any happiness in marriage. This back-and-forth represents a negotiation between the pilgrims—the formation of *discourse*. Thus *The Canterbury Tales*, a work of literary fiction, can be a fertile resource for analyzing the many distinct methods employed in the production of texts. Writing is not whole without reading.

The Rhetorically Savvy Student: Melissa W.

Rhetorical theory courses encompass several components that are critical to a writing major, from the history of rhetoric and the application of rhetorical theory to multiple (and alternative) perspectives on understanding writing and language. For example, I used Jean Baudrillard's theory of symbolism from *Spirit of Terrorism* to analyze how the actions of the characters in the movie *The Help* were shaped by symbols. Symbolism theory helped me see deeper character development in the text. It made me appreciate theory and the different lenses that I never knew I had at my disposal to understand texts all around me.

Furthermore, rhetoric courses should be accessibly described to students so that they can understand rhetoric's importance and versatility. Rhetoric is seen primarily as academic and civic, so it may be hard for students to grasp how it can relate to their future careers. In a study by Weisser and Grobman, several graduates of our major explained how they use rhetoric in their professional lives. Stephanie, a publications manager at a regional hospital, "emphasized the importance of rhetoric in interviewing, asserting that being rhetorical is an 'art' that includes written language and body language" (50). What strikes me about Stephanie's remarks is how rhetoric can be applied in interviews, not just in texts.

Fiction Writing: Extending Creativity beyond the Page: Michelle

A fiction writer uses his or her imagination to create stories, but this cultivation of imagination is also beneficial in many fields such as advertising or marketing, where selling products and getting out ideas require innovative strategies and designs. Furthermore, according to a survey report in the *Washington Post*, "While 57 percent of students said they were creative and innovative, for example, just 25 percent of employers agreed" (Selingo). My creativity expanded when I took my first fiction class. I wrote short stories and then longer pieces and was able to use my imagination to appeal to multiple readers. Beyond fiction writing itself, I was able to view my own creativity in a different light and bring it with me when writing articles for the online magazine *Her Campus* and doing my internship at The Reading Public Museum.

Sending Messages through Design: Kristy

Communication design is central to a writing major. With knowledge of communication design, students can use components such as contrast, repetition, alignment, proximity, and images to make their documents visually appealing, thereby drawing the attention of the audience. Graduates are also likely to enter a job where visual design is a requirement, whether they work with website design and layout, office documents like newsletters or memos, public relations writing like press releases, or magazine or newspaper layout.

Designing documents came to my attention through publishing my own poetry blog. I have posted poems that are left aligned, plain black text on white background and poems that include design components like different font colors and related images. Poems that are designed for visual appeal get about 50% more "reblogs" or "likes" than those that have a basic layout. As Tracey Bowen and Carl Whithaus contend, "Within college writing courses, the emergence of a wide array of information and communication technologies (ICTs) in the past twenty years has opened up new possibilities for the types of compositions that students can create" (1). Communication design courses should teach students how to increase the visual appeal of all kinds of texts, from online blogs to resumes and academic papers, through the use of Microsoft Word, Adobe Photoshop, or Adobe InDesign.

Grass Roots Writing: African American Scholarship and the Writing Major: Melissa D.

Professional writing courses should develop skills to obtain a job, infuse a desire to promote change, and develop students' capacities to fight against injustice, especially those based on race, ethnicity, class, gender, or sexuality. The African American fight against white supremacy is an excellent example of the enormous power of writing. Abolitionists of the eighteenth and early-nineteenth centuries used rhetoric to spread information across the country.

As a young African American woman reading Geneva Smitherman's work in my Rhetorical Traditions course, I became aware of how Smitherman's scholarly commitments fought for the validity of my native language and against injustice. I realized then how courses in a writing major might contribute to the pursuit of social and moral justice. The idea of African American social justice as fundamental to a professional writing major is affirmed by what Grobman and Weisser say about wanting graduate students who are "ethical, open-minded, intelligent, and civically-invested individuals" (191) and "active, responsible citizens and rhetors" (192). By assigning African American writing in the curriculum, teachers encourage students to more closely tie the power of writing to social change. By getting back to what I want to call the "grass roots" of teaching and learning, there is the opportunity to develop courses that may not seem "useful" to a pre-professional focus of a professional writing major but are nonetheless important for citizenship.

Coauthoring the Writing Major

These seven curricular focal points embody our collective passion for writing and our desire to contribute student perspectives to the scholarly conversation regarding the undergraduate writing major. During the past six weeks of reading, talking, debating, writing, rewriting —sometimes arguing—we came to an understanding of the difficulties and issues facing those who design and teach these programs; there are obviously competing and diverse perspectives about what will best impact students as writers. After coauthoring this essay with one another, our professor, and all those invested in this major, we ask that faculty, scholars, and administrators invite students to "coauthor," to "co-own" the major. The continued maturation of our major hinges on a dialogue between instructors and students.

Works Cited

Balzhiser, Deborah, and Susan H. McLeod. "The Undergraduate Writing Major: What Is It? What Should It Be?" *CCC* 61.3 (2010): 415-33. Print.

Baudrillard, Jean. "Spirit of Terrorism." *The Spirit of Terrorism and Other Essays*. Brooklyn: Verso, 2002. 1-34. Print.

Bowen, Tracey, and Carl Whithaus. "Introduction: 'What Else is Possible': Multimodal Composing and Genre in the Teaching of Writing." *Multimodal Literacies and Emerging Genres*. Ed. Tracey Bowen and Carl Whithaus. Pittsburgh: U of Pittsburgh P, 2013. 1-12. Print.

Grobman, Laurie, and Christian Weisser. "Renegotiating Tensions between the Theoretical and the Practical in the B. A. in Professional Writing at Penn State Berks." *The Undergraduate Writing Major: Eighteen Program Profiles*. Ed. Greg Giberson, Lori Ostergard, and Jim Nugent. Logan: Utah State UP. 190-204. Print.

Porter, James E. "Intertextuality and the Discourse Community." *Rhetoric Review* 5.1 (1986): 34-47. Print.

Selingo, Jeffrey J. "Why Are so Many College Students Failing to Gain Job Skills before Graduation?" *Washington Post*. 26 Jan. 2015. Web. 17 Feb. 2015. <http://www.washingtonpost.com/news/grade-point/wp/2015/01/26/why-are-so-many-college-students-failing-to-gain-job-skills-before-graduation/>.

Swales, John. *Genre Analysis: English in Academic and Research Settings*. Boston: Cambridge UP, 1990. Print.

Weisser, Christian, and Laurie Grobman. "Undergraduate Writing Majors and the Rhetoric of Professionalism." *Composition Studies* 40.1 (2012): 39-59. Print.

Stone Soup: Establishing an HBCU Writing Concentration

Collie Fulford and Aaron Dial, North Carolina Central University

Collie Fulford is an assistant professor of English at North Carolina Central University (NCCU). Aaron Dial recently earned his B.A. in English with a writing concentration from NCCU. They offer insights on the concentration's unusual positioning, its relative strengths despite limited means, and its prospects for the immediate future.

Where Are We Now?

AD: For any program at our university, the question of *where* is linked to the question of *who*. Because blacks couldn't get into white schools, we made our own. Historically black colleges and universities (HBCUs) became bastions for black intellectualism, providing a classical education and an equally important education of identity. To quote W. E. B. DuBois, HBCUs provide black "youth [with] dawning self-consciousness, self-realization, [and] self-respect" (15). Yet unfortunately, the reputation of HBCUs is rooted in deficiency—especially when compared to predominantly white institutions (PWIs). The meta-narrative of blackness combined with the mechanics of white supremacy mean that HBCUs can never measure up. When considering the *where* of our university, our physical location doesn't begin to explain our hierarchical position within the mainstream narrative of the academy. For us, the term *black* not only identifies our origins, but also marks us as other: Duke, North Carolina State, and UNC–Chapel Hill are the academic standard in the Raleigh-Durham area, and NCCU is always in their shadow.

CF: Ours was among the first public universities for African Americans, so these complex cultural contexts have bearing on our writing concentration.

Writing majors and concentrations are rare at HBCUs. An analysis of websites for 83 four-year HBCUs demonstrates that advanced writing curricula—writing minors, majors, concentrations, and graduate programs—are all in short supply.[1] We were able to find only three offering writing concentrations.

Our writing concentration was initiated in 2007 by English faculty from diverse specializations. The exigency—the stone for this soup—was fear of extinction; our department had been flagged for low productivity.

The department had no luxury to create an ideal version; we instead assembled a frugal curriculum almost entirely from courses on the books. The resulting concentration was grounded in literature out of necessity, yet its combination of writing, communications, and linguistics courses differentiated it sufficiently from the literature concentration. After five years of slow growth, we recently experienced a marked increase and graduated twenty-seven students in the past two years. Ours is a small program, yet it fills a need and is now growing at a robust rate.

AD: Yes, the blood is pumping.

CF: I think the goodwill across specializations enabled such growth. This phenomenon is at odds with the longstanding narrative about the rift between literature and composition (Bergmann). Our literature faculty recognize the value of the concentration for the survival of the department. All faculty teach composition and several teach upper-division courses outside their scholarly areas to help maintain the concentration. This abundant versatility stands in contrast to our austere financial resources.

Our university has been subject to recent relentless budget cuts on top of the underfunding that characterizes our entire history. The State of North Carolina reduced per student spending by 24.9% between 2008 and 2014 (Mitchell, Palacios, and Leachman 4). UNC system schools are expected to absorb another 2% cut in 2015 (UNC Board of Governors 2). Unfortunately, these are familiar constraints for HBCUs (Gasman 2). This climate results in scarce tenure lines and an absence of reassigned time for program development. Creating a concentration under these conditions is exactly the sort of underresourced move Kelly Lowe cautions about in "Against the Writing Major." Yet the risk is paying off. Our committee sponsored two periods of robust curriculum development in 2010–11 and 2014–15, sparked by three strategic hires. In five years we created ten new courses, including theory courses, per recommendations from the CCCC's Committee on the Major (Balzhiser and McLeod 427–28). Student requests prompted us to add two creative writing courses and an African American linguistics and rhetorics course.

AD: The financial burden of the department is one I think students carry as well—at least I do. For me, there is a sense that the department is scrambling and that its goals are outpaced by its stark financial reality. However, I think these budgetary challenges have inadvertently led to our department's biggest strength: an incredible sense of intimacy that permeates student and faculty interactions. When walking the halls of Farrison-Newton—the building writing-concentrators call home—the buzzing of student discovery is palpable. The cramped design is a result of constricted resources rather than pedagogical intent, yet it creates a hive-like atmosphere in which the hierarchal gap between student and professor has flattened. Our learning environment has become a space where evaluation is conversational and learning is communal.

CF: Yes, I like how narrow the power distance can become between faculty and students.

AD: Our writing concentration isn't perfect, far from it. But, I see people who generally care about each other, and in an environment where resources are scarce, goodwill becomes currency. The lifeblood of this program isn't just students or just teachers. The spirit of our program is found in the multitude of ways we come together.

Where Are We Heading?

AD: I think the future of the program lives and dies with student interaction. While the concentration makes a point to bridge the gap between student and faculty, there remains a pressing need for community between students. Whether it's through student-led publications, seminars, or the formation of work-groups within the department, the focus has to be on empowering students to be vocal. Student interests and passions, cultivated through this community, should guide curricular decisions.

CF: If we are to sponsor a writing community, not just a curriculum, we will need to be resourceful.

Our literary magazine's patchy history shows how pressed we are to sustain community-building projects, however. The literary magazine was published periodically from 1965 until 2010 when it abruptly lost funding during fallout from a state budget crisis ("History"). An effort to revive the magazine in 2014 as a class project yielded a one-off digital issue. We don't know if we'll be able to sustain further student publications like this, though, unless modest resources for space and leadership are reinstated.

In the meantime, the student work-group idea sounds flexible and right for us. Having Aaron join our committee has been eye-opening, but he shouldn't be the only student among us. It was his suggestion that led to development of an African American language course. A student advisory group might help us articulate a concentration that is even more responsive to our unique cultural and geographical "place and space," as Hill Taylor argues is vital for HBCUs (105).

AD: Along with a focus on student interaction, our university has an opportunity to serve a cultural niche. The tradition of black intellectualism is rooted in writing. Our writing concentration has the chance to develop into a place for young, black writers to thrive. But teaching students to write well isn't enough. Curriculum that explores blackness within writing should be the standard. We have to incorporate identity not as a label but rather as a tool for discovery.

Note

1. 2009 data from the CCCC Committee on the Major in Writing and Rhetoric do not thoroughly catalog writing curricula at HBCUs. Therefore, we thank graduate assistant Carole Montgomery who investigated all four-year HBCU websites for evidence of advanced writing curricula. Websites may lag actual curricular developments, so we consider these findings ballpark rather than gospel.

Works Cited

Balzhiser, Deborah, and Susan McLeod. "The Undergraduate Writing Major: What Is It? What Should It Be?" *CCC* 61.3 (2010): 415-33. Print.

Bergmann, Linda S. "What Do You Folks Teach over There, Anyway?" Introduction. *Composition and/or Literature: The End(s) of Education.* Ed. Linda S. Bergmann and Edith M. Baker. Urbana: NCTE, 2006. 1-13. Print.

CCCC Committee on the Major in Writing and Rhetoric. *Writing Majors at a Glance.* National Council of Teachers of English. Jan. 2009. Web. 15 Feb. 2015. <http://www.ncte.org/library/NCTEFiles/Groups/CCCC/Committees/Writing_Majors_Final.pdf >.

DuBois, W.E.B. *The Souls of Black Folks.* 1903. Rockville: Arc Manor, 2008. Print.

Gasman, Marybeth. *The Changing Face of Historically Black Colleges and Universities.* Philadelphia: Penn Center for Minority Serving Institutions, 2013. Print.

"History." *NCCU Ex Umbra.* North Carolina Central U. 2014. Web. 20 Feb. 2015. <https://nccuexumbra.wordpress.com/history/>.

Lowe, Kelly. "Against the Writing Major." *Composition Studies* 35.1 (2007): 97-98. Print.

Mitchell, Michael, Vincent Palacios, and Michael Leachman. "States Are Still Funding Higher Education Below Pre-Recession Levels." *Center on Budget and Policy Priorities*. Center on Budget and Policy Priorities. 1 May 2014. Web. 20 Feb. 2015. <http://www.cbpp.org/research/states-are-still-funding-higher-education-below-pre-recession-levels>.

Taylor, Hill. "Examining the Writing Major at an Urban HBCU." *Composition Studies* 35.1 (2007): 99-112. Print.

UNC Board of Governors. *2015-17 Operating and Capital Budget Priorities*. The University of North Carolina. Dec. 2014. Web. 20 Feb. 2015. <https://www.northcarolina.edu/sites/default/files/documents/final_bog_2015-17_budget_priorities.pdf>.

If You Build Online Classes (And Empower Faculty to Teach Them), Non-Traditional Students Will Come: One Student's Journey through the Professional and Technical Writing Program at the University of Arkansas at Little Rock

Heidi Skurat Harris and Wendy McCloud, University of Arkansas at Little Rock

Writing programs consistently face pressure to recruit and retain online students. Non-traditional students are the perfect target audience for such programs because non-traditional writing students often encounter work and family constraints, needing to fit the rigors of a college education into an already tight schedule. This article describes the experience of one non-traditional undergraduate in the Professional and Technical Writing Program at the University of Arkansas at Little Rock, a program focused on excellence in online education as well as building close ties between students and faculty. Wendy's experiences demonstrate how supporting tenure and non-tenure track online faculty allows those faculty to, in turn, support and challenge students in their pursuit of an online education.

As a writing faculty member, Heidi has seen writing programs struggle to recruit and retain majors while fighting increasing pressure to "adjunctify" writing faculty (Modern Language Association). Some programs build enrollment through online programs serving time- and place-bound students. The 2014 Babson Survey of Online Learning notes that 70.8% of chief academic leaders view online learning as critical to their long-term strategy (Allen and Seaman 4). In 2012, one quarter of college students enrolled in at least one online course with 10% of those students enrolled exclusively in online courses (U.S. Department of Education).

In the summer of 2011, I (Wendy) was one of those students working full time. I enrolled at the University of Arkansas at Little Rock (UALR) to complete a degree in business, the degree I believed that a forty-year-old married veteran with a full-time job, mortgage, and car payments *should* get. I had worked for over twenty-five years in a variety of businesses, always playing some type of administrative role. A business degree was the logical, practical choice. The UALR business degree was not fully online, but by taking one or two night classes each semester, I could graduate with a BA in Business around the summer of 2018.

Growing up, I wanted to write. Starting at age eight, I amassed scores of notebooks filled with my thoughts, my life, and my fantasies. I dreamed of the day my life story would fill the shelves of Barnes & Noble. I documented every moment. In the fall of 2012, I checked out the UALR English Department class options. Unfortunately, only one online creative writing class was available. My dream of being a writer remained a dream.

The next semester, my online Composition I & II teacher, a non-tenure track (NTT) instructor named Mary Henthorn, introduced me to the Rhetoric & Writing Department (R&W), which houses technical writing, editing, rhetoric, and creative nonfiction courses.[1] The R&W faculty, both tenure-line professors and non-tenure track instructors, are involved in all aspects of the department; all have access to professional development funds and sabbatical leave, and all participate equally in departmental committees, teaching, and governance. Before I had even declared my major in Professional and Technical Writing (PTW), Betty Freeland and Dona Bailey, NTT faculty in the department, helped me navigate the process of declaring my major and getting accepted into the program. They introduced me to the Oliver Breeze Kennedy Scholarship for Undergraduates in Technical Communication and Digital Literacies ($1,500 towards my tuition), and I won it twice.

Most importantly, these faculty helped me chart the online courses I needed to get my BA. With nearly all the classes I needed available online, my graduation timeline shrank from six or seven years to three-and-a-half years. Out of the thirty-eight classes I've taken at UALR, only TWO of them have been on campus.[2]

Recent data from the Noel-Levitz Survey of Online Student Priorities shows that Wendy is not alone. In my research, I (Heidi) have found that students completing the Noel-Levitz survey indicated that their primary reasons for selecting online education were "convenience, flexible pacing, and their work schedules" (4). Online writing instructors surveyed in the Conference on College Composition and Communication's Online Writing Instruction State of the Art report said the flexible qualities of online education gave students a "clear advantage" over face-to-face students, and that online courses helped build students' self-directedness and self-discipline.

In my (Wendy's) case, the flexibility allowed me to excel in my courses and gave me time to start writing again. By the end of my *first* year as part of the PTW program, I had four essays ready for publication in *Quills & Pixels*, R&W's peer-reviewed student journal. Three of those essays became pieces of a memoir I had been writing for years but never completed due to doubt and self-deprecation. In my third year, I took the online class "Publishing Inside/Out." Michael Greer, an adjunct faculty member who works in publishing, showed me how to target publishing companies to find the best match for my writing style. He taught me how to craft a book proposal guaranteed to make an editor sit up in her chair with excitement. I learned that marketing my book required harnessing the power of social media to self-promote. I was already a published author, but Professor Greer taught me how to become an *effective* published author.

In May 2015, I graduated from UALR with my BA in Professional and Technical Writing. In fall 2015, I began the PTW Masters program, continuing my full-time job/full-time class schedule and becoming one of the 22% of graduate students who are completing online masters degrees (U.S. Department of Education). The MA in PTW is completely online and includes courses in online writing instruction.[3] Perhaps I will follow Charles Anderson, my mentor and chief editor of *Quills and Pixels*, who said I should become an online writing instructor, inspiring online students just as the UALR faculty inspired me.

As writing studies moves forward as a field, I hope stakeholders consider that these programs are only as good the students and faculty invested in them. In classes with Mary Henthorn, Charles Anderson, and Michael Greer—instructors and professors who constantly engaged me through discussion, writing and editing feedback, reading suggestions, brain teasers, and Google searches—I became the self-directed, self-disciplined WRITER my eight-year-old self imagined.

Fledgling writers, by their very nature, are hungry for knowledge in any form. We will flourish the most when our professors actively, attentively, and articulately feed that hunger. The delivery method is not as important as the message. My experience in the Professional and Technical Writing Program at the University of Arkansas at Little Rock exemplifies how a writing program can challenge non-traditional students with engagement from the faculty, tenured and non-tenure track alike. The CCCC's "Principles for the Postsecondary Teaching of Writing" position statement says that "Writing instructors perform most effectively—and students writers learn best—when instructors are treated as professionals and provided with resources that allow them to focus on their students' development as writers." When a program invests in its faculty, and those faculty invest their time and energy in developing and facilitating engaging online courses, students will flourish.

Notes

1. The Rhetoric and Writing program split from English in 1993, in part because of a dispute over the place of non-tenured faculty in departmental governance. For a description of the split, see Barry Maid. For a description of the program, see Barbara L'Eplattenier and George Jensen.

2. Those two classes were not well received by my boss. He was unhappy that I had to leave work early every Tuesday and Thursday for sixteen weeks. He was so irritated with this work disruption that he made me sign an agreement that I would not take any other classes that could interfere with my regular work hours despite the fact that I came in early and stayed late on other days to make up the time and keep my absence from affecting the company.

3. These courses, part of a new Certificate in Online Writing Instruction, exemplify the CCCCs "Position Statement on Principles and Example Effective Practices for Online Writing Instruction" and can also be completed as an elective track in the MA in PTW.

Works Cited

Allen, I. Elaine, and Jeffrey Seaman. "Grade Level: Tracking Online Education in the United States." Babson Survey Research Group. 2014. Web. Feb. 2015. <http://onlinelearningconsortium.org/read/survey-reports-2014/>.

CCCC. "A Position Statement of Principles and Example Effective Practices for Online Writing Instruction." March 2013. Web. 3 March 2015. <http://www.ncte.org/cccc/resources/positions/owiprinciples/>.

---. "Principles for the Postsecondary Teaching of Writing." November 2013. Web. 3 March 2015. <http://www.ncte.org/cccc/resources/positions/postsecondarywriting>.

CCCC OWI Committee for Effective Practices in Online Writing Instruction. "The State of the Art of OWI." April 2011. Web. 3 March 2015. <http://www.ncte.org/library/NCTEFiles/Groups/CCCC/Committees/OWI_State-of-Art_Report_April_2011.pdf>.

L'Eplattenier, Barbara, and George Jensen. "Reshaping the BA in Professional and Technical Writing at the University of Arkansas at Little Rock." *Writing Majors: Eighteen Program Profiles.* Ed. Greg Giberson, Jim Nugent, and Lori Ostergaard. Boulder: Utah State UP, 2015. 22-35. Print.

Maid, Barry. "Non-tenure Track Instructors at UALR: Breaking Rules, Splitting Departments." *Moving a Mountain: Transforming the Role of Contingent Faculty in Composition Studies.* Ed. Eileen Schell and Patricia Lambert Stock. NCTE: Urbana, 2001. 76-90. Print.

Modern Language Association. "MLA Issue Brief: The Academic Workforce." Updated July 2014. Web. 3 March 2015. <www.mla.org/awak_issue_brief_pdf>.

Noel-Levitz. "2014-15 National Online Learners Priorities Report." Ruffalo Noel-Levitz: Coralville, 2014. Web. 3 March 2015. <https://www.noellevitz.com/papers-research-higher-education/2014/2014-15-national-online-learners-priorities-report>.

U.S. Department of Education. "Enrollment in Distance Education Courses by State, Fall 2012." Washington: NCES. June 2014. Web. 3 March 2015. <https://nces.ed.gov/pubsearch/pubsinfo.asp?pubid=2014023>.

Looking Into Writing

Cami Sylvia and Michael J. Michaud, Rhode Island College

Looking Into Writing: Cami

In my second semester of college, I took my first writing course, Writing 100. My section, I soon learned, was unlike any of the other sections of the course because my instructor, Dr. Michael Michaud, was using what I later learned is called a writing about writing (WAW) approach to teaching the course. Whereas my friends in other sections all seemed to be writing narratives or short stories or those awful five paragraph essays, there I was, learning about rhetorical situations through the work of a writing scholar named Keith Grant-Davie. My head was spinning. What are these terms? Who are these scholars? What are their goals? And what is the purpose of learning all of this?

It was in Writing 100 where I first realized that writing is more than something you do. It's also something you study, something you can actually look into. When I finished the course, I decided I wanted more. I took another writing course with Dr. Michaud and then signed on for the English Department's minor in Rhetoric and Writing (RAW). I have since taken four additional writing classes and am currently completing a writing internship, the capstone course for the RAW minor. I have been exposed to the work of Donald Murray, Mike Rose, Nancy Sommers, among others, and have used their research to understand both the ways in which one can look into writing and the many components of writing. Never before did I realize that one's composition process could be recorded and analyzed, that the approach one takes when writing could be so fascinating or so informative, and that to be a good writer, one must be aware of audience, purpose, genre and many other factors.

Without looking into writing, I feel I would be at a disadvantage as I approach graduation and the transition into "the real world." I appreciate that Rhode Island College has enabled me to enter this field. Writing well goes beyond knowing where to place commas and knowing the purpose of the semi-colon. As a peer tutor in our writing center, I am able to apply the knowledge I have gained in my own coursework directly to my tutoring sessions. I use the time I spend with my clients as opportunities to witness the issues beyond grammar that those in the field of writing discuss and look into. It is hard to run without knowing how to walk, and I feel that without recognizing components like genre, rhetorical situation, and discourse community, which make up the building blocks of writing, how can one ever write well?

The Fruits of "Looking Into Writing": Michael

Working with students like Cami, I have come to see what's possible when undergraduate students, via writing majors, minors, and concentrations are given the opportunity, as Cami memorably puts it, to "look into" writing. In his articulation of the rationales for WAW pedagogy, Doug Downs identifies *inquiry* as a key component of WAW, because this approach "[r]ender[s] writing 'study-able,' [. . .] help[ing] [to] demystify it for students, removing it from the realm of pure gift or talent, and making it 'knowable'" (21). Making writing knowable is the chief aim of our RAW minor. Cami's words above embody Downs' rationale for teaching students about the work of our field. What Cami has learned via her engagement with our minor is that writing is not just something you do but also something you investigate, examine, and look into. For many undergraduate students, this is a new kind of stance towards writing. Some, like Cami, find that they are both surprised by and attracted to the opportunities made available to them via this position and this work. What do they learn to know and do via their engagement with our field? What does it look like when undergraduates think with us, using our terms? To illustrate, I'd like to share a few passages from Cami's work in my classes over the past few years.

In a professional writing course, Cami learned about workplace literacy and about the ways in which writing functions in professional organizations. In the passage below, she makes a connection between the program notes she is writing at her internship and an article we read by Deborah Brandt several semesters earlier which introduces the metaphor of "the production line" for understanding the circulation of texts in knowledge organizations ("Writing"):

> This week at my internship I've been able to experience the "production line" side to workplace writing. Each week, once I have finished writing sections of my program notes or the final "rough" drafts of them, I have been submitting the notes to my supervisor for suggestions and proofreading. When he has finished reading them and we have discussed his feedback, I make revisions and I then send my work to the director/conductor of the ensemble for which I am writing the notes. From there they are sent to the person for each organization involved with printing. In sum, the notes start with me, head to my supervisor, make their way to the ensemble director, and then move on to printing. I suppose the process will finally end when the notes make their way to the audiences for each of the performances. It's pretty cool to be able to experience this type of process that I have up until now only read about in your class before. I really didn't expect when I started this minor to see myself in the position I'm in

now, where I can see aspects of workplace writing apply to me with my music background and interests, but here I am!

During her internship, Cami also ran into difficulties while trying to learn the genre of concert program notes. As the passage below illustrates, to sort through her experience, she drew on the concept of writer's block, which we discussed in great detail a few semesters earlier while reading Mike Rose's article "Rigid Rules, Inflexible Plans, and the Stifling of Language":

> I'm finding that I am experiencing more writer's block while writing for this internship than with other writing I have done in the past. With the type of writing I'm doing, program notes, there is a portion of background information I need to provide my readers before I can begin to analyze the piece on the program. There are only so many ways you can state facts, so having to rework the same information many people have already said before me is part of what causes me to have difficulty writing. Then, when I get to the section of the notes where I am to analyze the piece of music and incorporate my own ideas based on the compositional techniques used and what I am hearing I find myself struggling with being able to vary my language so that I don't use the same phrases over and over again. I'm going to try to do some more reading of sample program notes for pieces I am not writing on to see what other terms and vocabulary other authors use that I can add to my arsenal and be able to utilize in the future.

Finally, in this third passage, again taken from Cami's internship journal, she reflects on the transition from academic to professional writing that she is currently experiencing, prompted by her reading of Chris Anson and L. Lee Forsberg's "Moving Beyond the Academic Community." Specifically, she shares a tentative (and accurate) sense of how audiences function differently in academic and professional settings:

> Many of the interns from the article mentioned how they found it difficult to communicate with and understand their supervisor because of their lack of familiarity with their workplace and the limited help offered by their bosses. When they finally received feedback, the interns, especially Jim, noted how it was usually negative. "You just have to come to the conclusion that it's not a personal attack," Jim explains. "It's just, you know…an attack on your writing" (215). I find that it might feel like a personal attack on one's writing because it seems that students don't experience this type of situation in school. Usually, we are given an assignment, complete it to the

best of our ability (because it's probably finished the night before), hand it in, and when we get our papers back (usually) with feedback, as long as the grade was similar to what we expected, we shove the comments under the rug. We typically don't need to apply those suggestions to that assignment in order to "pass." We just move on. But in workplace writing, a supervisor's comments and revisions need to be understood and applied in order for that piece to be considered acceptable enough to be sent out.

As these passages demonstrate, undergraduate students have a great deal to gain from "looking into" writing. As their "sponsors" (Brandt, "Sponsors"), we can guide their inquiry as they examine the role that writing plays in their personal, communal, academic, and pre-professional lives. We can mobilize over fifty years of writing research to illuminate the influence of literacy and literacy instruction on their experiences. We can teach our ways of thinking, seeing, speaking, writing, doing, questioning and knowing. In doing so, students and faculty experience literacy in richer, more meaningful, and more engaged ways.

Works Cited

Anson, Chris, and L. Lee Forsberg. "Moving Beyond the Academic Community: Transitional Stages in Professional Writing." *Written Communication* 7.2 (1990): 200-31. Print.

Brandt, Deborah. "Sponsors of Literacy." *CCC* 49.2 (1998): 165-85. Print.

- - -. "Writing for a Living: Literacy and the Knowledge Economy." *Written Communication* 22.2 (2005): 166-97. Print.

Downs, Doug. "Teaching First-Year Writers to Use Texts: Scholarly Readings in Writing-About-Writing in First-Year Comp." *Reader: Essays in Reader-Oriented Theory, Criticism and Pedagogy* 60 (2010): 19-50. Print.

Rose, Mike. "Rigid Rules, Inflexible Plans, and the Stifling of Language: A Cognitivist's Analysis of Writer's Block." *CCC* 31.4 (1980): 389-401. Print.

The Evolving Identity of an Undergraduate Major in Writing and Linguistics

Barbara Jayne McGaughey and Aleyna Rentz, Georgia Southern University, and Jessica Nastal-Dema, Prairie State College

In the fall of 2014, Aleyna and Jayne found themselves in Jessica's Introduction to Writing Studies, a required course for writing and linguistics majors. Throughout the semester we interrogated foundational texts and considered what writing is. In many ways, this article began in that class, especially as we looked for—and found very few—student voices in the scholarship.

Aleyna—

Jessica's class asked us to reflect on, among other topics, the definition of writing. It made me realize that the scope of writing is enormous, which is why I love the loose structure and wide breadth of subject matter covered in Georgia Southern's writing and linguistics department.

I think the goal of our department, put simply, is to mold students into well-rounded writers. But I do not think one can achieve expertise in writing simply by focusing on one specific area or studying writing alone. Regardless of one's specific focus, it is important to study craft from every angle. For example, in our major, students can learn firsthand how intertextuality shapes writing in a class called Retellings and Retelling, just as they can explore how creativity informs even the most mundane experiences in Everyday Creative Writing. The wide variety of material covered in our writing program prepares us for any career in writing and linguistics.

I chose to major in writing and linguistics because I'm interested in writing fiction, and I feel that my non-creative writing classes are just as important to the development of my craft as is the fiction workshop I am currently taking. Our writing studies class, for example, made me question the fundamental aspects of my writing, such as whether meaning precedes writing, how writing shapes or defines one's identity, and what effect writing has on an audience. Such considerations are essential to a fiction writer—or any writer, really—for they determine what your work means and where it is going. While this course did not ask me to produce creative pieces, it made me consider my writing's purpose and how that purpose reflects my own values and beliefs. And, while I have not yet taken my required linguistics course, I am glad that one is required for students focusing on writing. When working with words, it only makes sense that one should understand their history, meanings, and etymologies. Understanding how languages work and are formed is imperative knowledge for the writer, because language is the writer's primary, if not only, tool.

Jayne—

For current students in our writing and linguistics department, I think there is a great deal of horizontal growth, but because of the do-it-yourself (DIY) nature of the program, there is little direction. There is room for self-directed growth, but not all students flourish in that atmosphere. Overall, writing can be an individual process at times, but the writing field grows from ongoing conversations between disciplines like writing studies, creative writing, technical and professional writing, and linguistics. Our primary concern should be the continued dialogue across the disciplines. That dialogue is precious, and has the power to inform and direct our field—and students' experiences within it.

We should draw on the range of perspectives in our department to ensure that we students do not get too comfortable with our writing. No matter the individual brilliance of our professors in creative writing, technical and professional writing, writing studies, or linguistics, when students take classes in only one genre, we cannot make gains as writers. We become comfortable by not venturing out of our discipline. As a result, we become unprepared for the pushback we are likely to receive from the broader audiences we will encounter in our genre and careers, as well as the writing community at large.

Our faculty are embroiled in conversations about how the disparate fields that make up our major can exist in one department. I believe the concern that writing and linguistics do not belong together is mostly founded in classes that enact a classical distinction between each discipline, classes that do not expose students to interdisciplinary work. This holds us back in our creative writing classes as much as it does in our technical classes, and even more so in our introductory courses. Such divisive thinking also seems to halt the possibility of collaboration between writing and linguistics, or cross-departmental collaboration at the university. Students could benefit from considering how we might break those forms and create new frameworks—how we might take what we learn in writing studies, for example, and apply it to the writing we hone in a creative nonfiction workshop or in a professional editing course.

Most students in the writing and linguistics program at Georgia Southern are not new to writing, but we are new to its disciplines. The majority of us students have found our way into the program from other academic walks of life. I think we should capitalize on students' versatile abilities and consider building a mentorship program into introductory FYW classes that introduces students to the major through current writing majors. If students came earlier to the department, more writing, mentoring, and academic opportunities could be realized. This would be positive for students, and it could be radical for the department itself. Not only would it illuminate the professional skills of current writing students, it would also create a nurturing environment for prospective students and highlight the department's capacity for inter- and cross-departmental partnership.

Jessica—

Teaching Introduction to Writing Studies during my first semester in a department of writing and linguistics was more complicated than I had anticipated. No student in the class had previously been exposed to the field, and most students identified as creative writers. As Jayne and Aleyna indicate, the DIY nature of our major certainly affects the identity of the department. Faculty have no unifying terminology to identify our various disciplines: are we areas, modules, or tracks? While a loose structure may invite a broad understanding of writing, does it minimize disciplines, or even minimize what a degree in writing and linguistics is? Would adding concentrations allow students to focus their still-flexible program of study? How can we encourage more collaboration across the disciplines? Clearly, these are questions the department needs to continue to address. And, like Jayne suggests, I think it behooves those of us in independent writing programs to continue pushing the boundaries, to relish the opportunity we have to define writing in our programs, in our local institutions, and in the field.

English Majors are Professionals, Too: Liberal Arts and Vocation in the English Writing Major

Michelle Smith and Michelle Costello, Marist College

Undergraduate writing majors have grown over the past few decades, and they can be housed in or across many disciplines and departments (Estrem 14). For writing majors or concentrations in English departments, the persistent view of English as an impractical major can discourage would-be majors and encourage them to seek other, more explicitly vocational programs. The first wave of scholarship on writing majors has focused largely on dynamics within English departments, such as the historic tensions between rhetoric and composition and literature (see Balzhiser and McLeod; Giberson and Moriarty). Yet these tensions may not be equally significant for our students. I met Michelle Costello two years ago, when she switched her major from journalism (in Marist College's School of Communication and the Arts) to English with a concentration in writing (in the School of the Liberal Arts). Her narrative demonstrates that for many students, the pivotal choice is not between studying literature or writing within English, but between studying writing in English or in communication (or similar programs). Michelle's trajectory—from English to communication and back—confirms some things the field already knows, provides reasons for hope, and offers productive avenues for departmental or curricular strategy.

This Much We Know Is True

> I applied to college as an English Literature major, hoping to at least enjoy my college courses since I didn't yet have a career in mind. However, being the only liberal arts major I knew, I worried about what kind of job an English degree would qualify me for. I switched my major to undecided via an online portal before even stepping foot on campus, planning to settle on a "practical" major once at school. During my first semester, I was placed in a Freshman Forum class for undecided majors that briefly reviewed general information about the majors at Marist. The communication major (pursued by 18% of all undergraduates at Marist, according to U.S. News & World Report) sounded appealing because of its emphasis on internships and practical career training, so I declared a communication major with a journalism concentration.

The scholarship on undergraduate writing majors has rarely explored the consequences of the content overlap between English writing majors and communication majors. At Marist, many of the courses housed in interdisciplinary writing studies majors at other schools (journalism, magazine writing, and writing for advertising, for example) are located in our School of Communication (Weisser and Grobman 42). So what leads a student to choose a writing-intensive major in communication versus a writing major in English? Hearing the "What can you do with an English major?" chorus all too clearly, Michelle chose a path to suit her passion for writing, as well as her vocational concerns. That she selected communication is not shocking; one difficulty plaguing undergraduate writing majors is that "job titles for writers often do not contain the word 'writing'" (Weisser and Grobman 55), whereas other writing-related areas like journalism, advertising, and marketing "claim an immediate application of disciplinary knowledge and professional skills" (Brooks, Zhao, and Braniger 36). In other words, like other popular majors—accounting and management, for instance—these majors sound like they lead directly to specific jobs. When students' or parents' career concerns take center stage, English enrollments suffer.

Seeing the Light

> *During the fall of my sophomore year, I quickly realized that my journalism courses were less about creativity and more about learning the "rules" of journalistic style. To find a creative outlet, I declared an English writing minor. In my first English courses the following spring, I felt like I was finally getting a collegiate academic experience. I liked having control over my writing style, and it was refreshing that everyone in my English courses actively wanted to be there. Encouragement and guidance from Dr. Smith helped me realize that this was where I had belonged from the start, and I made my final switch, becoming an English writing major with a journalism minor. This time around, I chose the writing over the literature concentration, because the writing major had built-in literature requirements, which allowed me to take courses in both areas.*

While Michelle's earlier narrative highlights the dangerous but commonplace opposition between liberal arts education and vocational preparation, her eventual switch suggests that at least some students value the liberal arts approach of writing majors housed in English departments. Using the heuristic offered by Lee Campbell and Debra Jacobs, which maps writing majors along trajectories from general to specific and liberal to technical, the English writing major at Marist falls primarily in the general and liberal quadrant (280). In contrast, the writing coursework in communication seemed, to Michelle, to have too strong a specific and technical emphasis, treating writing as a "skill divorced from context" (Baker and Henning 154). In fact, writing majors housed in English should be an ideal fit for students like Michelle, who enter college "with a mixture of affection for writing (and the liberal arts more generally) and a desire for career and personal rewards" (DelliCarpini 16). In this light, one of our major challenges is to undermine the mythical liberal arts/vocational split. As Randy Brooks, Pailing Zhao, and Carmella Braniger presciently ask, "How can English faculty bridge this supposed gap between general liberal arts skills and vocational preparation?" (37).

The Places We'll Go

> *The writing and editing skills I've learned as an English major have helped me immensely in my work as editor-in-chief of our campus newspaper. As a second semester senior, I'm seeing that lots of entry-level jobs do want English majors, contrary to what I was told in high school. High schools should be doing more to combat these "English major myths." Further, undecided college freshmen should be educated on the benefits of English as a legitimate major, perhaps by being assigned to interest-specific academic advisors. Most college freshmen don't understand that job titles aren't objectively linked to majors, and it is important to remind them of all the possibilities an English major can allow. The switch to the English writing major was the best decision I made in college, and it could easily have never happened.*

Our scholarship perpetuates the liberal arts/vocational binary when we sort writing majors into opposed camps: one recent example divided liberal arts writing majors (that required literature courses) from professional/rhetorical writing majors (Balzhiser and McLeod 418). As an alternative, Campbell and Jacobs' "trajectories" might more accurately depict the blend of "critical and career thinking" in our programs. In fact, while the writing concentration at Marist (as elsewhere) has always required upper-level literature courses, our newly revised literature concentration will now require that literature students take upper-level writing courses for the first time. Such changes recognize the flexibility and variety of our programs as strengths, not as indicators of overly abstract programs with no real-world applicability. Other solutions will of course depend on institutional context. At Marist, we need to consider the Freshman Forum and other venues for reaching undecided students. What are these students hearing about our majors online and in person, before or after coming to Marist? What promotional materials might we offer to more accurately depict our current curriculum and pedagogy? Finally, we must remember that our primary channel for reaching first-year students is the classroom: if we want to recruit the strongest writers, we need to teach composition, where most students have their first exposure to writing studies at the college level. In the end, we must take responsibility for identifying and reaching out to those students, like Michelle, who do not want to choose between a liberal arts or a professionally oriented major.

Works Cited

Baker, Lori, and Teresa Henning. "Writing Program Development and Disciplinary Integrity: What's Rhetoric Got to Do with It?" Giberson and Moriarty 153-73. Print.

Balzhiser, Deborah, and Susan H. McLeod. "The Undergraduate Writing Major: What Is It? What Should It Be?" *CCC* 61.3 (2010): 415-33. Print.

Brooks, Randy, Pailing Zhao, and Carmella Braniger. "Redefining the Undergraduate English Writing Major." Giberson and Moriarty 32-49. Print.

Campbell, Lee, and Debra Jacobs. "Toward a Description of Undergraduate Writing Majors." Giberson and Moriarty 277-86. Print.

DelliCarpini, Dominic. "Re-Writing the Humanities: The Writing Major's Effect on Undergraduate Studies in English Departments." *Composition Studies* 35.1 (2007): 15-36. Print.

Estrem, Heidi. "Growing Pains: The Writing Major in Composition and Rhetoric." *Composition Studies* 35.1 (2007): 11-14. Print.

Giberson, Greg A., and Thomas A. Moriarty, eds. "Introduction: Forging Connections Among Undergraduate Writing Majors." *What We Are Becoming: Developments in Undergraduate Writing Majors.* Salt Lake: U of Utah P, 2010. 1-10. Print.

"Marist College." *U.S. News & World Report: Education.* U.S. News & World Report, 2015. Web. 27 May 2015. <http://colleges.usnews.rankingsandreviews.com/best-colleges/marist-college-2765>.

Weisser, Christian, and Laurie Grobman. "Undergraduate Writing Majors and the Rhetoric of Professionalism." *Composition Studies* 40.1 (2012): 39-59. Print.

Major Affordances: Collaborative Scholarship in a Department of Writing and Rhetoric Studies

Christie Toth, Mitchell Reber, and Aaron Clark

Christie—

Like many new PhDs in writing studies (see Giberson et al.), I went on the job market having given little thought to the undergraduate major. I loved working with first-year writers, and I was interested in graduate education, so the opportunity to teach upper-division courses in the University of Utah's new Department of Writing and Rhetoric Studies was more bonus than deciding factor when I accepted my position. Now, as I finish my first year at the U, I realize our major is one of the most exciting aspects of my job. It has given me the opportunity to collaborate with undergraduates on digital scholarship that pushes the boundaries of my own knowledge and abilities. Two of those students—Mitchell Reber and Aaron Clark—decided to write with me about our experiences for this special issue of *Composition Studies*.

Mitchell—

When I entered the U, my major was philosophy. As the completion of my philosophy coursework grew nearer, I entertained the prospect of pursuing a career in academia. I first chose to minor in Writing and Rhetoric Studies to improve my grammar and style. One of the minor's requirements, Intro to Rhetoric, exposed me to the large body of theory in writing studies as well as its interdisciplinary nature. The program's union of applied knowledge, high theory, and diverse topics quickly seized my interest. After some deliberation, I decided that I wanted to study digital rhetoric in graduate school and switched my minor to a major.

Aaron—

As a nontraditional student making the difficult decision to go back to school in my mid-thirties, my expectations are somewhat different from my first attempt at the old college try. At my age, it is as much about the journey as it is the destination, and thus the university experience is as important as the degree itself. Although it may have made more sense from a career perspective to attain a communications degree, I chose writing and rhetoric because I love to write and am fascinated with the world around me and the rhetoric that often defines it.

Christie—

Our majors clearly bring intellectual agendas to their coursework. While many compositionists nod to undergraduates' contributions to our scholarship, only a few have discussed the possibilities the major presents for collaborative faculty-undergraduate research. Joyce Kinkead argues for including research methods courses in writing major curricula, calling on the discipline to assert greater presence in the national undergraduate research movement (see also Grobman). She focuses on the benefits of scholarly collaboration for *students*, stating, "Our goal is to move the novice to an apprenticeship through mentorship, helping the naive student become an expert" (154). While I do not discount the value of such mentorship, I have found my undergraduate co-authors to be far from naive; on the contrary, they possess "funds of knowledge" (Moll et al. 133) that I lack, and they have helped me understand and push the limits of my own expertise.

In Fall 2014, my first semester on the job, I taught a new upper-division course on Native American rhetorics. In line with Hill Taylor's arguments for situating writing majors in social, political, and geographical contexts, I believed it was important to ground our conversations about the exigencies of settler colonialism in our local scene. So, for their first assignment, I asked students to write rhetorical analyses of This Is the Place Monument, a public park near the university that commemorates the settlement of the Salt Lake Valley. When I created the assignment, I viewed the monument as a textbook example of how ongoing settler colonialism legitimizes the dispossession of Indigenous peoples (see Veracini). While my students were quick to identify such dynamics, they also brought to their essays a great deal of local knowledge—personal, historical, cultural, and political—that helped *me* begin to understand the monument's rhetorics in richer, more situated terms.

Aaron—

I will admit that the only reason I signed up for a class about Native American rhetorics was because it fit nicely into my desired schedule, but what started as a class of convenience turned into the type of experience I crave as a university student. While I had visited This Is the Place Monument several times while I was growing up, I was challenged to view it with a more critical eye and was surprised to see it in an entirely different perspective.

Christie—

The students' analyses of the monument were so insightful that I began wondering how we might share their work with a wider audience. Some kind of nonlinear webtext seemed like the best way to capture their compelling polyvocality. From the outset, however, it was clear that this *had* to be a collaborative project: I had neither the local knowledge nor the technological know-how to compose the piece on my own. A team of five students committed to pursuing the project with me during the Spring 2015 semester.

Aaron—

When the opportunity came up to work on this project, I immediately jumped at it. This type of project is exactly the kind of experience I want to have as a university student. The chance to research a specific topic and introduce new perspectives into the academic community is what the university experience should be about.

Mitchell—

I, too, was excited by the opportunities presented by this project. I was privy to Christie's beliefs and attitudes about collaborating with undergraduates and knew that working with her would yield an invaluable glimpse into academic publishing. But I have also benefited in unanticipated ways. One of my primary contributions to our project is building and executing the group's imagined design for our webtext. Taking on this task has been an enormously educational experience. I have become more proficient and knowledgeable in HTML, CSS, and Adobe Dreamweaver—much desired given my interest in digital rhetoric. A major rhetorical constraint we encountered is that the code for our entire webtext must be exportable for submission to online digital journals. Navigating this challenge led me to scour internet forums, how-to videos, and on-campus resources seeking technical tutelage.

Aaron—

Being freed of the drudgery of the normal classroom workload has allowed me to grow not just as a student but also as an academic, and my excitement for learning has never been higher. Working together with my classmates and professor as teammates with a singular vision has created the type of university experience that I always envisioned having, and the result is that I hope the journey never ends.

Christie—

As of this writing, our journey is still in progress; in fact, we just returned from a follow-up visit to This Is the Place, during which we photographed statues and plaques and continued to spin out our collaborative analyses. This time, as I circled the monument, it was layered with snow and the stories my co-authors have told me about their childhoods, their families, and their faiths. When I crouched to take a photo, I was furthering the multimodal vision we had scrawled together in boxes and arrows across the whiteboard in the department's conference room. To me, this is the unexpected reward of our undergraduate major: the opportunity to make knowledge with students who are interested not only in the object of our analysis, but also in writing, its technologies, and the process of collaboration. Together, we're undertaking scholarly work I could never have done on my own.

Works Cited

Giberson, Greg, Lori Ostergaard, Jennifer Clary-Lemon, Jennifer Courtney, Kelly Kinney, and Brad Lucas. "A Changing Profession Changing a Discipline: Junior Faculty and the Undergraduate Major." *Composition Forum* 20 (2009): n. pag. Web. 27 May 2015. <http://compositionforum.com/issue/20/changing-profession-discipline.php>.

Grobman, Laurie. "The Student Scholar: (Re)Negotiating Authorship and Authority." *CCC* 61.1 (2009): 175-96. Print.

Kinkead, Joyce. "Undergraduate Researchers as Makers of Knowledge in Composition in the Writing Studies Major." *The Changing of Knowledge in Composition: Contemporary Perspectives*. Ed. Lance Massey and Richard C. Gebhardt. Logan: Utah State UP, 2011. 137-60. Print.

Moll, Luis C., Cathy Amanti, Deborah Neff, and Norma Gonzalez. "Funds of Knowledge for Teaching: Using a Qualitative Approach to Connect Homes and Classrooms." *Theory into Practice* 31.2 (1992): 132-41. Print.

Taylor, Hill. "Black Spaces: Examining the Writing Major at an Urban HBCU." *Composition Studies* 35.1 (2007): 99-112. Print.

Veracini, Lorenzo. *Settler Colonialism: A Theoretical Overview*. New York: Palgrave Macmillan, 2010. Print.

Book Reviews

Multimodality in Composition, Rhetoric, and English Studies: Praxis and Practicalities

Cultivating Ecologies for Digital Media Work, by Catherine C. Braun. Carbondale: SIUP, 2014. 224 pp.

Multimodal Composition: A Critical Sourcebook, edited by Claire Lutkewitte. Boston: Bedford/St. Martin's, 2014. 548 pp.

Remixing Composition: A History of Multimodal Writing Pedagogy, by Jason Palmeri. Carbondale: SIUP, 2014. 194 pp.

Reviewed by Kirsti Cole, Minnesota State University

As the Director of Writing Across the Curriculum (WAC) at my institution, I found Jason Palmeri's *Remixing Composition: A History of Multimodal Writing Pedagogy*, Catherine C. Braun's *Cultivating Ecologies for Digital Media Work*, and Claire Lutkewitte's edited collection *Multimodal Composition* extremely useful. These authors make visible the long history of composition scholars using multimedia technologies (even prior to the "digital turn"), provoke broad pedagogical questions including assignment design and assessment practices, and explore technological ecologies and sustainable environments. Lutkewitte, in particular, serves as a useful primer for instructors unfamiliar with multimodal composition. Building on the work of Victor Villanueva and Geoffrey Sirc, who are not normally cited by multimodal scholars, Lutkewitte points to the argument that "multimodal composition allows for many voices—even those new, marginalized, or unpopular voices—to be heard" (5). She argues that this is evidenced not only in traditional scholarship but also in the kinds of texts and examples shared by the authors in her collection.

We live in a digital age, one that provides access to a multiplicity of voices. How then can we best cultivate supports for working with, teaching with, and researching digital media, digital scholarship, and multimodal composition that create access to potentially unheard voices at department, college, and university levels? Though these authors do a convincing job arguing that issues of multimodal composition and digital media work are relevant and pressing for composition scholars, and for English studies as a whole, WAC scholars will also benefit from reading these books because they touch on deeply relevant issues to cross-curricular and university-wide writing and reading practices.

Braun, Lutkewitte, and Palmeri write at an opportune moment in digital and multimodal literacy studies, which, while still a relatively young area of research, calls on a well-rooted intellectual tradition. The list of scholars engaging in pedagogical questions about the possibilities of the digital is extensive and growing (Folk; McKee and DeVoss; Szabady, Fodrey, and Del Russo), and yet as Braun and Palmeri each convincingly argue, digital content is still undervalued, feared, and ignored by more traditional, or "print-centric" departments.

Catherine Braun's *Cultivating Ecologies* is a book that should be on the shelves of every department chair in English studies because of the ways that it cogently examines how the digital influences department life. She gives an in depth study of three departments: the "print-centric department," the "parallel cultures department," and the "integrated literacies department" (22). In profiling each department, Braun provides a series of tables based on her research that could lead a department struggling with the place of digital media through a series of heuristic activities focused on digital media and teaching, digital media and departmental culture, and the potential value of digital media research and digital scholarship. Her heuristic tables are comprehensive, and the questions grow, shift, and become more complex as the discussion of each department profile points to a series of issues surrounding digital media scholarship in the humanities. As she argues, "[d]igital media work often emerges as a solution to the problem or as an efficiency that is problematic, when it can better be conceived as a site to reconceptualize the work of scholarship and teaching" (5). In order to launch her reconceptualization, she outlines three "big questions" about the definition of text and how we read and write (9), which she argues lay the groundwork for digital media teaching and scholarship. Braun introduces a matrix that plots these questions against the different contexts in which digital media work can occur and uses the profiles of the three departments to explore the technological ecologies for digital media. Her use of "ecology" comes from the introduction to *Technological Ecologies and Sustainability* edited by Dànielle DeVoss, Heidi McKee, and Dickie Selfe. They use the concepts of ecology and sustainability to argue that "richly textured technological environments" enhance teaching and learning (1). However, instead of focusing just on composition programs or writing studies departments, Braun extends her analysis to English studies as a discipline. Her focus on the larger discipline is particularly useful for those of us who may work in comp/rhet programs that are part of an English department offering multiple undergraduate and/or graduate degrees.

Braun cites the work of Meredith Graupner, Lee Nickoson-Massey, and Kristine Blair, who conclude in "Remediating Knowledge-Making Spaces in Graduate Curriculum: Developing and Sustaining Multimodal Teaching and Research" that "reciprocal mentoring, particularly involving both graduate students and faculty" (147) can foster developing technological ecologies and further professional development in digital media teaching and research. Braun argues that reciprocal mentoring and "rough spaces" for experimentation and learning-by-doing activities can promote a safe space for those faculty members who may feel ill equipped to mentor students in digital media work (147). The rough spaces not only promote a community culture, but also allow for professionalization activities that can be hugely beneficial for graduate students and faculty members. Braun's book provides an entry point for faculty who assert that, because they were not trained in multimodal and digital practices, they do not feel comfortable engaging in them. The ability to work in a rough space, to foster ecologies and promote reciprocal mentoring, is key to her argument and compelling for departments that do not have faculty trained in digital media. A rough space can do what I would argue is the work of the academy: create conditions for continual learning through reflexive praxis.

For those faculty members and graduate students looking for more than learning-by-doing activities, however, Claire Lutkewitte's *Multimodal Composition* sourcebook proves an invaluable tool. Learning-by-doing activities such as those outlined in the sourcebook are of particular use to faculty teaching in WAC programs because they emphasize tools through which a variety of content can be taught. Learning-by-doing allows instructors who may not be writing experts to begin incorporating writing activities to promote content learning. Although Lutkewitte's collection is focused on the composition classroom, and populated with authors who do cutting edge scholarship in multimodal and digital media scholarship, I believe that it is a useful text for departments that house a variety of diverse subdisciplines including literature, rhetoric and composition, linguistics, and creative writing. The first chapter of the collection, the National Council of Teachers of English position statement on multimodal literacies, includes a section on building a sustainable environment for multimodal composition that intersects new media pedagogies with diverse institutional environments. It is an excellent starting place for anyone who wants to learn more about the practicalities of design, assignment activities for the classroom, assessment models for evaluating multimodal writing, and the dynamics of multilingual and multimodal frameworks. It is clear, however, that like Braun, Lutkewitte feels pressed to justify why multimodalities in composition matter. She includes a chapter from Claire Lauer who contends with the terms "multimodal" and "multimedia" in both the academic and public spheres (22), and a chapter on the value of new media scholarship by Cheryl E. Ball (163). Lutkewitte argues that her sourcebook attempts to address questions and interrogate answers such as what we should call multimodal composition, exploring the integration of projects in courses, and the implications of multimodal scholarship (1). These basic questions seem, after reading Braun and

Palmeri, to have obvious answers. However, for the broader interdisciplinary community, and for scholars unfamiliar with Braun and Palmeri's work, the questions remain significant because of the entrenched resistance to multimodal scholarship that each author confronts. In Lutkewitte's introduction she summarizes resistance to engaging in such work, making her collection important for scholars who may resist incorporating multimodal pedagogies in their classrooms or as they train TAs. She draws on Jody Shipka's *Toward a Composition Made Whole* to argue that "recognizing the multimodal practices and behaviors that take place throughout the entire composing process" can encourage students to experiment in a way that "broadens their understanding of what effective communication entails" (Lutkewitte 3). Lutkewitte ends her introduction to the sourcebook by arguing that the selected chapters represent a diversity of theories and pedagogies because depending on a singular "Theory or a Pedagogy can be dangerous" (8).

Instructors in multidisciplinary WAC programs are, frequently, new faculty who are assigned writing intensive courses, some without experience teaching writing. If composition scholars, as Lutkewitte suggests, find the prospect of building a unitary multimodal theory or pedagogy dangerous, it may well seem impossible to newcomers from different fields. However, Lutkewitte's selections, and the multiple entry points the theories and pedagogies provide, complement the work done by WAC scholars. In other words, instructors in other fields who already teach with technology will likely find common ground with multimodal composition pedagogies. In addition to emphasizing the multiple possible approaches to multimodal composition, Lutkewitte also briefly foregrounds what Palmeri does a masterful job of arguing: that there is a long history of multimodal writing pedagogy in composition.

Palmeri's *Remixing Composition* draws attention not only to this evolution, but also to the classic texts of composition theory from the 1960s, 1970s, and 1980s in order to examine how compositionists respond to new mediums. Palmeri traces the use of multimedia technologies in teaching composition before the personal computer and the graphic Web. For those interested in contending with Braun's print-centric departments that claim technology and multimodality as something new, Palmeri's work provides a rejoinder. Palmeri's argument is powerful and evocative because he revisits the core theories of process pedagogy in order to examine what is arguably the foundational (and often taken for granted) pedagogy of our field. He looks at what he calls three core tracks and how they engage the forgotten multimodal aspects of the process movement.

Palmeri uses what he refers to as an associative remix, drawing on Joseph Harris's *A Teaching Subject* and Lisa Ede's *Situating Composition* to create a useable past that productively acknowledges but also expands the use of accepted teaching paradigms in relation to multimodal texts. In revisiting the work of such foundational scholars as Janet Emig, Linda Flower and John R. Hayes, Nancy Sommers, and Ann Berthoff, Palmeri provides a series of three "macrotheoretical principles—that can potentially help us reimagine what it means to study and teach composing in the contemporary digital moment" (44). From the first page of the introduction he re-sees and retells the history of composition, challenging recent announcements of a "multimodal turn" in the midst of "tectonic change" (Yancey 298). Palmeri explains that though the multimodal progress narrative can be useful, it can also conceal a dynamic multimodal past in our field (5). So as to avoid the progress tale, and craft a richer and historically informed text, Palmeri sets up his book as a reclamation project of sorts, hoping to show that compositionists in the '60s, '70s, and '80s "studied and taught alphabetic writing as an embodied multimodal process that shares affinities with other forms of composing (visual, aural, spatial, gestural)" (5). It is the invisibility of the past that Palmeri seeks to make seen—and in some cases heard, as there is a rich set of resources from multimedia textbooks in the early 1970s.

His purpose and aims for the book are threefold: (1) to demonstrate compositionists' unique expertise in multimodality, (2) to discuss the ways in which students can benefit from multimodal composing, and (3) to critique the fear that accompanies new technologies in the field (6). Palmeri accomplishes these ambitious goals. The first and third goals seem to speak in the most explicit terms to the calls for action in Braun and Lutkewitte's books. Palmeri does a convincing job of demonstrating the ways in which compositionists (and therefore, in some ways, scholars in English studies) are qualified to work in multiple modes and across digital media. He also outlines the reciprocal nature of our relationship to new technologies: that they are always met with both trepidation that they will expand and hope that they will fix our problems.

One of the underlying goals of this book, I believe, is to engage university educators across the curriculum in multimodal pedagogies. In his epilogue, Palmeri's first of three goals calls explicitly for the involvement of WAC directors in two ways. The first is to "actively resist the common tendency to present alphabetic writing as inherently the best tool for promoting active learning in disciplinary courses," instead calling for a vision of "'composing to learn' that emphasizes how the integration of informal writing, speaking, and visual-production activities can enhance students' understanding and application of concepts" (150). Instead of writing to learn, composing to learn gives space for multimodalities and engagements in the composing process that could support content engagement across disciplines. As far as the second goal, Palmeri calls for WAC directors to

[D]evelop workshops or institutes that bring together instructors from "allied art" fields—providing opportunities for teachers of writing, theater, visual arts, film, music, graphic design, and architecture to collaboratively develop and share multimodal strategies for promoting creative invention in their disciplines. In so doing, we will work to expand beyond the consideration of multimodality as course or seminar specific—specialized—skill set, and instead integrate informal and formal composing practices into classes that do not necessarily focus on technology. (151)

Palmeri also notes the possibility for administration to work with a group of teachers to design and engage low and high stakes multimodal assignments and activities in order to incorporate the engagement of technology across classroom spaces (153).

Because I work regularly with WAC faculty and scholars, I read all three of these texts through a terministic screen that is predisposed to see the possibilities for applying multimodality to WAC programming. I see a direct line of intervention between multimodal composing, digital media, and cross-curricular and interdisciplinary pedagogical practices. One of the significant commonalities between Braun, Lutkewitte, and Palmeri's books is a focus not just on the composition classroom, but also on the discipline as a whole, and on the praxis of being an academic in the midst of the ever-evolving contemporary digital turn, one in which all scholars, regardless of discipline, are implicated. These books, particularly Braun's, take on a significant project: How do we see ourselves? How do we best engage with the available resources? What does this kind of engagement mean? I think for the WAC community we could easily add: How might these available resources affect interdisciplinary writing pedagogies?

Mankato, Minnesota

Works Cited

DeVoss, Dànielle N., Heidi A. McKee, and Richard (Dickie) Selfe, eds. *Technological Ecologies and Sustainability*. Logan: Computers and Composition Digital P/Utah State UP, 2009. *Computers and Composition Digital Press*. Web. 1 August 2015. <http://ccdigitalpress.org/ebooks-and-projects/tes>.

Ede, Lisa. *Situating Composition: Composition Studies and the Politics of Location*. Carbondale: SIUP, 2004. Print.

Folk, Moe. "Multimodal Style and the Evolution of Digital Writing Pedagogy." *The Centrality of Style*. Ed. Mike Duncan and Star Medzerian Vanguri. Fort Collins: WAC Clearinghouse and Parlor P, 2013. 213-37. Print.

Graupner, Meredith, Lee Nickoson-Massey, and Kristine Blair. "Remediating Knowledge-Making Spaces in Graduate Curriculum: Developing and Sustaining Multimodal Teaching and Research." *Computers and Composition* 26 (2009): 13-23. Print.

Harris, Joseph. *A Teaching Subject: Composition Since 1966.* Logan: Utah State UP, 2012. Print.

McKee, Heidi A., and Dànielle Nicole DeVoss, eds. *Digital Writing Assessment & Evaluation.* Logan: Computers and Composition Digital Press/Utah State UP, 2013. Web. 12 July 2015. <http://ccdigitalpress.org/dwae/foreword.html>.

Shipka, Jody. *Toward a Composition Made Whole.* Pittsburgh: U of Pittsburgh P, 2011. Print.

Szabady, Gina, Crystal N. Fodrey, and Celeste Del Russo. "Digital (Re)Visions: Blending Pedagogical Strategies with Dynamic Classroom Tactics." *Kairos* 19.1 PraxisWiki (2014): n. pag. Web. 5 July 2015. <http://praxis.technorhetoric.net/tiki-index.php?page=PraxisWiki%3A_%3ADigital_Revisions>.

Yancey, Kathleen Blake. "Made Not Only in Words: Composition in a New Key." *CCC* 56.2 (2004): 297-328. Print.

Embracing the Challenges of Conventional Practices, Program Inquiry, and New Media in Writing Center Theory and Research

Peripheral Visions for Writing Centers, by Jackie Grutsch McKinney. Logan: Utah State UP, 2013. 150 pp.

Building Writing Center Assessments that Matter, by Ellen Schendel and William J. Macauley, Jr. Logan: Utah State UP, 2012. 207 pp.

The Routledge Reader on Writing Centers and New Media, edited by Sohui Lee and Russell Carpenter. New York: Routledge, 2014. 297 pp.

Reviewed by Harry Denny, Purdue University, and Cara Messina and Michael Reich, St. John's University

All three of us utilize different lenses to perceive the world. We enter spaces as gendered, sexualized, racialized, and nationalized people, yet too often those identities are not foregrounded in the everyday work we do in writing centers. As a result, our everyday becomes easily hegemonic, unchallenged. For us, questioning the pedagogy and process of how we operate in sessions should be just as ubiquitous as the stories we share and the practices we employ in writing centers. Three recent books in writing center studies—Jackie Grutsch McKinney's *Peripheral Visions for Writing Centers*, Sohui Lee and Russell Carpenter's *The Routledge Reader on Writing Centers and New Media*, and Ellen Schendel and William J. Macauley Jr.'s *Building Writing Center Assessments that Matter*—offer theoretical frameworks, technological innovation and program inquiry to re-imagine and critically explore how we think and practice in the ordinary (sometimes exceptional) spaces where one-to-one mentoring happens. We approach this review attuned to the distinct standpoints from which we look. Too often scholarship for/on writing centers flattens its audience, rarely addressing the intellectual demands necessary for participating in disciplinary conversations or the process for a diverse range of interlocutors to join these communities of practice.

Harry approaches these texts as a faculty administrator and researcher of writing centers; Cara as a recent graduate student and current professional writing center consultant; and Michael as a second-year doctoral candidate in writing center and composition studies. Our orientations to these texts reflect different degrees of experience—as purveyors of stories of writing centers (the good, the bad, and others), as tutors struggling with (and through) new media to collaborate with writers, and as scholars engaged in everyday and formalized assessment of our mentoring practices. The texts under review speak directly to our experiences and our needs, and they also speak past us, presuming a sort of exteriority that makes us wish they each had a better sense of us as their audience. Harry's scholarship has focused on a deep awareness of how writing centers promote domination but create spaces for opposition and activism and how assessment offers promise to transform and devastate programs. He is just recently beginning to embrace new media as an arena through which to produce and disseminate research. Cara and Michael, however, live in fully digital worlds—academic, writing center, and otherwise. They too often have been excluded from conversations about assessment and grand narratives about writing centers. Although consultants/tutors/coaches are central agents in program reflection, development, and inquiry, more often than not, they are the objects, not viewed as collaborators.

In Jackie Grutsch McKinney's *Peripheral Visions for Writing Centers,* we see that the stories told about writing centers by directors, consultants, and others revolve around a central story or, as McKinney refers to it, a grand narrative: "[W]riting centers are comfortable, iconoclastic places where all students go to get one-to-one tutoring on their writing" (3). She produces this argument about the grand narrative using well-known writing center lore and an online survey filled out by writing center professionals—the participants' answers are located in the appendix. One problem for McKinney is that this grand narrative does not reflect the actual complex work performed by consultants and directors alike. Deconstructing it, she focuses chapters on the narrative's constituent elements that come to signify writing centers as "cozy homes," "iconoclastic," and inclusive (3). In her chapter on debunking the narrative that writing centers are "cozy homes," McKinney argues that the decor of writing centers, although typically filled with plants and open space to parallel with the "cozy home" aesthetic, curtains the more complicated narrative about writing centers (20). As writing center professionals challenge colleagues, the students they work with, and themselves, the notion of "cozy home" fades because thinking critically, questioning, and revising—all important elements of writing center work—are not "cozy." After complicating the oversimplified "cozy homes" myth, McKinney tackles the notion that writing centers are "iconoclastic," or a marginalized space separated from institutional values and expectations (35). The problem with marking the writing center as marginalized is it implies "victimhood;" McKinney believes writing center work has moved past that notion, yet this marginalization may be used as a subversive tactic to be critical of writing center work and scholarship. McKinney also argues that the claim of marginalization undervalues and under-complicates the navigation that writing center directors do; she claims, "writing centers and the institutions they are found in are always both—marginal and not marginal, emancipatory and regulatory" (54). Finally, McKinney challenges the third part of the grand narrative about how writing centers are for "all students" (57). In this chapter, she turns to her data set—the survey answers—to show how writing center professionals view their work. The grand narrative suggests inclusivity, but McKinney argues that the narratives writing center professionals create about "normal and abnormal tutoring sessions" suggest an anxiety about working with a diverse student body (70). She concludes by emphasizing the importance of looking past the grand narrative: "Peripheral vision," or "trac[ing] the... negative space to see the actual dimensions of writing center work and operational beliefs" combats the generalized—often incorrect—story told about writing center work (84). McKinney calls on scholarship to celebrate and learn from individual stories, techniques, and ideologies.

As an undergraduate when she first read McKinney, Cara began to critically examine her own writing center and its reliance on creating a "cozy home" for students. Cara noticed how she and other consultants foregrounded values of comfort and inclusivity for the students they worked with, yet what was lost in that mindset was an interrogation of how and why making space for discomfort might be productive. The "cozy home" thinking was dangerous and seductive because it became a stock, even easy, formula for approaching every student in every context rather than the more complicated dynamic of engaging with students where they were intellectually and emotionally, as part of the students' own journey of learning to write and express themselves. Working from similar instances invoked in her research, McKinney points to the reliance on comfortable and already-known narratives that can stifle challenge in everyday thinking. We had hoped for a more comprehensive exploration of the individual experiences and interpretations writing center professionals share, perhaps seeing her dig further into what her survey data reflected as opposed to the extended analysis of lore. For example, we are interested in the comparisons and insight that might be made from the responses to her questions about work definitions and the positioning of writing centers within institutions. Although McKinney demonstrates the necessity of challenging the grand narrative and celebrating individual writing center stories, we wonder how this critical analysis translates to the everyday work between consultants and clients. We thought *Peripheral Visions* begged the question of the "micro" narratives that consultants and clients might share, not just the more abstract or grand versions that directors circulate. By exploring what McKinney names as "negative space," that discursive domain beyond the grand narrative, she challenges us to imagine stories that take/make space for interrogating social justice and identity politics activism that writing center work can transform, whether through individual interaction or institutional challenge. This spurring toward more and sustained critical inquiry in writing centers makes *Peripheral Visions* useful for a variety of audiences because such believing and doubting (as well as research projects that take up such intellectual questioning) need to be integrated into the practices of directors, graduate students, and peer consultants alike, wherever they find themselves mentoring and learning.

Like the questioning and challenging of writing center hegemony in *Peripheral Visions*, Ellen Schendel and William Macauley's *Building Writing Center Assessments that Matter* argues that effective assessment protocol begins with introspection and turns outward, bridging assessment insights to larger institutional goals. Such reflection integrates and complicates the role writing centers play in executing and challenging systemic forces. Assessment, Schendel and Macauley suggest, can promote greater understanding of writing center practices beyond the usual stakeholders of staff and clients. As Macauley advises, "writing centers don't work in a vacuum; centers live and breathe within institutions, in relation to other academic entities. . . . [I]t behooves writing center directors to acknowledge this reality and work with it" (57). *Building Writing Center Assessments*' first of six chapters orients readers to writing center assessment through a comprehensive literature review of wider scholarship in composition studies and provides a structure for developing local assessment protocol. Over the subsequent chapters, Schendel and Macauley suggest writing centers document their own local values and goals, from which measurable outcomes can be shaped for eventual data gathering (39-51). Institutional documents, like mission statements or accreditation reports and self-study documents, should guide writing center assessment thinking and practices. Such linking work bridges gulfs between the everyday work of writing centers and the various stakeholders, making the links more concrete and tangible and expanding the scope of potential audiences for the work specific to writing centers, which can provide meaningful assessment strategies that link back to the institution (59). In addition to mining from and integrating local institutional values and statements for individual assessment protocol, Schendel and Macauley note that professional associations, like the MLA, CWPA, and NCTE, have policy documents and position papers that can further guide or nuance assessment principles and practices. To capstone the linking of center and institution, the end of the first section highlights the reach of writing assessment reports to larger audiences beyond those who work at writing centers. The authors describe how this process of integration can educate institutions on the role writing centers play in operationalizing shared goals (83). Neal Lerner's interchapter, "Of Numbers and Stories," provides a historical and conceptual overview of empirical research methods in a writing center context. The true goal of such scholarship, in Lerner's view, is to capture, map and understand observable dynamics as well as to "understand significance and meaning from the participants' perspectives and their social actions" (111). The last two chapters document Schendel and Macauley's experiences with research methods for gathering info for assessment by already fitting it into the work that writing centers do (126-131) and with writing effective reports rooted in audience awareness that will invite ongoing conversation (140). Brian Huot and Nicole Caswell point out in their afterward that the intellectual labor of writing center assessment can grow the disciplinary profile of the field and can nuance the discourse of the community. Schendel and Macauley's coda reminds readers that assessment is an iterative and recursive process (171-72).

While they share experiences with assessment through concrete examples from their institutions, the local nature of Schendel and Macauley's lessons makes generalizing to other contexts difficult. How might writing center assessment be inherently different (or similar) in a research-intensive university, a regional comprehensive, or a small liberal arts college? If writing center assessment is to matter, we were left wondering for whom and to what end, and the authors leave us with too little to latch on to. Harry wondered how the samples exclusive to Schendel and Macauley's local institutions foster cross-institutional scholarship or dialogue between peer and aspirant institutions. When he was on faculty at St. John's University, the writing center produced volumes of the sorts of data for which *Building Writing Center Assessments* advocates, but he found no mechanisms or networks of mutual support to compare data sets with other large Catholic or similar peer institutions. Likewise, Michael and Cara have struggled to parlay their own individual assessment research projects to larger conversations that cut across institutions; instead, they feel confined to the anecdotal. Michael wondered about the assumption in the book that the coordination of values and goals between larger institutions and writing centers must happen and how those "shared" values might, in practice, operate at cross purposes with one another. What happens when common ground between the writing center and the institution cannot be found so easily or is illusive? In their advocacy of appropriation of institutional values for assessment purposes, Schendel and Macauley implicitly advocate a subversive mindset that does not address the complicated politics of institutions or the differential positioning of professionals directing writing centers (lacking security of employment or tenure). By coordinating (even accommodating) institutional values with the writing center's, assessment can be made to matter and resonate with the culture of power in the institution, but it still does not displace power differentials between stakeholders that can lead many writing center professionals to adopt a bunker mentality, endlessly staving off threats to their leadership and unit autonomy or tirelessly bending to institutional currents. Regardless, the lesson from *Building Writing Center Assessments* remains especially critical for new directors or graduate students learning about the field: Effective program evaluation requires a careful reading and understanding of institutional systems.

McKinney, Schendel, and Macauley offer useful lenses through which we review our final text, which argues that writing center practices need to adapt to a changing rhetorical and technological landscape where students and other writers seek support with genres and media. In *The Routledge Reader on Writing Centers and New Media*, editors Sohui Lee and Russell Carpenter reprint a set of foundational and historical essays on multimedia, multiliteracy, and multimodality. The nineteen chapters build awareness of and provide tools for tutors and directors alike to address contemporary literacy demands and innovative outlets through which writers can express themselves. Tutors and administrators no longer exist in a world of academic expression where thesis-driven essays are the norm and where hard copy printouts of term papers dominate; instead, consultants and students are likely to encounter blogs, digital portfolios, multimedia, or multilingual projects in everyday sessions. Lee and Carpenter's thesis across their anthology is that we require a more complicated sense of the history, theory, and discursive conventions and possibilities that "traditional" writing center practice does not provide. The chapters from the New London Group and John Trimbur are critical for re-imagining the place of media and literacies, especially in the contexts of the one-to-one mentoring that happens in writing centers. Michael Pemberton's essay on hypertextuality calls for writing centers to break from the mindset and practices confined to an exclusively textual, non-linked world of writing and to embrace an environment where communication is inherently multimodal. Jackie Grutsch McKinney sounds a similar call in her chapter, pushing for writing centers to explicitly train staff on the unique experience of tutoring for new media and digital document design; quite simply, pedagogical practices rooted in another era ill-equip tutors and poorly serve their clients. Andrea Lunsford and Lisa Ede's chapter complicates notions of audience in a digital age influenced by the presence of social media, while Cynthia Selfe makes a case for the rhetorical impact of hearing and listening in multimodality.

While we applaud *The Routledge Reader* for its packaging of a critical collection of essays that potentially re-orient writing center practitioners, we wondered what different insights would have emerged if the collection had operated on the assumption that peer consultants, graduate students, and perhaps even writing center administrators and faculty are already well-immersed in the everyday practices of multiliteracy and multimodality. Instead, the editors seemed to write from a notion that writing centers are deficient and just now responding to the challenge of and integrating pedagogical practices to respond to new media: "most writing and learning centers are only recently considering how they will offer tutorials for students creating multimodal arguments" (xv). Neither the editors nor any of the contributors in the collection offer any empirical data or insight on any adoption of technology or the prevalence of multimodal, multiliteracy tutoring in writing centers. In our own writing centers, we have been struck by how our colleagues and staff tap diffuse literacies and engage in numerous modalities in their personal lives beyond their writing center work, all the while being reluctant to embrace a more complicated, nuanced view of literacy, modality, and argument in typical tutoring sessions. Apart from raising consciousness and building theoretical and technical knowledge, *The Routledge Reader* does not help them (or enable us to train them) to transcend the disconnect between everyday practices and the teaching and learning that happens with students. Lee and Carpenter's introduction begs for a follow-up empirical study that documents and assesses the very questions the collection's essays hope to address: How and to what degree do writing centers address multimodality and multiliteracy? The editors do not offer an adequate survey of actual mindsets and practices of writing centers. As the editors acknowledge, writing centers are as diverse and locally contingent as is education within and beyond the United States. Reflecting our own local bias toward diversity, we were also struck by how the collection defines and portrays multiliteracy as primarily technological and media-driven, but does not take up how multiliteracy varies by discipline, by access to technology and media, and by linguistics. In addition to exploring different ways of arguing and writing through/with (new) media, we had hoped that a post-millennial discussion of literacy might take up what languages and Englishes are supported and marginalized, how disciplinary conventions and faculty development complicate writing center outreach and programming needs, and how different sorts of institutions embrace and presume student bodies with dramatically different access to technology. Like *Building Writing Center Assessments that Matter*, Lee and Carpenter's *Writing Centers and New Media* serves as an excellent primer for those new to the conversation and will spur more experienced professionals to seek out advanced or grounded literature on the debates surrounding literacy, new media, and peer-to-peer mentoring.

    These texts testify to a difficult reality for our work: How do we transcend our impulse to tell stories, collect lore, and share recipes for best practices? Just as Dana Driscoll and Sherry Wynn Perdue have charged writing centers to take up Richard Haswell's now-famous call for replicable, aggregable, and data-driven (RAD) research, we wonder what significance these texts might have had if they were to share empirical data, results, or findings from qualitative and quantitative research. McKinney comes the closest to performing the very research discussion we hoped for, but we craved a more sustained discussion, a dialogue across these three books. Instead, she and the others end up returning to lore and story-telling, narrative reflection as an end to itself rather than as launching points to more generalizable, empirical research. For a field so self-aware of its own politics and political implications (like the efficacy of our work and the populations that we reach/fail to reach), we had hoped for a more sustained challenge to the orthodoxy of how we circulate our research, our stories, our assessments.

However these texts fit in the field's broader disciplinary debates and evolution, they offer writing center studies promising research for practitioners to consider the importance of creating a new space for researching, innovating, and revising. Each writing center possesses unique narratives layered with the stories of participants, of the space and its institution, as well as the local and global sociopolitical dynamics. Both McKinney's and Schendel and Macauley's texts remind us to create space for individual stories and assessments to mold, support, and rethink our own writing center's role in relation to other writing centers, clients, and institutions. Lee and Carpenter's collection emphasizes the importance of creating a space for new media to take advantage of and celebrate the potential of technology—especially since the virtual world has become an integral part of this generation. As we create space for new media, narratives, and assessment, we think about how to borrow from other writers' texts and critically imagine in our exuberant (early) adoption whose stories become standard, how access is differential and too often reinscribes domination and oppression, and where and for whom possibilities exist for better understanding the efficacy of everyday practices. With each of these books, writing center studies continues down a promising path, where directors, consultants, and students have rich opportunities to continue dialogue through inquiry-based research that explores, experiments, interrogates, and challenges, especially what seems customary or inventive, wherever it happens.

West Lafayette, Indiana and Jamaica, New York

Works Cited

Driscoll, Dana, and Sherry Wynn Perdue. "Theory, Lore and More: An Analysis of RAD Research in *Writing Center Journal*, 1980-2009." *Writing Center Journal* 32.1 (2012): 11-39. Print.

Haswell, Richard. "NCTE/CCCC Recent War on Scholarship." *Written Communication* 22.2 (2005): 198-223. Print.

Christian Rhetorics: Toward a Hopeful Future

Mapping Christian Rhetorics: Connecting Conversations, Charting New Territories, edited by Michael-John DePalma and Jeffrey M. Ringer. New York: Routledge, 2015. 305 pp.

Renovating Rhetoric in Christian Tradition, edited by Elizabeth Vander Lei, Thomas Amorose, Beth Daniell, and Anne Ruggles Gere. Pittsburgh: U of Pittsburgh P, 2014. 211 pp.

Reviewed by T J Geiger II, Lamar University, and Melody Pugh, United States Air Force Academy

In this dialogic review, we hope to highlight some of the vibrant work being done on religious rhetorics. Christianity is a topic that frequently provokes suspicion in higher education—and not without reason. Its complicity with normalizing and dominating discourses should give all critical observers pause. At the same time, *Mapping Christian Rhetorics: Connecting Conversations, Charting New Territories* edited by Michael-John DePalma and Jeffrey M. Ringer and *Renovating Rhetoric in Christian Tradition* edited by Elizabeth Vander Lei, Thomas Amorose, Beth Daniell, and Anne Ruggles Gere are two collections that invite scholars of rhetoric and composition to consider nuanced contributions of Christian rhetorics to diverse political, social, and pedagogical projects. These collections provide scholars and teachers with tools for connecting interests in religious rhetorics to concerns shared by disciplinary and departmental colleagues: notions of agency, instances of performativity, historical inquiries, gendered norms, methodological issues, classroom dynamics, and representations of students. While we would like to have seen more examinations of living rhetors both within and outside of the United States included in both books, and attention to religious rhetorics within conversations about human sexuality, taken together, *Mapping* and *Renovating* present rich historical investigations, inquiries into gender, studies of rhetoric within institutions, and considerations of religious rhetorics in writing, rhetoric, and literature classrooms.

Melody: I'm so glad that I have the chance to read these two collections with you, T J. They are both so rich that it's almost hard to know where to begin. So, as a starting point, I find myself wondering what, if anything, can be learned from the verbs that are used in the titles of these respective books?

T J: In some ways, the titular verbs (renovating and mapping) both rely on what came before and offer fresh expressions that enable new opportunities. Both terms carry a kind of Socratic energy—one that seeks to explain where we've been and predict where we're going with regard to Christian rhetorics. In *Mapping*, the editors highlight the map's ability to acknowledge, connect, and chart—a cartographic trinity. The familiar/fresh dynamic seems especially pronounced around questions of research methodology and theory. In "Coming to (Troubled) Terms: Methodology, Positionality, and the Problem of Defining 'Evangelical Christian,'" Emily Murphy Cope and Jeffrey M. Ringer take up familiar research concerns, but they explore them in the context of rhetorical inquiry about evangelical Christian identity. Their thoughtful self-examinations and inquiries into participants' self-identifications provide valuable resources for other investigators. Rich considerations of standard theoretical terms also prove fruitful: Richard Benjamin Crosby shows how religious terrain and performances offer complex grounds for agency, and William T. FitzGerald compellingly demonstrates that studies of prayer yield insights into the very nature of rhetoric.

Melody: Explorations of theory and method are two of the major contributions that *Mapping* brings to the table. This collection offers us a vision of not only how composition and rhetoric as a field has arrived at a place where religion can be an integral part of rhetorical inquiry, but also how distinctive elements of religious practice can offer us new pathways forward. As you rightly point out, FitzGerald's assertion that rhetoric *is* a form of prayer is a wholly original way of thinking about the work of rhetoric. Similarly, I found my thinking challenged by Richard Benjamin Crosby's articulation of dual agency in the preaching of Henry Yates Satterlee, the first Bishop of the National Cathedral. Crosby examines the complexities that arise when an individual locates (and even perhaps fully invests) him or herself within a religious institution, and in so doing, develops a creative agency that is beholden to a higher power. I find that this conceptualization of agency—a concept so vital to the current work of the field—adds a layer of nuance that clearly distinguishes agency from mere individualism.

T J: Yes, this issue of understanding where religious rhetorics have been in order to freshly understand rhetorical power seems especially evident in two threads woven together throughout these two collections: historical work and Christian women's rhetorical activity. I was struck by the vibrancy and scope of chapters dealing with these issues. For example, I found Aesha Adams-Roberts, Rosalyn Collings Eves, and Liz Rohan's "'With the Tongues of [Wo]men and Angels': Apostolic Rhetorical Practices Among Religious Women" especially thoughtful and engaging (*Renovating*). The coauthors take the approach of analyzing several rhetors inhabiting various identities side-by-side, an approach that illuminates multiple complex dynamics simultaneously.

Melody: This is a striking commonality between the collections. In *Mapping*, Lisa Zimmerelli and Lisa Shaver each reflect on how female preachers and deaconesses in the 19th and early 20th centuries used rhetorical strategies to craft agentive spaces by which women could shape and expand the activities of the church within mainstream society. *Renovating* includes related discussions—by Vicki Tolar Burton; Karen K. Seat; and Adams-Roberts, Eves, and Rohan—of somewhat more reluctant (but no less effective) Christian women who adapted and subverted traditional religious rhetoric in an effort to craft public leadership roles within church structures that resisted the full significance of their work.

In fact, this complexity of individuals locating agency both within and in response to institutional power structures and belief systems is one of the common threads I see uniting the chapters in *Renovating*. Renovating, of course, means restoring, but the word also carries connotations of reinvigorating and refreshing. To that end, I appreciate the way that this collection opens by paying close attention to the rhetorical work accomplished by lesser known religious sects, such as the Latter Day Saints and Seventh Day Adventists. The authors of these chapters, Anne Ruggles Gere and Lizbeth A. Rand (respectively), offer a vision of the complexities, clashes, and contradictions that can exist within and among the adherents to a single religion.

T J: You're absolutely right. And this attention to individuals operating within institutions also appears in contributors' analyses of school scenes. I find myself wondering about the implications of these collections for rhetorical education and the teaching of writing. *Renovating* provides a significant contribution to the way I think about Christian rhetorics in the classroom. Elizabeth Vander Lei's "'Ain't We Got Fun?': Teaching Writing in a Violent World" shares nuanced reflections on the nature of the pedagogical enterprise, the affective lives of students and teachers, and the role of writing classrooms in furthering deliberative and participatory democracy. She challenges me to imagine ways to forge a classroom—and dream of a world—where as many voices as possible are encouraged and valued and where participants feel not only an obligation to deliberative conversation but also take delight in each other and the work before them (and to acknowledge when those efforts fall short). In a similar way, Beth Daniell's "A Question of Truth" opens up new avenues for dialogue about the rhetorical nature of religious belief. By engaging with historical biblical criticism by figures like Marcus Borg as well as central rhetorical concerns about knowledge construction, Daniell helps writing teachers build a vocabulary for talking about faith in complex ways.

Melody: I agree. One of the most powerful things about Vander Lei's chapter is her unflinching willingness to turn a critical lens on her own assumptions about what constitutes appropriate academic engagement and her willingness to be reflexive about the subjectivities that we—as instructors—privilege. I think we see a similar self-reflectiveness in her chapter, "'Where the Wild Things Are': Christian Students in the Figured Worlds of Composition" (*Mapping*), where she examines the conceptual metaphors that have so longed served to divide religious and academic rhetorics. I see in Priscilla Perkins's "'Attentive, Intelligent, Reasonable, and Responsible': Teaching Composition with Bernard Lonergan" a similar willingness to acknowledge the possibility that can arise when we ask students to engage religious belief, even if students are not always able to fully realize that potential in their own thinking (*Renovating*). In calling our attention to the ways that students Tina, Sara, and Shruti all grapple with discussions of religion in very personal and individualized ways, Perkins does a great service to those of us who are trying to expand our vision of the ways that students may be operationalizing their religious commitments within the writing classroom.

T J: While I found myself not thinking quite so much about the classroom as I read *Mapping*, I did find myself challenged by Thomas Deans' "Sacred Texts, Secular Classrooms, and the Teaching of Theory" (*Mapping*). When I teach, I tend to assign texts about religion or contemporary statements from religious individuals and communities, but not primary sacred texts. When Deans describes his use of Gospel scenes to teach literary theory, I began imagining how to use such texts to engage students around questions of interpretive practice and argument making. He asks students to keep in mind their initial reading reactions when they encountered a story from one Gospel as they read a different story from another Gospel, which works to make clear the value of reading from multiple vantage points—even those texts that students hold dear or that are held sacred by many—and to make clear the idea that their understandings of texts can change.

Melody: You know, I had to think hard about whether or not it would be appropriate for me to use the sacred text in ways similar to Deans (*Mapping*) and Daniell (*Renovating*). Similarly, I've thought hard about when it might be appropriate to use Bruce Herzberg's exploration of the Jewish roots of the Apostle Paul's rhetoric (*Renovating*) to help Christian students think more expansively about the interconnections between the rhetorics of many different religious traditions. Like you, I am inspired by the successes of these teachers and scholars, but I also worry that I might not be as successful as they have been were I to include sacred texts in the classroom. These articles rightly suggest that religious texts are (to use the language of Scripture) a "two-edged sword," and I think they are correct: Deans points out that use of sacred texts in the classroom "can provoke anxiety" (86), and Daniell argues that when people are concerned about questions of the "truth" of Scripture, "the underlying issue is more often than not how people read" (106). In particular what I found myself wondering is this: how can we ensure that students understand that we are not trying to threaten or change their belief systems, but (as both Vander Lei and Daniell point out) trying instead to be hospitable through our use of these texts? Can we invite student engagement in ways that emphasize exploration and discovery so as to renovate and invigorate students' thinking about their own rhetorical and religious practice, whatever that may be? Such clarity about our purposes has never seemed more important to me than it does now, at a time when students from many religious faiths, and even those who do not have a religious faith, are struggling to understand how (and whether) their spirituality is welcome within the classroom.

T J: Your wondering, I think, will be shared by many readers. You raise such an important point. Answers to questions about student uptake of teachers' efforts around religious rhetoric in the classroom (if, indeed, there are any real answers) are necessarily partial. But I find potential answers in the spirit of the collections. There's a gracious capaciousness contained in the songs sung by these choirs of contributors. There's room enough at the table (or in the edited collection pages or in the classroom) for many voices and stories, and differences can be held in creative tension. More practically and specifically, I think these chapters model an intellectual honesty that is critical if students are to buy into any project teachers would have them undertake, so being honest with students about our own commitments and how we come by them may be one important way forward. Vander Lei, Daniell, Deans, and others share glimpses of their own stories, their experiences with religion in their own lives. I enjoyed Deans sharing in his chapter his experience of presenting on a Gospel passage at an academic conference, hearing a homily on the same passage, and receiving a novel and creative interpretation of the passage from Deans' ten-year-old son. While these occasions could have produced interpretive whiplash, because Deans adds these experiential moments to his chapter, readers are graced with fruitful and still-too-rare accounts of writing teachers' own diverse experiences with religious discourse.

Melody: If I hear you correctly, you're suggesting that the chapters in these collections model a productive openness to examining and acknowledging the ways that religious rhetorics can be both limiting and liberating. Am I right?

T J: Exactly!

Melody: I walked away with a similar sense that the authors of these pieces are very realistic about the potential and the limitations of the rhetorical moments they explore. Both collections demonstrate that religion (and systematic theologies in particular) is a multifaceted and complex rhetorical agent that works simultaneously on and alongside its adherents. Religion can manipulate and interpolate; it can be an exigence, a tool, and even a partner in accomplishing particular social and spiritual ends. Certainly religion can limit its adherents, but if the authors in these collections are to be believed, religious discourses can also be a tool that rhetors use to accomplish their social goals—some of which may run counter to the expectations and desires of the very religious systems that produce these discourses.

T J: At the same time, in the case of both collections, I yearned for greater attention to religion's capacity to construct rhetorical boundaries that exclude and expel. Readers of these books will acquire a strong sense of Christianity's rhetorical power and of how individuals, communities, teachers, and others may be formed—or may themselves act—within religious contexts that make available certain life options and persuasive possibilities. However, it's not possible for me to watch the news or skim my Facebook newsfeed without seeing religious warrants mobilized to oppose the rights of lesbian, gay, bisexual, or transgender folks. You mentioned earlier the idea of sacred texts as a "two-edged sword," and for many, that is exactly how they have experienced Christian scripture: not as texts that encourage adherents to, as the old spiritual goes, "lay down [their] swords and shields down by the riverside," but as a sword wielded against them. While both collections tackle the civic implications of Christian rhetorics and pay special attention to their connection to gendered ideologies, no chapter within either book takes up LGBTQ-Christian issues in a direct way, and that seems a missed opportunity—even a heartbreaking absence.

Melody: I think this is a really important point, and one that may be connected to the largely historical and methodological emphases of these collections. You rightly point out that LGBTQ-Christian issues are one of the most pressing concerns faced by Christian churches in the U.S. today, and these issues are one factor that shape how North American Christianity, particularly

Christianity in the U.S. defines itself in relation to other global Christianities. To really grapple with the questions raised by these tendencies toward exclusion and embrace (to extend Vander Lei's use of Miroslav Volf in her article in *Renovating*), I think we need to be ready to look more closely at the rhetorical activities of living Christian rhetors, both in the United States and globally—those who use religion to liberate or oppress, either publicly or in the course of their daily lives. Current research shows that among religious adherents in the U.S., attitudes toward LGBTQ individuals (particularly with regard to marriage equality) are rapidly changing, but this may not be true globally. To better understand the role that rhetoric plays in facilitating these complex trends, and to better understand what these changing attitudes can teach us about how individuals craft idiosyncratic beliefs in relation to theological systems, we need to examine not just historic religious trends, but also the activities of those who are using and transforming religious rhetorics in contemporary life.

T J: Right! My own religious tradition, the Episcopal Church, has been undergoing a renovation regarding what it believes about human sexuality, a renovation that has unfolded through debate and discussion since 1976 when its decision-making body, General Convention, passed a resolution affirming the pastoral claims of gays and lesbians. In summer 2015, I was present when that renovation resulted in General Convention overwhelmingly voting to make the sacrament of marriage available to same-sex couples, a vote that came only days after the Supreme Court decision establishing civil marriage equality as a fundamental right. The morning of that decision, friends and I were gathering for the daily worship that takes place during General Convention when it was announced that a change to the musical prelude would let us mark with dance and celebration the good news from the Supreme Court. Clapping and dancing with joy in the aisles and rows, with many others, I sang, "We are marching in the light of God." A secular, civil court's affirmation of marriage equality provoked a profoundly spiritual experience among several participants in a Christian community preparing for worship. To share this story in this review is not an attempt to privilege my own experience, but to suggest that, for a long time, I think such a moment would be illegible within dominant frameworks for analyzing Christian practice and belief within composition and rhetoric. And if it were legible, it might be primarily rendered by rhetorical scholars as a moment celebrating liberal social gains, and the quality of the experience that participants might understand as distinctly spiritual could be lost.

Melody: What a powerful story. It's a timely reminder to be vigilant in seeking what Matthew W. Althouse, Lawrence J. Prelli, and Floyd D. Anderson, in their article "Mapping the Rhetoric of Intelligent Design: The Agentification of the Scene" (*Mapping*) call the "dialectic between both perspectives" (177), the academic and the religious. By using Kenneth Burke's pentad, these scholars show that spiritual and academic practice of rhetoric can be mutually illuminating: just as distinctively religious approaches to religious inquiry can open up new methodological and theoretical approaches to thinking about the academic practice of rhetoric, so existing rhetorical theories can offer us very useful ways of thinking anew about the spiritual claims made by rhetors.

T J: The collections we're reviewing do offer resources that could aid scholars in understanding the rhetorical ecology in which these kinds of religious dynamics are taking place. Two pieces in *Mapping* strike me as especially useful for considering the issues surrounding my desire for more scholarly engagement on rhetoric and Christian thinking about human sexuality. The question of why and how Christian rhetors are witness to social realities and how that witnessing changes is an issue William Duffy helps me think about in "Transforming Decorum." His historical and sophistic evaluation of Walter Rauschenbusch's efforts to promote a socially and economically progressive Christian stance may support others who seek to chart changes within contemporary Christian communities, changes with implications for our political life. Also, Beth Daniell's "More in Heaven and Earth" surveys both social science research and historical biblical criticism to argue that the religious landscape in the U.S. is more textured (and that Christian identifications are more diverse) than is typically imagined.

Melody: Absolutely! *Texture, diversity, nuance*: this is the nature of religious practice, and I am so thankful that these collections do the work of capturing that variety. Since 2011, Vander Lei and Michael-John DePalma have been encouraging scholars to look for places where religion can be a resource in rhetorical education, and in *Mapping*, Heather Thomson-Bunn calls for more scholars to do what Daniell has done, to combine empirical research and existing scholarship. Yet, as someone who studies the ways that religiously engaged students (many, but not all, of whom favor marriage equality, believe in evolution, and support progressive social causes) understand their academic literacy practices, I found myself longing for a discussion of how students are agentive in the classroom, and how they may be both mirroring and enacting changes in what constitutes normative religious belief. The religious students that I've talked to interact with social groups and popular cultures more diverse and multifaceted than at any time in history. They are working to make sense of their own faith commitments within these diverse environments, and in so doing, they are accruing rhetorical expertise and simultaneously creating new conversations—new rhetorics—about what it means to practice religious faith in U.S. I wonder if perhaps these collections have given us license to make normative something previously novel: the rhetorical and the religious constantly in conversation, mutually constitutive rather than always already competitive?

T J: That seems a beautiful way to put it. These collections offer a vision that seeks to make normative the generative interaction of religion and rhetoric, a vision that is fundamentally hopeful about where this interaction can lead.

Beaumont, Texas and Colorado Springs, Colorado

Teaching Arguments: Rhetorical Comprehension, Critique, and Response, by Jennifer Fletcher. Portland, ME: Stenhouse Publishers, 2015. 264 pp.

Reviewed by Glen McClish, San Diego State University

Jennifer Fletcher's *Teaching Arguments: Rhetorical Comprehension, Critique, and Response* is intended to empower its audience—high school language arts teachers and those who train them—to help students develop a distinctly rhetorical perspective on reading and writing arguments. Rhetorical training, she argues, provides the essential tools for understanding and composing texts, or, in Kenneth Burke's terms, "equipment for living." It is no wonder, therefore, that Fletcher, building on the work of Jan Meyer and Ray Land and a growing number of composition scholars, characterizes key rhetorical ideas as "threshold concepts" that constitute not merely one more set of literacy skills, but a dynamic way of being and acting in the world.

Fletcher's Introduction, "Crossing the Threshold," makes the general case for teaching language arts rhetorically and fleshes out "threshold concepts" of argumentation. She declares, "This book is about opening doors for deeper learning for all our students through a rhetorical approach to arguments—an approach based on situational awareness and responsiveness instead of rules and formulas" (xiv). Chapter one, "Starting with Open-Minded Inquiry," employs Peter Elbow's concept of "the believing game" to explore the pedagogical value of reading arguments on their own terms (Elbow 147–91). Chapter two, "From Comprehension to Critique," complements the previous chapter by presenting reading against the grain via Elbow's "doubting game" (Elbow 147–91). Fletcher explains that applying both of Elbow's orientations to reading assists students in discovering their own positions on the issues at hand. "Fostering a Deeper Understanding of the Occasion," Fletcher's third chapter, features the rhetorical situation in which an argument is embedded. Building on issues of context, chapter four, "Fostering a Deeper Sense of Audience," focuses specifically on the interplay of values, assumptions, and beliefs between the text and its audience. "Fostering a Deeper Understanding of Purpose," chapter five, features Aristotle's deliberative, forensic, and epideictic genres of rhetoric as a way of discussing the rhetor's motivation. Chapter six, "Analyzing and Integrating Ethos, Pathos, and Logos," which to my mind forms the heart of the book, presents a useful approach to argumentation based on Aristotle's triune appeals and other concepts, including Toulmin's famous model. (This material is so important that I recommend reading it between chapters two and three, rather than in the order Fletcher places it.)

Fletcher has designed *Teaching Arguments* as a gateway to college and career readiness for students, particularly those from the lower reaches of the socioeconomic spectrum. Facility in rhetoric, she urges, is a key step in the journey toward college, meaningful work, and informed citizenship, which makes the subject at hand all the more important for students who do not benefit from privilege. Nowhere is her motivation to equip students who struggle with the "next steps" after high school more evident than in her final chapter: "Aristotle's Guide to Becoming a 'Good' Student." Here, Fletcher provides specific methods for helping such students imagine and effect success.

One of the most notable characteristics of *Teaching Arguments* is Fletcher's decision to build on the rhetorical learning of the ancients. She draws most heavily on Aristotle, particularly his *Rhetoric*, but she also enriches her discussion of student success by drawing on the *Nicomachean Ethics*, a less obvious, but inventive source. *Phaedrus*, Plato's best-known dialogue concerning rhetoric, is insightfully featured, as are the ancient rhetorical concepts of *kairos, decorum*, the common topics (or *topoi*), and stasis. For the most part, her reliance on classical rhetoric is welcome, for it grounds contemporary reading and writing instruction in the long tradition of humane learning. Cultural differences aside, the classical terminology Fletcher introduces has great explanatory power and remarkable transferability.

Furthermore, Fletcher conscientiously articulates her pedagogical program of rhetorical education with current trends in language arts instruction, most significantly the Common Core State Standards (CCSS). She convincingly demonstrates that the widely adopted national pedagogy invites a rigorously rhetorical approach to high school language arts instruction. Fletcher's links to the CCSS demonstrate the value of the rhetorical approach to reading and writing instruction to those with a strong interest in the CCSS and, alternatively, suggests the value of the CCSS to those heavily invested in rhetorical education. It is important to note, however, that although *Teaching Arguments* operates comfortably *within* the structure of the CCSS, it is not truly *of* the CCSS. Fletcher makes her own way, emphasizing links to Common Core anchor standards and grade-specific standards when they make sense, but not slavishly. For teachers operating beyond the boundaries of the CCSS, the pedagogical advice offered here is sufficiently general and portable to remain relevant. A similar line of argument could be made about *Teaching Arguments*' links to developments in California's public school system, in which Fletcher has served as a high school teacher and a California State University professor. The book frequently references California's rhetorical Expository Reading and Writing Course and the California State University's English Placement Test, which are both germane to California teachers and their students. Nonetheless, one need not have ties to California's educational system to benefit from the book's overall pedagogical program.

In addition to providing high school language arts teachers with a distinctly rhetorical perspective grounded in both ancient and twenty-first-century pedagogy, Fletcher expertly blends theory and application. For every set of terms or concepts introduced, she provides specific exercises that can be directly incorporated into the classroom. In many cases, she reproduces students' responses to featured activities that render the process of rhetorical education all the more concrete. In addition to these activities and responses, Fletcher concludes each chapter with a generous list of "Prompts for Quick-Writes or Pairs Conversations"; and, over the course of the book, she includes seven argumentative essay prompts and four readings. (She also features a compilation of the principal readings and exercises as twenty-five appendices.)

Fletcher's skillful combination of the abstract and the concrete calls to mind an additional act of blending that significantly enhances *Teaching Arguments*—namely, her inclusion both of K–12 and university-level pedagogy and scholarship. Thus, on the one hand, the book's foreword is produced by Carol Jago, longtime California high school teacher, and Fletcher draws upon many others who contribute to K–12 pedagogy: scholars such as George Hillocks and Kelly Gallagher, as well as many practicing high school teachers. On the other hand, she features rhetoricians better known in university circles such as Kenneth Burke, Charles Bazerman, and Carolyn Miller, as well as prominent college textbooks such as Sharon Crowley and Debra Hawhee's *Ancient Rhetorics for Contemporary Students*, John Gage's *The Shape of Reason: Argumentative Writing in College*, and the contributions of Peter Elbow. And several of her influences, such as Gerald Graff and Cathy Birkenstein's *"They Say/I Say": The Moves that Matter in Academic Writing*, operate in both realms. Through this blend of high school and college scholarly and pedagogical traditions, Fletcher demonstrates that the differences between K–12 and college pedagogy should not be viewed as a matter of kind, but of degree.

My concerns about *Teaching Arguments* fall within the realm of minor limitations—for no book can do all things for all people. Fletcher's treatment of support for claims (Toulmin's concept of data or Aristotle's minor premise for an enthymeme) seems rather narrowly focused on "evidence" (information, statistics, and so forth), whereas in the larger historical discussion of argumentation, support is conceptualized more broadly in terms of reasons and reason-giving. The data or minor premise, in effect, answers the question "why?" by forming the "because clause" for the thesis. Supplementing *Teaching Arguments* with something like Gage's discussion of supporting arguments in *The Shape of Reason* (chapter six, "Giving Reasons") may be a useful workaround here. Furthermore, I would have appreciated a more precise handling of the term "purpose," which varies in meaning throughout the book, from claim or central argument, to motive (in contrast with the argument), to something like generic goal. My final concern is Fletcher's rather vague use of the term "essay" to describe most of the writing assignments introduced in the book. Given her commitment to providing very concrete applications and exercises for learning rhetorical concepts, it would be a relatively easy matter to render in more precise terms the generic and rhetorical expectations for the papers she discusses. This increased specificity is particularly important given the growing importance of genre awareness in composition studies.

These minor quibbles aside, I wish to conclude by praising what is perhaps the defining feature of *Teaching Arguments*, Fletcher's highly persuasive teacherly *ethos*. Throughout the book, she models for her reader the public persona of a knowledgeable, principled, caring instructor of rhetoric who both explains and exemplifies the principal elements of Aristotle's notion of rhetorical character: *phronesis*, *arête*, and goodwill. Thus, *Teaching Arguments* epitomizes Aristotle's ancient assertion that "character is almost, so to speak, the controlling factor in persuasion" (38). I heartily recommend this book for K–12 language arts educators—and those who prepare them—drawn to the ranks of that ancient, civic-minded profession: the teacher of rhetoric.

San Diego, California

Works Cited

Aristotle. *On Rhetoric*. Trans. George A. Kennedy. New York: Oxford UP, 1991. Print.

Crowley, Sharon, and Debra Hawhee. *Ancient Rhetorics for Contemporary Students*. 5th ed. New York: Pearson Longman, 2011. Print.

Elbow, Peter. *Writing Without Teachers*. New York: Oxford UP, 1973. Print.

Gage, John T. *The Shape of Reason: Argumentative Writing in College*. 4th ed. New York: Pearson Longman, 2006. Print.

Graff, Gerald, and Cathy Birkenstein. *"They Say/I Say": The Moves that Matter in Academic Writing*. 3rd ed. New York: Norton, 2006. Print.

Rewriting Success in Rhetoric and Composition Careers, edited by Amy Goodburn, Donna LeCourt, and Carrie Leverenz. Anderson, SC: Parlor Press, 2013. 240 pp.

Reviewed by Beth L. Hewett, Defend & Publish, LLC

If rhetoric and composition as an advanced degree field is enveloped by what Amy Goodburn, Donna LeCourt, and Carrie Leverenz call "narrowness and elitism typical of other disciplines" in higher education institutions (xii), then who does it serve? How does this field fulfill rhetoric's ancient Aristotelian promise of providing a voice for the people from the people, of the Ciceronian good man speaking well? Although *Rewriting Success in Rhetoric and Composition Careers* is advanced as a book about reconceiving professional careers and opportunities, the above questions are at the heart of the authors' stories that comprise the text. In other words, what is the use of a disciplinary field whose primary purpose in educating graduate students appears to be to get people academic jobs—just like those of their academic grandparents—when they finish? To what end the making and remaking of the scholarly self if only to beget new scholar-teachers for higher education—and for traditional research institutions at that? What does the future of higher education hold for those who identify themselves with the discipline of rhetoric and composition? More importantly, what do those who identify themselves as rhetoricians and compositionists offer to the world?

The editors of *Rewriting Success* issue "a call to action by suggesting how institutions can do a better job of supporting and encouraging *alternative* career paths, by welcoming adjuncts and term instructors as full members of the profession, and by actively mentoring in ways that honor all kinds of career options" (xvi, emphasis added). The issues raised in this book make sense in light of a dreadful economy and a greatly changing face of postsecondary education. Let's be real: English studies educators have limited potential to be hired for traditional tenure-track jobs, as the recent "Report on the MLA *Job Information List*, 2013-2014" clearly shows. In the 2013-2014 hiring season, the *JIL* announced merely 1,046 English-language jobs, a number that had fallen by 96 (8.4%) over the previous year; fewer of these were tenure-track, assistant professor positions (another 8.4% decrease). It is not that English studies educators are underprepared; many are incredibly accomplished thinkers, scholars, and teachers. It is that the need for traditional scholarly humanities-based skills has not grown in the academy, and the economics of higher education will not accept an old model that no longer fits. To its credit, *Rewriting Success* does not bemoan that fact; rather, it critiques the old model and those in the professoriate who bemusedly wipe their sleepy-dust-filled eyes and say, "What? Not *my* graduate students. They want and get jobs just like mine" (xiv). Such critique is necessary, and that is what makes this volume worth reading.

Yet the book could have had a greater impact with a different perspective. Certainly it rightly considers the lack of (traditional) jobs and the reality that rhetoric and composition PhDs are unique individuals who require the right job and the right fit for their personalities and life styles—meaning that not just any job will do, despite tight economic constraints. The challenges go deeper, however, and a less fully addressed but significant problem for rhetoric and composition professionals is an unclear identification of what it is to be a working, engaging, publishing, and/or teaching rhetorician and compositionist. For that understanding, I suggest returning to earlier conceptions of rhetoric and composition—once oral and now written and image driven. When John Quincy Adams was the first Boylston professor of rhetoric and oratory at Harvard in 1806, rhetoric was a practical field. Students studied rhetoric primarily for their work in law, religion, and politics. However, by 1876 the department was no longer called "Rhetoric and Criticism" but "English Language and Literature" (Heinrichs), something Donald Stewart called the "'Harvardization' of American English" (Edwards 696). The focus changed from one of applying rhetoric to other disciplines to being a topic solely for the study of language and literature, leading to the field being too engrossed with the subject itself and not enough with the doing of the subject. Although in recent years the field has started to return to its roots, there remains a good bit of attention to mitosis evidenced in graduate programs where the end goal is to get a job in the professoriate. The authors of this book's collective chapters seem to focus and function counter to the historical model of the past two hundred years precisely because they describe an action-oriented rather than reproductive rhetoric and composition approach. Indeed, some of the authors of this volume offer powerful narratives of career work that engage the notion of applied rhetoric (Yeats 111), which is the understanding that rhetoric is about something larger than itself and that it can contribute to the world in myriad ways—pragmatically and in relation to the work of other disciplines.

Applied rhetoric as action certainly is something that engages teaching, as Mya Poe, Malkiel Choseed, Ildikó Melis, Sue Doe, and Heather Graves describe in section one, "Redefining Work in Academic Institutions." By taking jobs that enable supple definitions of productivity, they have rejected the requirement to publish just to keep a job. Choseed makes a particularly strong point about flexibility when he describes the empowering work of a community college teacher who can elect to write and publish—or not—depending on whether "I believe I have something to add to the conversation, not because a tenure-review clock is ticking like a time bomb" (22). His point is well-taken since the purpose of research and publication should be to address real questions and not merely to punch a ticket on the way to tenure and peer acclaim, as is the case in a publish-or-perish mindset (see Barbara Fister regarding the need for selectivity in scholarly publication, for example).

Applied rhetoric as action—maybe most helpfully and engagingly—disrupts the academic beaten path, erupting new and fertile ground, as Moria K. Amado-McCoy, Dave Yeats, Benjamin Opipari, Shannon Wisdom, and Nick Carbone explain. In the second section of the book, titled "Redefining Valuable Knowledge Beyond Academe," they offer fascinating stories of people with rhetoric and composition PhDs, or with graduate work, who elected to work outside academia. Yeats' chapter is especially helpful because he outlines ten specific ways that English studies applies directly to varied careers, which in his case involves user-experience research. Opipari writes in especially clear prose about lawyers' stark need to learn to write well; this chapter's emphasis on teaching strong writing skills to lawyers, who have a particularly obfuscating vocabulary, underscores that rhetoric and composition professionals can model and teach practical writing to workers in varied settings. Carbone's chapter illuminates the satisfaction that scholar-educators can achieve when they work for such educational venues as textbook publishers, which are badly in need of the knowledge that rhetoric and composition specialists can provide.

"Working for Change," the third section of this book, examines some ways to bring about the kinds of changes our profession needs if it is to accommodate the exigencies of contemporary higher education economy. Cindy Moore, Jennifer Ahern-Dodson, Stacey Pigg, Kendall Leon, Martine Courant Rife, Lara Smith-Sitton, and Lynée Lewis Gaillet write of projects aimed at professionalizing students for potential careers outside the academy. Because of its focus on collaboration and learning "in the moment" (199), the Writing in Digital Environments (WIDE) research project that Pigg, Leon, and Rife discuss is particularly interesting. This collaborative project prepares students for jobs outside the academy by addressing learning as an ongoing and metacognitively rich experience. (These chapters would be even more helpful if they were to point readers to such outside-the-academy resources as "PhDs at Work," an online collaborative where PhD-holding professionals network and share career building experiences.)

I very much wanted to like *Rewriting Success* because I, too, have struggled with an academic identity. My scholarship solidly lives in the academic arena while my thinking, writing, and work reject its borders—hence, my alter egos as a dissertation coach and bereavement author, trainer, and coach.

I also wanted to like this book because its publication is a necessary first step toward overturning an outdated perspective of what it means to have a rhetoric and composition advanced degree. That perspective fails to acknowledge the economic realities of the academic job market and the diverse life choices available to those with PhDs. Yet, while I admire the contributors' efforts and believe they offer a path to important dialogue, I sensed a patronizing attitude about walking such a nontraditional path born of the very editorial collaboration that created the book. The editors—all accomplished, smart, well published, and *well situated* academics—fail to include on their team even one of the individuals whose voices they purport to support. This failure to include a non-tenure track academic or non-academic professional on the editorial team creates the impression of the *haves* showcasing the poor *have nots*. To their credit, the editors admit that they hail from privileged positions and, as a result, their "own stories . . . are perhaps overly influenced by the very model we sought to question" (viii). However, to offer people a voice in a book while not including them (or someone like them) in the book's planning and construction removes self-determination about the story being told from those whose writing and lives comprise the book itself. To paraphrase from the important messages in James I. Charleton's *Nothing About Us Without Us: Disability Oppression and Empowerment*, a book about rewriting rhetoric and composition careers cannot do its work well without collaboration with those whose careers are, in fact, different from the traditional norm. In trying to explain others' career choices as legitimate, the editors trip over an implicit core assumption that those alternative choices are *not* legitimate and, therefore require traditional academics to legitimize them through publication in a book such as this one. Operating even unconsciously from such a core assumption is to participate in the very milieu that afflicts the professional lives of those who are not recognized as PhDs in full regalia when their work setting deviates from traditional academe. Sadly, the approach is condescending. The collaborative inclusion of even one editor who was not so traditionally situated could have changed the trajectory of the entire volume, inspiring a different, exciting set of questions and responses from the authors. For example, those who choose alternative rhetoric and composition careers might have framed the book around such questions as "Why do you (not) publish and what does publication mean from your career perspective?" and "What does the academic notion of service mean when it is not required for the job?" or "What is the nature of a rhetoric and composition career when one's work has global, practical applications?"

Despite my sense that the editors have offered a somewhat limited view of legitimacy in the rhetoric and composition profession, I realize that, without such initial conversations as they provide, the status quo cannot change. To what degree it will change in the academy—where the triumvirate of research, teaching, and service still reigns—is unclear, but change it must, particularly for the many professional rhetoricians and compositionists who should see themselves as free to create meaningful lives of which their careers are but one part. Ultimately, *Rewriting Success* is a book about *alternative paths* in rhetoric and composition rather than *paths*. Yet when we stop looking at the mainstream path as the ideal and begin seeing all paths as legitimate, something this book can help us learn to do, we will make progress toward encouraging graduate students and seasoned rhetorician and compositionists alike to choose applied careers that make personal and professional sense—and about which no apologies need to be made.

Forest Hill, Maryland

Works Cited

Charleton, James I. *Nothing About Us Without Us: Disability Oppression and Empowerment*. Oakland: U of California P, 1998. Print.

"Connecting PhDs Working Across Industries." *PhDs at Work*. N.p., n.d. Web. 12 June 2015. <http://phdsatwork.com/>.

Edwards, Bruce L. "Stewart, Donald C. (1930-1992)." *Encyclopedia of Rhetoric and Composition: Communication from Ancient Times to the Information Age*. Ed. Theresa Enos. New York: Garland, 1996. 696-97. Print.

Fister, Barbara. "Publish Research. Not Too Much." *Inside Higher Ed* 18 May 18, 2015. Web. 12 July 2015. <https://www.insidehighered.com/blogs/library-babel-fish/publish-research-not-too-much>.

Heinrichs, Jay. "Why Harvard Destroyed Rhetoric." *Figures of Speech*. N.p., 2005. Web. 30 July 2015. <http://inpraiseofargument.squarespace.com/harvard>.

MLA Office of Research. "Report on the MLA *Job Information List*, 2013-2014." *ADFL* (2014): 1-30. Fall 2014. Web. 12 June 2015. <http://www.mla.org/pdf/rpt_jil_1314web.pdf>.

Other People's English: Code-Meshing, Code-Switching, and African-American Literacy, by Vershawn Ashanti Young, Rusty Barrett, Y'Shanda Young-Rivera, and Kim Brian Lovejoy. New York: Teachers College P, 2014. 192 pp.

Reviewed by Jenny Krichevsky, University of Massachusetts Amherst

I'm sitting in an auditorium in Bryant University, listening to Vershawn Ashanti Young open up the floor for questions after his keynote address to the 2014 Northeast Writing Centers Association Conference. Young had just finished arguing that through a pedagogy of "code-switching," the burden of discourse assimilation invariably falls on African American students. Instead of positioning students to switch between codes based on setting and audience, Young had proposed to the audience his term, "code-meshing." Code-meshing, he explains, is an approach to writing and interpreting texts that advocates for blending language codes in the classroom, rather than switching from one set of linguistic codes to another, depending on the "appropriate" social and discursive contexts. Young wraps up his slides, and there is an energy in the big room, like the moment before you take a deep breath. The first question is a familiar one, almost boilerplate: "But how can I let a student, who had come to see me for help, walk out without my having shown them the way the school wants them to write?" At least a dozen hands shoot up. The responses that follow, some echoing this anxiety, some responding critically to the implicated assumptions, are indicative of a tense, decades-old pedagogical impasse in language and writing studies. In *Other People's English: Code-Meshing, Code-Switching, and African American Literacy*, published in 2013, Young and his co-authors Rusty Barrett, Y'Shanda Young-Rivera, and Kim Brian Lovejoy offer a new way into this tension, unprecedented in its translation of theory into a practical teaching road map.

While teachers and scholars in language and writing fields are trying to understand the viability of code-switching, *Other People's English* unpacks the fluidity, mobility, and heteroglossia of English through the possibilities of code-*meshing*, and outlines what structures of racism code-switching reconstitutes, despite the good intentions by which it is deployed. Blending linguistics and composition theory with curricular applications in K-12 and higher education, this four-part book is "a conversation," as Victor Villanueva puts it in the foreword, "not in your face, not in demand of a conversion, but a conversation based on personal experiences, classroom experiences, and decades of research and scholarship" (x-xi). The goal of *Other People's English*, a direct reference to Lisa Delpit's *Other People's Children,* is to give readers "analytical snapshots" of how code-meshing is already being used in classrooms at several levels of education, as well as to present the exigency of code-meshing as an alternative to code-switching, as effective and inclusive as the latter may seem. Young continuously points to the elision of the ways in which code-switching is connected to racial self-understanding, and suggests further that code-switching is not just an isolated school practice, a necessary way into success, but rather another social construct "perpetually thrust upon Blacks to prove themselves when communicating, particularly in the mainstream and/or with non-Blacks" (5). Code-switching is then an act of racial compromise for African American English users, one that code-meshing pedagogy desires to move beyond.

In the following four sections, the book sets up theoretical, personal, and pedagogical approaches to code-meshing. In "African American English and the Promise of Code-Meshing," linguist Rusty Barrett lays the groundwork for the subsequent, pedagogically oriented sections by articulating two organizing ideas related to language and power: first, the *who*—the physical body doing the writing and speaking—matters a great deal in terms of how much value is assigned to undervalued codes like African American English; and second, no language, Standard English included, is a static, neutral, code. In "Code-Meshing or Code-Switching?", Young argues that code-switching, despite well-intended goals of inclusion, is in practice a vestige of legalized segregation, and "an educational strategy that forces African Americans to view their language culture and identity as antithetical to the U.S. mainstream" (9). It is not enough, then, to "value" African American English in schools. The system is such that black students must constantly "limit their display of African American cultural styles and use of African American language to sites that are near exclusive to African American people, and they must keep these out of the academic, economic, and professional spheres" (59). Indeed, that Black English is often seen merely as a way to inflect writing with some sort of "authentic" but always marginal identity obfuscates the ways in which this undervalued discourse influences and spills over into other forms of English, including Standard Academic English. It is imperative, Young says, that we ask whom this narrow notion of English serves.

Most notably, this collection builds on and complicates Delpit's notion of a "culture of power" in a pedagogy that enables students to learn the discourse they will be asked to master while at the same time incorporating undervalued English into learning spaces and school texts to demarginalize it (Delpit 24). In "Code-Meshing and Responsible Education in Two Middle School Classrooms," Y'shanda Young-Rivera offers an elementary education perspective on how code-meshing works on the ground, within several classroom contexts. Young-Rivera, previously a skeptic of code-meshing, offers revealing articulations by fourth-, fifth-, and eighth-grade students of the terms "code-meshing" and "code-switching." She includes daily lesson plans, as well as images of the students' written homework responses, in which the young writers identify and interpret the code-meshing they encounter in their world. This chapter serves to not only emphasize how easily implemented the frame is but also how flexible the code-meshing curriculum can be, given the imperative of a state-wide accountability project like Common Core requirements. In "Code-meshing and Culturally Relevant Pedagogy for College Writing Instruction," Lovejoy speaks from his teaching experience as a white man in a first-year college writing program and English department that are predominantly African American. By sharing assignments, student writing, and most tellingly, conversations he has had with colleagues initially resistant to any code-meshing content in the curriculum, Lovejoy teases out the multifarious implications that African American English carries especially in a post-secondary education context. Both Young-Rivera and Lovejoy fundamentally re-frame writing as an activity rooted in community and embodiment of daily experiences. The authors' narratives tackle the quandary of what we "owe" our students: we must work toward showing that "a culture of standard language ideology" exists, and moreover, that we can work to change it from the ground up (122).

That this change can happen in the classroom, as the authors of the book maintain, shifts the epistemology of writing and teaching. In *Other People's English*, the pedagogical imperative moves beyond solely teaching students what the languages of academic institutions are and how to use them. It also moves beyond Delpit's imperative to give students access to the "language of economic success" (Delpit 68). Rather than building a language curriculum that assumes a Standard Academic English code deficiency in students, educators can work with students from a space that emphasizes how their language experiences are *already* engaging with different linguistic codes, both standard and disenfranchised. As Young-Rivera demonstrates, by helping students investigate the ways in which different language codes work in the world around them, especially the ways their home languages are actively influencing languages of power, a code-meshing curriculum can work against the ongoing historical elision that languages spoken by people of color in the United States experience, and take historically disenfranchised linguistic codes out of the marginalized Other space.

The exigency of *Other People's English* should be clear: this, as Vershawn Young puts it, is a "'learning and teaching' book" (10). The goal of the text is to illustrate code-meshing theories and practices accessibly. Each chapter offers visually distinct glosses reminiscent of a textbook in that each sets up an anticipated "concern" that a reader might have, offers "guiding inquiries" that raise frequently asked questions about code meshing, suggests "teaching tips" for classroom use, and presents a prompt at the end—"What are your thoughts?"— that invites readers to engage with ideas from their own perspectives. These visual aids invite readers to make code-meshing a "shared project, one that will not only inform instructional practices, but possibly intervene into the culture of prejudices against African American English as a mainstream language variety" (10). How we, composition and language scholars and instructors, are implicated in these power systems around language is an old question. Moreover, both Delpit and Young persistently position all educators to consider what is at stake when teaching the "culture of power." Yet through this book, Young, Barrett, Rivera-Young, and Lovejoy suggest that the project before us is about more than exposing ideologies or hidden histories. To promote the "power of language rather than codes of power" (156) means we must make space for "standard" and undervalued codes to exist right alongside each other, to mesh on the pages, and in the classrooms, and in institutions that, despite their rhetoric, go out of their way to exclude codes uttered by non-white bodies. The time for change is now, Young insists, and while code-switching offers one approach to opening up access in the classroom, it does not alleviate the marginalization of African American English. *Other People's English* positions us to consider the ways we are inscribed by the tools we use despite our good intentions, to question our current pedagogical epistemologies and the terms we use, and to consciously extend our theory into practice.

Amherst, Massachusetts

Works Cited

Delpit, Lisa D. *Other People's Children: Cultural Conflict in the Classroom*. New York: New Press, 1995. Print.

The Open Hand: Arguing as an Art of Peace, by Barry M. Kroll. Logan: Utah State UP, 2013. 176 pp.

Reviewed by Rachel Griffo, Indiana University of Pennsylvania

While "mindfulness" has been a buzzword across disciplines and beyond, in *The Open Hand: Arguing as an Art of Peace*, Barry Kroll grounds some of the tenets of mindful practice, which include active listening, favoring the present moment, and exercising nonjudgmental behavior, in a cross-cultural, embodied, and kinesthetic approach to Rogerian argumentation. Based on a course he taught over a period of six semesters, entitled "Arguing as an Art of Peace," Kroll's book includes student writing on, and in response to, deliberative, conciliatory, and integrative approaches to argument. Using the image of an open hand, as opposed to a closed fist, Kroll juxtaposes these approaches alongside Chinese cosmologies, yin and yang. Returning to these terms of difference throughout the book, Kroll reveals the way that a mindful approach to argumentation requires an awareness of the interplay between resistance and reception where moments of balance may occur.

The intention behind Kroll's book is understood through the concepts he uses as the basis of his students' projects and in the way he structures the book itself. Each of the five sections of *The Open Hand* may be read as five individual chapters, or, as a practice not unlike aikido or judo. For instance, the opening chapter, "Clapping In," does what it says and says what it does: it calls the reader to attention. Reminiscent of Japanese martial arts, Kroll explains that he and his students began their class sessions with three claps. Being mindful of practicality and readability, Kroll enacts a mindful approach to the transmission of the book's intentions by keeping "focus on projects and activities" students completed in the course and avoiding "strings of in-text references and citations . . . using notes for most references" (8). What results is an accessible and practical example of a mindful approach to argumentative writing pedagogy.

The second chapter, "Reframing and Deliberative Argument," includes kinesthetic examples of activities that further explicate the interdependent nature of yin and yang transitions in argument. To facilitate an embodied understanding of the implications for yin and yang in deliberation and redirection, students participate in a version of push hands based on tai chi and an aikido movement called *irimi* (entering). Some important questions that guide this section of learning include: "When does redirection feel soft and when does it become aggressive? When, that is, does a redirective push become an adversarial shove?" (51). These questions direct students toward the kind of thinking that LuMing Mao encourages in "Returning to Yin and Yang: From

Terms of Opposites to Interdependence-in-Difference." These kinesthetic exercises ask students to examine and be aware of the subtle transitions within and between assertive, redirective, and receptive approaches to push and pull activities and to reflect on the ways they may relate to verbal argumentation.

Chapter three, "Attentive Listening and Conciliatory Argument," describes the second unit of Kroll's seminar, "Arguing as an Art of Peace." Having developed and become aware of mindful approaches to argumentation, this next unit asks students to consider "[h]ow is it possible to use arguing as an art of peace when a clash of views appears to be inevitable?" (61). To support connections between kinesthetic activities and argumentation, Kroll assigned his students sections of George Thomson and Jerry Jenkins' *Verbal Judo*. While karate is based on an offensive system of movements, judo, by contrast, is all about redirection and non-hurtful approaches to conflict. When used as a verbal approach to argumentation, the precepts of judo provide an opening for a conciliatory argument about a controversial issue in a way that practices reciprocity.

Circumventing the traditional "taking sides" approach, in chapter four's "Mediating and Integrative Argument," Kroll pairs editorials that implement mediation strategies with a Zen Buddhist koan, "Nansen Cuts a Cat." In this koan from the sacred text *The Gateless Gate*, monks on east and west ends of a hall argue over a cat. Lost in their words, neither side is able to find a middle ground, so Nansen cuts the cat in half. Revealing the problem with binary logic, students commented that Nansen was a mediating figure who was trying to create a space for the monks to distance themselves from their own words and focus on shared viewpoints. Striving for a similar approach to argumentation, students chose topics on controversial issues and "talked about points of agreement or shared concern as a basis for mediating differences of view" (100), which created a space for them to enact yin and yang logic in their papers.

Finally, in chapter five's "Bowing Out" Kroll closes an analogical loop. Like the *enso*—a circle painted in one single breath—that appears in chapter three and on the cover of the book, Kroll's subtitle, *Arguing as an Art of Peace*, comes full circle. Returning to some of the contemplative practices that students enacted throughout the seminars, Kroll is explicit about the gaps between mindful practice and argument. While painting an *enso*, slowly eating raisins, and sitting in a Japanese garden were meaningful for students in the seminar, some of them were skeptical about what direct connections there were between these practices and argumentation. In response, Kroll explains that "mindfulness is not a *model* for arguing differently but a *practice* that supports arguing with an open hand" (116, emphasis in original). In other words, the relationship between mindfulness and argument is best understood by looking at where our contemplative life and our material life meet. For instance, one would not sit around in a Japanese garden all day or spend all of his or her time painting *enso*. That kind of thinking and acting would be extreme. Drawing instead on yin and yang logic, it is possible to understand the way that these practices simply create a foundation, making argument as an art of peace more accessible.

As a practitioner of contemplative practice, I have been attracted to composition scholarship by Mary Rose O'Reilley, Gesa Kirsch, Claude Hurlbert, LuMing Mao, and Kurt Spellmeyer—among others—who value, to use O'Reilley's words, the way "contending elements of the self . . . nudge us toward living a more integrated life" (33). I would certainly add Kroll's book to this important list of contemplative scholarship. The challenge with applying contemplative practices and concepts to the teaching of rhetoric or argument is often explaining how and why they translate into useful rhetorical strategies. In this regard, what some readers might like to see more of in this book is an even greater level of transparency that would reveal how difficult it is to teach and practice argument as an art of peace, when arguing to win or to get a good a grade are, at times, more desirable options. There is a lot to be learned from the kind of teaching moments described in chapter four when Kroll shares students' concerns about the relationship between mindful practice and argument. Without these moments of honest reflection on the role of contemplative practices in rhetorical strategies, the benefit of such practices might be lost. Having said that, one of the strongest aspects of Kroll's project is his inclusion of kinesthetic learning set beside written models of similar (rhetorical) moves. To make the kinesthetic examples he discusses palpable, he includes photographs of students enacting the practices he discusses in the index to the book. After reading, I am encouraged, and I think other compositionists might be as well, to write and develop work that not only talks or theorizes about contemplative practices but also provides transparent examples of how these practices (or concepts) may be enacted practically and critically.

Indiana, Pennsylvania

Works Cited

Hurlbert, Claude. *National Healing: Race, State, and the Teaching of Writing*. Logan: Utah State UP, 2012. Print.

Kirsch, Gesa E. "From Introspection to Action: Connecting Spirituality and Civic Engagement." *CCC* 60.4 (2009): W1-W15. Print.

Mao, LuMing. "Returning to Yin and Yang: From Terms of Opposites to Interdependence-in-Difference." *Symposium: Comparative Rhetorical Studies in the New Contact Zone: Chinese Rhetoric Reimagined* 60.4 (2009): W45-W56. Print.

O'Reilley, Mary Rose. *Radical Presence: Teaching as Contemplative Practice*. Portsmouth: Boynton/Cook, 1998. Print.

Spellmeyer, Kurt. *Buddha at the Apocalypse: Awakening from a Culture of Destruction*. Somerville: Wisdom Publications, 2010. Print.

Thompson, George J., and Jenkins, Jerry B. *Verbal Judo: The Gentle Art of Persuasion*. New York: HarperCollins, 2013. Print.

Yamada, Koun. *The Gateless Gate: The Classic Book of Zen Koans*. Somerville: Wisdom Publications, 2004. Print.

UNIVERSITY OF CENTRAL FLORIDA

TEXTS *and* TECHNOLOGY *Ph.D.*

ORLANDO, FL

UCF's Texts & Technology Ph.D. is part of a growing field combining scholarly study, creative production, and assessment of digital media texts. The future demands those who can analyze, synthesize, and produce new knowledge, and effectively communicate to a broad range of audiences.

Areas of Research Include:

- Digital Archiving & Editing
- Scientific & Technical Communication
- Social Media
- Information Architecture
- Digital Media
- Visualization
- Rhetoric & Composition
- Public History
- Game Design
- Digital Humanities

This flexible, interdisciplinary curriculum encourages communicators and problem solvers who strive for leadership positions as educators, consultants, employees, and administrators.

Find out more online at
TANDT.CAH.UCF.EDU

Contributors

Kati Fargo Ahern is Assistant Professor of English at Long Island University-Post and does all her work on soundscapes, auditory rhetoric, and composition theory. Some of her most recent work appears in *Convergence: The International Journal of Research into New Media Technologies* and *Computers and Composition*.

Kara Poe Alexander, Associate Professor of English, teaches writing courses in the Professional Writing Program at Baylor University. Her current research examines literacy narratives and social change writing. Her work has appeared in *CCC, Composition Forum, Computers and Composition Online, JBTC, Technical Communication Quarterly*, and several edited collections.

Erin Bradley graduated from Penn State Berks in May 2015 with a BA in professional writing.

Steph Ceraso received her PhD in English from the University of Pittsburgh, specializing in rhetoric and composition, pedagogy, sound and listening, and digital media. Steph is currently Assistant Professor at the University of Maryland, Baltimore County. You can find more about her research, projects, and teaching at www.stephceraso.com.

Aaron Clark is a recent graduate of the University of Utah, where he majored in writing and rhetoric studies and wrote regularly for the *Daily Utah Chronicle*. He is interested in journalism, particularly arts and culture, as well as travel writing.

Kirsti Cole is Associate Professor of Rhetoric, Composition, and Literature at Minnesota State University. She teaches in the Teaching Writing Graduate Certificate and Master's of Communication and Composition programs. She has published articles in *Feminist Media Studies, College English, Harlot*, and *thirdspace*, and her collection *Feminist Challenges or Feminist Rhetorics* was published in 2014.

D. Shane Combs PhD student at Illinois State University. His teaching philosophy, *the pedagogy of giving a shit*, is informed by liberatory, feminist, and social-expressivist pedagogies. He is currently researching affect and highly sensitive people in the academy.

Michelle Costello is a recent graduate of Marist College, where she was an English major with a concentration in writing as well as a journalism minor. This is her first published article.

Melissa Davis was a Penn State Berks senior when this collaboration was created. Davis uses writing to continue the tradition of storytelling within the black community in order to preserve the significant contributions of African Americans in American history and culture.

Harry Denny is Associate Professor of English at Purdue University, where he directs the Writing Lab. He is the author of *Facing the Center* and is at work on projects on writing center assessment, the politics of access, and the rhetoric of contemporary civil rights in the U.S.

Aaron Dial is a 2015 graduate of North Carolina Central Universitywith a BA in English and a concentration in writing. He is currently pursuing an MA in English at his alma mater.

Michelle Dierlof graduated from Penn State Berks in May 2015 with a BA in professional writing.

Keith Dmochowski, a student at Penn State Berks, will graduate in fall 2015 with a BA in professional writing. His work has been featured in campus news and creative publications; he will continue pursuing professional and creative writing interests after graduation.

Michelle F. Eble is Associate Professor of technical and professional communication and serves as graduate director in the department of English at East Carolina University. Her research and teaching interests include technical writing theory and practice, especially as it relates to rhetorical intervention, gender studies, and technology in medical, scientific, and academic contexts.

Erin A. Frost is Assistant Professor of technical and professional communication at East Carolina University. She teaches scientific writing, writing for business and graduate courses in her research areas. Her research centers on feminisms in technical communication, most often as they relate to healthcare policy and risk communication.

Collie Fulford is Assistant Professor of English rhetoric and composition at North Carolina Central University. Her research examines writing program and curriculum development from basic writing through graduate programs.

John Gangi is a professional writing major and is set to graduate in 2015. His passions include reading and hiking. He hopes to someday travel the world.

T J Geiger II is Assistant Professor of English at Lamar University. His research focuses on the writing major, writing studies pedagogy, and religious rhetoric. His work has appeared in *College English*, *Peitho*, and *CCTE Studies*.

Ian Golding is a PhD student in rhetoric and composition at the University of Cincinnati. His creative work has been published in *Mid-American Review, Salt Hill,* and *CutBank,* and other journals. To him, writing is like drawing a collage.

Rachel Griffo is a doctoral student at Indiana University of Pennsylvania working at the intersections of comparative rhetoric, literacy studies, and first year composition.

Dr. Laurie Grobman is Professor of English and Women's Studies at Penn State Berks. She has published four articles (three of them co-authored) on the undergraduate writing major and several articles and a co-edited collection on undergraduate research. Grobman and four former undergraduates co-authored a forthcoming article in *Community Literacy Journal* (2015).

Heidi Skurat Harris is Assistant Professor of Writing and Rhetoric at the University of Arkansas at Little Rock. She also serves on the CCCC Committee for Effective Practices in Online Writing Instruction. Her primary teaching and research interests are rhetorical theory, creative nonfiction, and online pedagogy and practice.

Beth L. Hewett is President and Senior Writing Coach with Defend & Publish, LLC, as well as a certified bereavement author, trainer, and coach. She has led the CCCC Committee for Effective Practices in Online Writing Instruction for more than seven years, and she has published numerous books and articles.

Jonathan Hunt is Associate Professor in the department of rhetoric and language at the University of San Francisco, where he teaches first-year writing and speaking courses.

Edward Jacobs began playing violin at age 8, later shifting to saxophone. He subsequently studied music composition at the University of Massachusetts, Amherst, the University of California, Berkeley, and Columbia University. In 2005 Jacobs' work as a composer of both instrumental/vocal and electronic music was recognized by a Charles Ives Award of the American Academy of Arts & Letters. Jacobs has taught at East Carolina University since 1998.

Elizabeth Kimball teaches writing, literacy, and linguistics, including community-based learning courses, at Drew University in Madison, NJ. She also directs the College Writing Program. Her research focuses on language and learning in communities, past and present. She has published in *Rhetoric Review*, *Reflections*, and *Community Literacy Journal*.

Sarah Klotz recently received her PhD from the University of California, Davis in English with an emphasis in rhetoric and composition. Her research focuses on indigenous rhetorics and anti-assimilationist pedagogy in higher education. She currently teaches writing at Butte College in northern California.

Jenny Krichevsky is a graduate student in the English department at the University of Massachusetts Amherst, specializing in composition and rhetoric. Her dissertation delves into the intersections between literacy, embodied subject positions, and national identity by investigating the ways in which individuals pass down language values in families through shifting temporal, political, and geographical landscapes.

Glen McClish is Professor and Chair of Rhetoric and Writing Studies at San Diego State University. His scholarly interests include eighteenth- and nineteenth-century British and American rhetoric (with a particular emphasis on African American discourse), as well as composition and communication pedagogy.

Wendy McCloud is a professional and technical writing graduate student at the University of Arkansas, Little Rock. She is a driven professional with a passion for writing. Wendy is a published author in several genres of nonfiction and is currently focusing on writing her tell-all memoir, "Her Mother's Madness: One Child's Journey out of Darkness."

Barbara Jayne McGaughey is a senior writing and linguistics major at Georgia Southern University. Her focus is nonfiction, working primarily on the intersection of girlhood, social politics, and mental illness.

Cara Messina recently earned her MA in English and currently holds positions as adjunct professor at St. John's University and writing tutor at Queensborough Community College. She has presented her research on writing centers at several conferences and is a recipient of an IWCA/NCPTW grant.

Michael J. Michaud teaches courses in composition and rhetoric at Rhode Island College in Providence, Rhode Island, where he is Associate Professor of English and chair of the campus writing board. His work has appeared in *CCC*, *Writing and Pedagogy*, *Teaching English in the Two-Year College*, *Open Words*, and is forthcoming in *Writing on the Edge*.

Jessica Nastal-Dema is Assistant Professor of English at Prairie State College and Associate Editor of the *Journal of Writing Assessment*. Her work focuses on writing pedagogy, writing assessment, and access in higher education.

Kristy Offenback graduated from Penn State Berks in May 2015 with a BA in professional writing.

Lori Ostergaard is Associate Professor and chair of the Department of Writing and Rhetoric at Oakland University. Her research examines contemporary writing programs and majors, as well as histories of writing instruction at Midwestern normal schools and high schools.

Melody Pugh is Assistant Professor of English at the United States Air Force Academy in Colorado Springs, CO. Her research interests include learning transfer, writing across the curriculum, and the literacy practices of religiously engaged college students.

Mitchell Reber is a senior at the University of Utah, where he is double majoring in philosophy and writing and rhetoric studies. His research interests include digital rhetorics and composition pedagogy.

Michael Reich, a doctoral candidate at St. John's University, has studied composition with Professors Harry Denny, Anne Geller, and Derek Owens. He is on the graduate student editorial board for the forthcoming journal, *The Peer Review*.

Aleyna Rentz is a junior writing and linguistics and English double major in Georgia Southern University's honors program. Her fiction and creative nonfiction have appeared or are forthcoming in *Black Fox Literary*, *Sanctuary*, and *Deep South Magazine*.

Emily Schnee is Associate Professor of English at Kingsborough Community College, City University of New York, where she teaches composition and developmental English. Her research focuses on issues of access and equity in urban public higher education. Her work has been published in journals such as *Teachers College Record*, *Community College Review*, *Radical Teacher* and *Thought and Action*.

Liesl Schwabe's essays have appeared in *Creative Nonfiction*, *The Common*, *Tricycle: The Buddhist Review*, *AGNI*, *Post Road*, *The Writer's Chronicle*, as well as several other journals and anthologies. Beginning in September 2015, she will serve as Director of the Writing Program at Yeshiva College.

Michelle Smith is Assistant Professor of English at Marist College, where she teaches public writing and rhetoric. Her research interests include feminist rhetorics, rhetorical theory, and the rhetorical gendering of work. Her publications include articles in *Rhetoric Society Quarterly* and *Peitho*, as well as several edited collections.

Cami Sylvia received her Bachelor of Music degree as well as a minor in rhetoric and writing from Rhode Island College. While at RIC, she also tutored in the writing center. Cami will pursue her Master of Music degree at SUNY Purchase in fall 2015.

Christie Toth is Assistant Professor of Writing and Rhetoric Studies at the University of Utah. Her work has appeared in *Assessing Writing, CCC, JBW, TETYC,* and *WPA*. She is co-editor of the collection *Teaching Writing in the Two-Year College* and is working on a book about locally responsive writing pedagogies.

Carl Whithaus is Professor of Writing and Rhetoric and Director of the University Writing Program at the University of California, Davis. His books include *Multimodal Literacies and Emerging* Genres (University of Pittsburgh Press, 2013) and *Writing Across Distances and Disciplines* (Routledge, 2008).

Melissa Wilk is a student at Penn State Berks and will graduate in December 2015 with a BA in professional writing and a BA in communication arts & sciences with a certificate in public relations. Her interests include reading and creative writing. She wishes to pursue a career in the field of public relations, specifically integrated marketing communications.

PARLOR PRESS
EQUIPMENT FOR LIVING

Congratulations to These Award Winners & WPA Scholars!

The WPA Outcomes Statement—A Decade Later
Edited by Nicholas N. Behm, Gregory R. Glau, Deborah H. Holdstein, Duane Roen, and Edward M. White
Winner of the Best Book Award, Council of Writing Program Adminstrators (July, 2015)

GenAdmin: Theorizing WPA Identities in the Twenty-First Century
Colin Charlton, Jonikka Charlton, Tarez Samra Graban, Kathleen J. Ryan, & Amy Ferdinandt Stolley
Winner of the Best Book Award, Council of Writing Program Adminstrators (July, 2014)

Mics, Cameras, Symbolic Action: Audio-Visual Rhetoric for Writing Teachers
Bump Halbritter
Winner of the Distinguished Book Award from *Computers and Composition* (May, 2014)

New Releases

First-Year Composition: From Theory to Practice
Edited by Deborah Coxwell-Teague & Ronald F. Lunsford. 420 pages.

Twelve of the leading theorists in composition studies answer, in their own voices, the key question about what they hope to accomplish in a first-year composition course. Each chapter includes sample syllabi.

A Rhetoric for Writing Program Administrators
Edited by Rita Malenczyk. 471 pages.

Thirty-two contributors delineate the major issues and questions in the field of writing program administration and provide readers new to the field with theoretical lenses through which to view major issues and questions.

www.parlorpress.com

Available now in the MLA series

Options *for* Teaching

Teaching Early Modern English Literature from the Archives

Edited by **HEIDI BRAYMAN HACKEL** and **IAN FREDERICK MOULTON**

"The volume brilliantly combines the visionary and the pragmatic and is a gold mine of great ideas about how to engage students in the production of knowledge. It is a remarkably timely project."

—*Michael Schoenfeldt*
University of Michigan, Ann Arbor

Teaching Early Modern English Literature from the Archives focuses on English literature and culture from 1473 to 1700.

xi & 274 pp. • 6 x 9
Cloth $45.00 • Paper $29.00

Teaching the Graphic Novel

Edited by **STEPHEN E. TABACHNICK**

"Professors and teachers thinking of introducing graphic narratives in their courses, or of creating a dedicated class for this popular genre, will do well to consult it and profit from the generous advice of its contributors."

—*Vittorio Frigerio*, Belphegor

Graphic novels are appearing in a great variety of courses: composition, literature, drama, popular culture, travel, art, translation. The essays in this volume explore issues that the new art form has posed for teachers at the university level.

vii & 353 pp. • 6 x 9
Paper $25.00

Join the MLA today and receive **30% off** the list price.

Modern Language Association

bookorders@mla.org ▪ www.mla.org ▪ Phone orders 646 576-5161

Modern Language Association | MLA

TEACHING
RESEARCH
CAREERS
COMMUNITY
ADVOCACY

The MLA Today

- Promotes language and literature study
- Advocates on behalf of the field
- Publishes scholarship and the *MLA International Bibliography*
- Hosts an annual convention of scholars where you can share your work
- Supports scholars in their careers through the *Job Information List* and other resources
- Creates opportunities for you to be part of a vibrant community on *MLA Commons*

Why Join?

◆ To add your voice to more than 25,000 colleagues who are working to strengthen the field and its outreach

◆ To support career services for you and your colleagues

◆ To help prepare doctoral students for the workforce through projects like Connected Academics

◆ To support research and reports on the job market, enrollments, and evaluating scholarship

◆ To participate in the MLA Annual Convention

The MLA Annual Convention
7–10 January 2016
Austin

The largest gathering of teachers and scholars in the humanities features

- roundtables, workshops, and discussions
- conversations with leading thinkers, artists, and critics
- reduced rates and special discounts available only to members

Visit **www.mla.org/convention** for more information.

 #mlanews
#mlaconvention

As a member, you'll receive a free copy of the forthcoming eighth edition of the *MLA Handbook*, a subscription to *PMLA*, convention registration discounts, and much more.

Join Now

- Visit www.mla.org
- E-mail membership@mla.org to request a membership packet
- Call 646 576-5151

www.ingramcontent.com/pod-product-compliance
Lightning Source LLC
Chambersburg PA
CBHW031316160426
43196CB00007B/553